Organisation studies

J. W. D. Glover

W. G. Rushbrooke

Lecturers in Advanced Business Studies,
Hammersmith and West London College

PITMAN PUBLISHING
128 Long Acre London WC2E 9AN

© JWD Glover and WG Rushbrooke 1983
Reprinted 1985, 1987

All rights reserved. No part of this publication may be reproduced,
stored in a retrieval system, or transmitted, in any form or by any
means, electronic, mechanical, photocopying, recording and/or
otherwise, without the prior written permission of the publishers.
This book may not be lent, resold, hired out or otherwise disposed of
by way of trade in any form of binding or cover other than that
in which it is published, without the prior consent of the publishers.

Produced by Longman Group (FE) Ltd
Printed in Hong Kong

ISBN 0-273-02562-7

Contents

Preface · vii

PART A

1 The organisation · 2
  1.1 Characteristics of organisations · 2
  1.2 Ways of classifying organisations · 4
  1.3 Miscellaneous classifications · 6
  1.4 The bureaucratic organisation · 7
  Self-test questions · 9

2 The historical development of organisation theory · 10
  2.1 The Classical approach · 10
  2.2 The Human Relations approach · 15
  Self-test questions · 17

3 More recent contributions to organisation theory · 18
  3.1 The Systems approach · 18
  3.2 The Action approach – an alternative view · 21
  3.3 The Contingency approach · 21
  Self-test questions · 23
  Chronological bibliography of the main writers on organisation theory · 23

PART B

4 Motivation and behaviour at work · 25
  4.1 Why study motivation? · 25
  4.2 Taylor and the concept of 'economic man' · 26
  4.3 Economic man becomes social man · 27
  Self-test questions · 31

5 Motivation: the importance of individual differences · 32
  5.1 External influences · 32
  5.2 Individuals' perceptions of their situation · 34
  Self-test questions · 38

6 The nature and significance of groups · 39
  6.1 Defining a group · 39
  6.2 Formal and informal groups · 40
  6.3 The characteristics of groups · 40
  6.4 Group membership · 41
  6.5 The uses of groups in organisations · 42
  6.6 Formal group effectiveness · 42
  6.7 Group cohesion · 43
  6.8 Group involvement · 43
  Self-test questions · 44

Contents

7 Leadership — 45
7.1 Early approaches to leadership theory — 45
7.2 More recent approaches to leadership theory — 46
Self-test questions — 51

8 Roles and role theory — 52
8.1 Basic role concepts — 52
8.2 Defining different roles — 53
8.3 Role theory and problem diagnosis — 54
8.4 Applications of role theory — 56
Self-test questions — 58

Case studies on Part B — 59

PART C

9 Power and authority in organisations — 62
9.1 Authority and power — 62
9.2 Sources of power — 63
9.3 Responses to different power sources — 65
Self-test questions — 67

10 Conflict at work — 68
10.1 Unitary and pluralistic views of organisations — 68
10.2 The dimensions and types of organisational conflict — 71
10.3 The underlying causes of conflicts — 72
10.4 Conflict management — 73
Self-test questions — 74

11 Employee participation in decision making — 75
11.1 Forms of participation — 76
11.2 Some varieties of employee participation — 78
Self-test questions — 83

12 Business communication — 84
12.1 The communication process — 84
12.2 The four communication media — 85
12.3 Channels of communication — 87
12.4 Designing an effective communication system — 90
Self-test questions — 93

13 The environment of organisations — 94
13.1 The nature of the business environment — 94
13.2 The interest groups of organisations — 95
13.3 Anticipating and responding to environmental conditions — 98
Self-test questions — 100

Case studies on Part C — 101

PART D

14 Capital structure and sources of finance — 105
14.1 Financing different business entities — 105
14.2 Financial management — 108
14.3 Finance for the small firm — 110
Self-test questions — 110

Contents

15 Budgetary planning and control — 112
   15.1 Budgets as a basis for planning and control — 112
   15.2 Budgetary planning — 113
   15.3 Human and motivational aspects of budgetary planning — 116
   15.4 Review — 116
   Self-test questions — 117

16 The marketing function — 118
   16.1 The marketing philosophy — 118
   16.2 The marketing mix — 119
   16.3 The marketing department — 120
   Self-test questions — 122

17 The production department — 123
   17.1 Production planning and control — 123
   17.2 Jobbing production — 124
   17.3 Batch production — 124
   17.4 Mass production — 125
   17.5 Process production — 126
   17.6 Woodward's research — 126
   Self-test questions — 127

18 The purchasing function — 128
   18.1 The scope of the purchasing function — 128
   18.2 Purchasing policies — 129
   18.3 Stores and stock control — 131
   18.4 The decision-making unit — 132
   Self-test questions — 132

19 Personnel management — 133
   19.1 The personnel function — 133
   19.2 Fulfilling manpower requirements — 134
   19.3 Staff appraisal — 137
   19.4 Training — 138
   19.5 Wage and salary administration — 139
   19.6 Industrial relations — 143
   19.7 Employee safety and welfare — 143
   19.8 Maintenance of records — 144
   Self-test questions — 145

Case studies on Part D — 145

PART E

20 The functions of management 'revisited' — 148
   20.1 Forecasting and planning — 149
   20.2 Organising — 152
   20.3 Leadership and direction — 155
   20.4 Control — 159

Index — 163

Contents

112	15 Budgetary planning and control
112	15.1 Budgets as a basis for planning and control
113	15.2 Budgetary planning
115	15.3 Human and motivational aspects of budgetary planning
116	15.4 Review
117	Self test questions

118	16 The marketing function
118	16.1 The marketing philosophy
119	16.2 The marketing mix
120	16.3 The marketing department
122	Self test questions

123	17 The production department
123	17.1 Production planning and control
124	17.2 Jobbing production
124	17.3 Batch production
125	17.4 Mass production
126	17.5 Process production
126	17.6 Woodward's research
127	Self test questions

128	18 The purchasing function
128	18.1 The scope of the purchasing function
129	18.2 Purchasing policies
131	18.3 Stores and stock control
132	18.4 The decision-making unit
132	Self test questions

133	19 Personnel management
133	19.1 The personnel function
134	19.2 Fulfilling manpower requirements
137	19.3 Staff appraisal
138	19.4 Training
138	19.5 Wage and salary administration
139	19.6 Industrial relations
143	19.7 Employee safety and welfare
144	19.8 Maintenance of records
145	Self test questions

| 145 | Case studies on Part D |

PART E

148	20 The functions of management revisited
149	20.1 Forecasting and planning
152	20.2 Organising
153	20.3 Leadership and direction
155	20.4 Control

| 163 | Index |

Preface

Organisations have many facets. The study of organisations must combine different subject disciplines and perspectives to achieve a rounded and overall understanding of problems and issues involved.

Some analyses of organisations are heavily 'structural', tending to attribute organisational success and failure primarily to structural factors – the appropriate or inappropriate design or allocation of work and responsibility within the organisation.

Other approaches emphasise 'people' as the key to organisational success. People's motives, priorities and aspirations, the effects of leadership and group memberships, have all been exhaustively studied in attempts to understand and explain deficiencies in organisations and to prescribe measures to remedy them.

A full awareness of the impact of technology and the environment external to the organisation is also offered in organisation theory as being fundamental to effective organisation design and functioning.

Each of these approaches is evident in this volume but none *alone* can be said to cause, or predetermine, organisational success. Success is unlikely wherever structure is inappropriate, where the needs and aspirations of any part of the workforce are ignored or frustrated, where environmental conditions are disregarded, or where the effects and implications of different technologies are misjudged.

Naturally, what many people want from their study of organisations, apart from a general understanding of the subject area and the issues it embraces, are practical remedies for common organisational problems – and these practical remedies are elusive. If they were not, then management would be a science in the true sense of the word and there would be no such thing as inefficiency or poor organisational performance. With a statistical or mathematical problem, there will be one correct solution, and it is rewarding to reach it through the application of proven methods. Regrettably, in a study area such as this one, there is no such certainty. Indeed, even the problems of organisations are often extremely hard to define, and there are no universal, proven solutions to them.

Throughout this volume, the many different theories and assertions which claim to offer insights and explanations of actions or situations within organisations are discussed. Often one conflicts with others, or has been superseded by them. Yet in many chapters, especially in the first three sections of the book, a *range* of theories has been included, not just the most recent or the most plausible. This is not an attempt on our part to make life unusually difficult for the student of organisations, but stems from two important facts.

First, current theories have been born, with few exceptions, of observed or logical deficiencies in their predecessors. It is essential that the process of evolution and refinement of organisation theory as a *body* of theory is quite clearly seen, and the origins of the particular theories appreciated.

Second, many theories relevant to the study of organisations are not strictly testable or verifiable. Where they conflict or are incompatible, clearly each should be discussed and compared if its relative worth is to be assessed.

Whilst we shall attempt to show which theories, in our view, are the most useful or insightful, we do not apologise for not having more or better answers to problems commonly arising within organisations. The book will have achieved its main purpose if, after reading it carefully, the student can understand why.

J. W. D. Glover and W. G. Rushbrooke, 1982

PART A

Managers, workers, politicians – in fact all people involved in any section of our society or economy – ask a lot from organisations – and therefore from organisation structures. How can we create and maintain structures to meet the demands placed upon them, when these demands often seem scarcely compatible?

This section lays the foundation for the study of organisations by examining what organisations are, how they may be structured and how they can be classified.

The structure of an organisation – the way work is divided and grouped and responsibility allocated – is a key factor in organisational success both technically and managerially. What principles, if any, exist for organisation and job design? How universal are these? What effects might different structures have on a workforce and on managerial effectiveness? Are certain structures better suited to particular external operating conditions or technologies?

Different organisation theorists have come up with differing answers to these questions. We chart those theories and principles which have been most influential and establish that organisation structure is not something inert, lifeless and inconsequential. It needs to be matched to its particular industrial context and it must be based on, and be responsive to, the wider context in which it operates.

1 The organisation

- Although organisations carry out different activities, they all share common characteristics and can be relatively easily categorised.
- Many modern business organisations show the features of a bureaucratic model that was first put forward as an idealised type of organisation.

1.1 Characteristics of organisations

In any field of human behaviour there exist organisations. In business, in politics, in sport, there are formal bodies of people engaged in some activity for some purpose. Although their activities may be completely different, it is possible to find similarities between the organisations concerned. At first sight

Table 1 Characteristics of selected organisations

Common Aspects	XYZ Bank	XYZ Manufacturing Company	XYZ National Corp.	XYZ College of Further Education	National Union of XYZ Workers	XYZ Owners' Club
Objective	Commercial	Commercial	Social/ commercial	Educational/ social	Social/ economic/ political	Social
Activity	Provision of banking services to business and private individuals	Production of goods for business and private individuals	Provision of state services to business and private individuals	Provision of education to local community	Representation of and service of members' interests	Representation of and service of members' interests
Management	Board of Directors	Board of Directors	Board of Directors	Board of Directors	National Executive	Executive Committee
Membership	Directors Managers Non-management staff	Directors Managers Non-management staff	Directors Managers Non-management staff	Principal and vice-principal Heads of departments Teaching and non-teaching staff	Full Time officials Part Time officials Ordinary members	Part Time officials Ordinary members
Party reported to	Shareholders	Shareholders	Central Government	Local Authority	Membership	Membership
Finance (excluding loan debt)	Shareholders	Shareholders	Central Government	Local Authority	Membership	Membership

Characteristics of organisations

the similarities between a bank, a college, a hospital, a trade union and a manufacturing company are difficult to identify. However, they all have certain features in common: each has an identity, such as a name; each has an objective – often in the form of a written constitution; they all have a list of employees so that it is known who works for the organisation; they have a method of replacing or recruiting new members to ensure continuity.

Technical criteria such as these distinguish an organisation from an informal group of people such as a crowd; and there are further characteristics that all organisations share. First, each is involved in a task of one kind or another. The task or job of work obviously relates to the organisation's objectives and can be broken down into supporting or sub-tasks, depending on the level of task complexity.

Second, each uses people in achieving the task. Without human resources, either employees or other members of the organisation, the concept of organisation is meaningless.

Third, each has some form of structure that co-ordinates the people who are engaged in achieving the task. The structure of people's duties and responsibilities in turn defines, to a large extent, the relationships between them. Management studies concentrate on this area.

Finally, every organisation both operates in, and itself constitutes, an ever-changing environment. The business organisation, for example, draws certain inputs from the external environment and, through a work process, converts them into outputs to send back to the external environment.

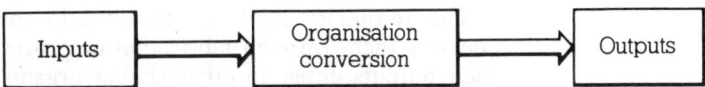

The inputs are usually referred to by the economists as the factors of production: land, labour, capital and enterprise. They consist of such things as money, machines and equipment, materials, labour and information. The outputs consist of goods or products (such as washing machines) and services (such as advice).

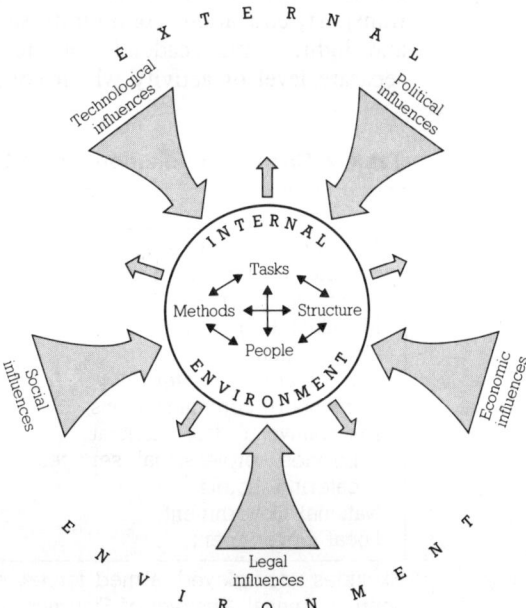

Figure 1
Organisational environments

The organisation

Each organisation has to handle the mutual influences of its external and internal environments. Legal, social, economic, political and technological influences will affect the choice of inputs and outputs and act as constraints on the organisation's operations. They will also influence the internal environment provided by the organisation itself, affecting its members. The organisation's operations will, in turn, have some impact on the outside world.

1.2 Ways of classifying organisations

Organisations are conventionally classified by three main categories: by level of economic activity, by legal structure, and by economic sector. Other, less conventional but nevertheless appropriate, categories are possible and will be discussed later; but first we shall look at the main classifications, concentrating on business organisations although some classes will apply to organisations without a profit motive.

Level of activity

This method of classification assumes that any economic activity can be broadly subdivided into levels of a macro-economic process. At the primary level of activity organisations are concerned with extractive operations based on natural raw material. Thus mineral ores, oil, unprocessed foodstuffs and timber are typical products at the primary level.

The secondary level of activity uses these primary outputs as inputs and converts them through fabrication or processing. Organisations at this level sell their outputs either to other similar organisations in the form of capital goods, e.g. machinery in industrial markets, or as consumer goods. The latter consist of durable products (cars, for example) or non-durable products (such as cigarettes). The term 'manufacturing industry' is often loosely used to describe this level of activity.

The final, tertiary level of activity consists of organisations that perform services. Activity at this level includes banking, insurance, hotels and catering, transport, education, community services and the utility industries such as heat and light. Some academics argue that it is useful to distinguish a further, separate level of activity which covers research and development.

Table 2 Changes in distribution of UK labour force* 1969–78

	1969	1978	Percentage change
Total population in employment	22,624,000	22,710,000	+0.3
Agriculture, forestry, fishing, mining, quarrying	928,000	730,000	−21
Manufacturing	8,356,000	7,298,000	−13
Construction	1,463,000	1,269,000	−13
Gas, electricity, water, transport, communications	1,965,000	1,796,000	−9
Distributive trades, financial, business, professional, services, catering, hotels	8,445,000	9,977,000	+18
National Government	595,000	659,000	+11
Local Government	872,000	977,000	+12

Excludes unemployed, armed forces, employers and self-employed.
Source: *Annual Abstract of Statistics*, 1980.

Ways of classifying organisations

It is interesting to note that the proportion of UK working population employed in these levels of activities has changed and is changing. Before the industrial revolution the majority of the UK population was rural and worked at the primary level. In 1980, the percentage at primary level was 3% and declining; some 40% of the country's workforce was occupied in the secondary level, the rest of those employed being mainly concerned with tertiary activities. Table 2 shows how employment in the various levels of the economy has changed in recent years. It is often questioned, rightly or wrongly, whether the expansion of activities in the tertiary level will create enough long-term wealth for the country.

Legal structure

In business, the most readily identifiable classification of organisations is by legal status. To a large extent the different legal types of organisations relate to the scale of operation involved.

In the private sector by far the majority of business organisations are small units run by self-employed persons, supported by family members or a few assistants. The easiest legal identity to adopt in these circumstances is that of the Sole Proprietor or the Sole Trader. Here, beyond a requirement to register a trading name, there are few if any peculiar legal restrictions. The Sole Trader is literally very often a 'one-person business', and factors such as control and liability for debt are totally personal. Typically, the owner of the small shop and the farmer fall into this category.

For various reasons, particularly those concerned with the desire to expand, raise finance, cover risk (see Chapter 4), the Sole Trader is not a significant business organisation in terms of scale of operation. A more formal but nevertheless still flexible and personal organisation is the Partnership. Between two and twenty people may combine under a Deed of Partnership, by which liability is shared equally as, usually, are profits and financial investment. Typically those in professional occupations such as doctors, solicitors, estate agents and management consultants combine in partnerships.

The third type of business organisation differs from the other two in one significant respect. The limited company is an incorporated organisation: that is, it has its own legal identity which is separate from that of its owners or members. In limited companies any owner's liability for the business's debt is limited to the value of his investment, or shareholding, whereas Sole Traders put all their personal assets at risk. Control of limited companies is often separated from ownership, because the shareholders appoint directors to manage the business (a point often forgotten when the word 'employer' is used). Many directors, however, are also shareholders.

Limited companies are of two types, Private and Public. Numerically, there are far more Private Limited Companies. Often family owned and run, they must have at least one director, and more than two members. There is a restriction on the right to transfer shares, and funds cannot be raised from the general public. Because the private company can find it difficult to raise capital it is the second type of organisation, the Public Limited Company, which accounts for most of the large household-name companies. The public company may sell shares to the public and borrow from it. For a price, a private individual can buy a share of such an organisation and become a shareholder, thereby becoming a part owner. Public companies must have at least two directors and more than two members. Both Private and Public Limited Companies are formed under the conditions of the Companies Acts (1948–81).

Each company has a basic constitution, the Memorandum of Association, which gives details of the registered name and the location of the registered office, the

The organisation

company's objectives and the amount of capital it may raise. Each must also draw up Articles of Association, the rules for electing directors and the rules for conducting meetings.

The last legally distinct group of business organisations are those such as the Co-operatives and Building Societies whose main formal aim is not maximum profit but whose main purpose is to benefit their members. They must register with the Registrar of Friendly Societies. Their importance should not be underestimated. The Co-op grocery, for example, still dominates the distributive trades in this sector.

Economic Sector

The organisations we have just been discussing are all within what is termed the private sector of the economy: private because there is no direct ownership or control by the Government. For various historical and political reasons however, there are many organisations that are owned and controlled by the State (and therefore indirectly, through the democratic system, are accountable to the voting public). These organisations are grouped together as the Public Sector. They include Government Ministries, the Law Courts, the Bank of England, the nationalised industries (such as coal, steel, railways), and local government bodies such as County Councils and Local Education Authorities. 'Civil Servants' is a term that applies to National Government employees such as clerks in Whitehall, but it could arguably apply also to local government staff such as the dustman, teacher, nurse and policeman. Thus in political debate, when public expenditure is referred to, it can cover anything from the cost of new nuclear missiles to allowing London Transport to reduce bus fares or to raising the cost of school meals. The extent to which the UK economy is mixed, i.e. that organisations in it can be in either the private or the public sector, has significant implications. For example the nationalised industries have the unusual role of having to operate on a self-financing basis but also of having to meet the social needs of their users. Should the Gas and Electricity Boards compete? Should British Rail Southern Region subsidise British Rail Scotland? Should, indeed, there be competition between private and public sector organisations? These are typical points of contention.

The Central Government has to deal with these problems. The creation of the National Enterprise Board as financial saviour of many private sector organisations who got into trading difficulty such as Rolls Royce, highlighted this involvement of Central Government in a mixed economy where free trade and political planning come together.

1.3 Miscellaneous classifications

To classify organisations by level of activity, legal structure or economic sector offers an acceptable but potentially limited framework. Organisations can be analysed in other ways. Three additional distinctions are offered for consideration.

Size

Organisations can be classified by size. Size can be interpreted to mean the amount of capital employed, the number of employees, sales turnover, market share, gross profit or even size of buildings. If size is related to economic efficiency, an analytical ratio is often used. Thus two ratios that would be significant are profit earned relative to capital employed and profit earned relative to sales turnover.

Technology

Organisations can be also classified in relation to the technology employed. Certain organisations are capital intensive. This means that the amount of money invested in the organisation's physical plant i.e. machinery, general fittings and equipment, is large compared to the labour costs. A petrochemical refinery costing £300 million might only employ 200 site workers. Other organisations are labour-intensive, where the opposite relationship occurs. The catering trades are such an example. Technology also relates to the type of work that goes on in the organisation. The office block offers working conditions totally different to those of the farmyard or the shop floor of the car factory.

Personal

It is also worthwhile considering how a single individual might classify organisations. Does the school leaver choose employment in one particular firm because it has a good reputation for welfare facilities? Is an employee happy to work for a firm not because it is successful, but because the work is enjoyable? Such rhetorical questions are not timewasting. Personal attitudes about any particular organisation do not usually draw on the formal classifications and distinctions that this chapter has concentrated on. Nevertheless they should be seen as equally valid. Consider the replies given on asking someone, 'Who do you work for?' The replies do not usually state, 'I work for a private limited company' but rather, 'I work for a good company that has a subsidised canteen'.

1.4 The bureaucratic organisation

The word 'bureaucratic' implies a degree of criticism; being associated with petty officialdom and large impersonal organisations, especially those in the public sector. These connotations are perhaps a jaundiced view of the way many organisations operate although they may be accepted as typical of certain inefficient organisations.

Max Weber, the writer who first coined the word 'bureaucracy', foresaw many of the problems of large organisation, but he saw Bureaucracy as an Ideal Type of organisation. Weber was a Berlin Professor who wrote at the turn of this century, although his works were not translated into English until the 1940s. He has a deserved reputation for being one of the earliest sociologists and his interests were wide ranging. He considered the relationship of capitalism to what he termed the 'protestant work ethic' in N.W. Europe and the social need for selection through an examination system.

Weber's particular interest was in organisations, and his ideas have had a significant influence on organisation theory. This interest was founded on his curiosity as to why people obey orders. To understand obedience, he suggested that two concepts should be distinguished. First power, which he saw as the ability to force obedience, and second authority, where orders are obeyed voluntarily. Authority where there is an acknowledged right to use power is, he suggested, based on three different sources, each of which determined the characteristics of an organisational type through the key function of its leader.

First, Weber saw a source of authority in charismatic power. Here the leader has a very magnetic personality. Charisma, literally the gift of divine grace, gave rise to organisations based largely on personality cults. The organisation was consequently only stable so long as the leader survived. On the leader's death it would become very unstable and would usually cease to exist. Sometimes this charismatic source of authority led to the second type, termed traditional authority. Here authority was rather arbitrary, because the role of leader was based on custom and tradition,

The organisation

often, in fact, on hereditary rulership rights similar to the feudal system or the monarchy. This second source of authority led to more stable organisations, but was open to abuse especially by tyrannical people. It was the third source of authority that, in theory, led to the most efficient type of organisation. This type he termed legal-rational authority. Leadership here is based on explicit rules of efficiency which both the leader and subordinate accept as being based on specific, acceptable (and therefore legitimate) objectives. This legal-rational type of authority led Weber to suggest the possibility of an ideal type of organisation which, although never existing in a pure form, was a constructive guide as to how all efficient organisation might eventually, in whatever field, be based. This type of organisation he termed Bureaucracy. A model showing the development of these ideas is shown in Figure 2.

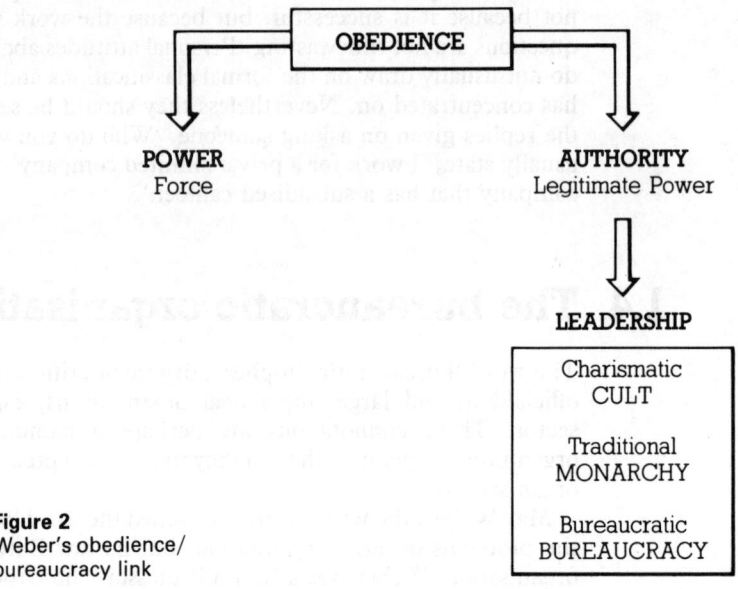

Figure 2
Weber's obedience/
bureaucracy link

The bureaucratic model

People working in this bureaucratic/ideal type of organisation Weber called officials. By looking at the role of officials within legal-rational authority structures he itemised the specific features of bureaucracy (features which bear a strong similarity to many large organisations today). These features were

1. There is a clear hierarchy of officials.
2. The responsibilities and sphere of authority of each official are clearly defined.
3. Officials are formally selected on the basis of examinable qualifications.
4. Officials are appointed on the basis of a contract.
5. The official's job is his main occupation.
6. The official has no ownership rights to any part of the organisation.
7. There is a clear career structure, with promotion through seniority or performance noted by the judgement of superior officials.
8. Officials have a money salary, graded primarily to hierarchical position and with pension rights.
9. All members of staff obey orders from above because of hierarchical position, not because of the influence of individual personalities. They never become emotionally involved with their work but maintain a bureaucratic professionalism.

The bureaucratic organisation

10 Everyone is subject to a strict, unified system of discipline and control which is based on a relatively fixed body of established rules and standardised procedures.

11 All transactions are recorded and eventually filed in a central bureau.

Evaluation

There is no doubt that Weber's bureaucratic model is, on first impression, convincing. In theory favouritism and discrimination are eliminated and formal specialisation is encouraged. The three elements of a career structure, a hierarchy, and employee expertise are common in the majority of organisations today. However, Weber's premise that 'the decisive reason for the advance of the bureaucratic organisation has always been purely technical superiority over any other form of organisation' cannot be fully supported, although he acknowledged that his model was only an idealistic yardstick. It has been justifiably argued that Weber concentrated too much on the role of the formal leader in the organisation, thus neglecting a full consideration of informal groups and informal leaders. We shall examine the significance of the informal elements found in every organisation in later chapters.

His bureaucracy assumes highly intelligent and well-trained officials and it therefore must remain an ideal type. Moreover, such a bureaucracy may well discourage personal initiative and encourage organisational inflexibility. It could degenerate to a situation where rules stop being a means to an end but an end in themselves, and then it is easy to sabotage the organisation's efficiency by 'working to rule'. Two current writers have pointed to the way in which bureaucracy can degenerate into incompetence. Peter with his Peter Principle stated:

'In a complex organisation everyone eventually reaches his level of incompetence, and stays there',

and Parkinson with Parkinson's Law stated:

'Work expands so as to fill the time available for its completion.'

Both these aphorisms should be looked out for in modern organisations.

Summary

This chapter has set out to create an awareness of what an organisation is, how it may be classified and how, ideally, it might operate. Weber's ideas have been looked at because he stimulated so much interest in organisations. His bureaucratic model offers a checklist against which many subsequent theories can be assessed. How well his ideas stand up to criticism should be considered after reading the views of other writers who have contributed to organisational theory and who are presented in the two following chapters.

Self-test questions

1 Which of the following are organisations?
   a a bus queue   b a youth club   c a football crowd   d a political party

2 Compare the different methods of classifying organisations. Which method would be appropriate for advising a school leaver on employment prospects?

3 Can you identify any charismatic leaders in today's business world?

4 What evidence is there that modern firms share similar features to Weber's Ideal Type?

5 Can you think of reasons why the Peter Principle is not really a serious proposition?

6 If Weber's bureaucratic checklist is convincing, why then do we nowadays use the term 'bureaucracy' to criticise organisational inefficiency?

2 The historical development of organisation theory

- The Classical approach includes the ideas of Taylor and his concept of Scientific Management, and Fayol, who was the first writer to define management and offer Principles of Management.
- The Human Relations approach was taken by two groups: the early writers, who were influenced by experiments into worker behaviour in a factory in Chicago, and the later writers, who developed the approach in different directions.

Organisation theory is a relatively new branch of the social sciences. Its origins are nineteenth century, and its writers mainly American. The next two chapters trace the development of the three main schools of thought or approaches to the study of organisations: the Classical approach, the Human Relations approach, and the Systems approach.

Within each of these broad approaches writers had different emphases and points of interest. For this reason we have provided a brief bibliography for easy reference (p. 23). This bibliography also illustrates the chronological development of ideas on organisation theory over the last century.

2.1 The Classical approach

The Classical writers, most of them practising managers, were among the first to concentrate attention on specific problems of management and organisation in large-scale industry. In doing so they laid the foundations of organisation theory. Two of the most influential were an American, Frederick Taylor, who introduced 'Scientific Management' and a Frenchman, Henri Fayol, who made the first detailed analysis of administrative practice.

Scientific Management　Taylor trained as an engineer and was a manager at a large American steelworks in the 1880s. He studied the activities involved in production, shovelling coke and operating lathes in particular. He attempted systematically to observe and measure the rate at which workers could work at maximum output, which in practice meant at maximum physical effort. Taylor recommended that wage rates should be set close to the workers' maximum possible rate of output through a payment scheme known as 'incentive piece-rate', which means that the harder an employee works the more pay he receives.

In association with these ideas, Taylor made some fundamental comments on formal organisational practice that led to his proposals for Scientific Management. He acknowledged that organisations are constructed on the concept of the division of labour: the more jobs are broken down into their constituent parts, the more specialised and skilled an employee could become. This should lead to greater efficiency. He claimed management was not efficient because it failed to realise this and to use it in conjunction with piece-rate payment schemes. Management's role was to select the right man for the right job and ensure the appropriate resources were available. Taylor summarised these ideas in his 'Four Great Underlying Principles of Management'. These were

1 The development of a true science of work.
2 The scientific selection and progressive development of the workman.
3 The bringing together of 1 and 2.
4 The constant and intimate co-operation of management and men.

Criticism of Scientific Management

Taylor's ideas were at first welcomed by many parties including some trade unionists. He suggested, for example, that there should be no upper limit on potential earnings. But although his ideas purported to bring fairness into organisations, his famous phrase 'a fair day's work for a fair day's pay' became highly controversial. He was nicknamed 'Speedy Taylor' and the press soon referred to him as the most hated man in America.

It had become clear that he had oversimplified both the work process and workers' motivations. He assumed it was possible to establish one best way of working, and that only this way would be 'scientific' and rational – but he was not a trained researcher and his measurement tests were later criticised. Furthermore, it is now accepted that not all employees are simply earnings maximisers. Too much task specialisation can easily lead to dull, alienating jobs and therefore excessive division of labour can be counter-productive. Taylor tended to forget that he was dealing with human beings and not with some inanimate resource. He also assumed that, as a manager, his perspective on work was automatically the correct one. His ideas centred on the formal structure of organisations and in particular on selected shop-floor workers. To assume that earnings and profit maximisation would be complementary and that managers and managed would co-operate was unrealistic.

However, Taylor's work did have an enormous influence on Organisation Theory. He started the traditional management school of writing that still continues its search for the best ways of doing things. Work study is still carried out today although its limitations are recognised. It is also too easy not to appreciate that many production workers do like piece-work, if wage rates are negotiated, as opposed to the alternative of a measured day rate based on time worked rather than output reached. Many workers feel that a direct reward to effort system is fair.

Fayol's Functions of Management

Fayol was a mining engineer who moved into general management in the early twentieth century. He is most famous for his definition of management which is still widely used today. Fayol looked at the sorts of activity which went on in a business organisation: he suggested that there were six areas.

1 Technical – production.
2 Commercial – buying and selling.
3 Financial – capital acquisition and use.
4 Security – protection of assets.
5 Accounting – cost and stock control.
6 Managerial – 'to manage is to forecast and plan, to organise, to command, to co-ordinate and to control.'

Later writers have added communication and motivation to this longstanding definition of managerial activity.

The historical development of organisation theory

Fayol's other main claim to fame is in offering General Principles of Management as fundamental maxims for organisational administration. Many of them now appear rather quaint, e.g. The Principle of Equity – the need for kindliness and justice in business. However, several of them were widely accepted and added to by other Classical writers and have become known as the 'Principles' of Organisation or of Management.

The Principles of Management

The Principles of Management, as put forward by Fayol and other Classical writers like Mooney and Urwick, were seen as recommendations for reaching maximum efficiency in the organisation. They were:

1 **The Principle of Objectives** The hierarchy should suit the aims of the organisation which must be consistent and have a unity of direction to ensure full co-ordination and co-operation.
2 **The Principle of Specialisation** Each job should be linked to one main function; employees should be formally grouped into sections, departments and divisions.
3 **The Scalar Principle** There should be clear lines of authority in the hierachy. The chains of command should be represented in an organisation chart (see page 13).
4 **The Principle of Unity of Command** Each employee should have only one superior to report to.
5 **The Delegation Principle (or the Principle of Correspondence)** Responsibility should always be commensurate with authority.
6 **The Principle of Definition** The degree of responsibility and authority for every position should be clearly specified, preferably in writing.
7 **The Principle of Span of Control** Limits should be set to the number of subordinates for each superior, four to six being the suggested optimum number.
8 **The Principle of Primary Task** Line functions should be distinct from advisory staff functions (see page 14).
9 **The Principle of Communication** The number of levels of authority in the hierarchy should be restricted to ease the flow of communication.
10 **The Principle of Exception** Management should only be concerned with non-routine decision making and should only be notified when results are off target.
11 **The Principle of Simplicity** The organisation should stay simple to stay effective.
12 **The Principle of Flexibility** The organisation should be able to adjust to change.

These were the main principles put forward by Fayol and other traditional management writers. Fayol advised that his principles be treated as guidelines only, but many saw them as a set of golden rules. In fact this remains their major weakness: they prescribe without clearly explaining how they can be easily followed in practice, and in fact they seldom are followed. In practice they are useful only if treated as management proverbs. Underlying many of the principles is the theme of a formal organisation structure, without which management would not be able to operate effectively. This structure is often called a hierarchy.

The Classical approach

The hierarchy and organisation charts

The word 'hierarchy' has been mentioned several times. It occurs constantly in Organisation Studies. The word derives from the Greek for 'sacred rulers' and today means a structure with grades or classes linked one above the other. Very few, if any, organisations do not have a hierarchy. Sometimes the grades are formally designated by job title linked to a letter or number as in the Army or Civil Service. In other instances the pecking order of personnel is not formally constituted, e.g. in a commune.

The Classical writers assumed that a hierarchy was inevitable and indeed many of their ideas were based around it. Although hierarchies vary tremendously in size (a case of an organisation with thirty-five levels has been recorded), they tend to average around six or seven levels. They are usually represented in model forms called *organisation charts*.

Four main types of formal structure are charted below. They are drawn in the common vertical format although charts may also be drawn horizontally or in the form of overlapping circles of responsibility. The lines on the charts represent the line of command and consequently the lines of formal communication. The outline shape is almost always that of a pyramid, and the fact of having one boss at the top and ever increasing numbers of subordinates below leads to the term the 'pyramid of power'.

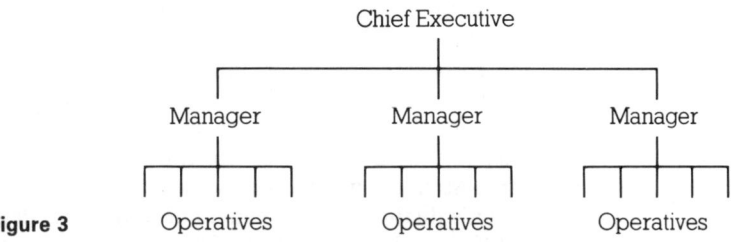

Figure 3

Line structure

The line structure is the fundamental basis of nearly every type of organisation design. It follows from a simple military analogy – in theory there is an unbroken line of delegated authority from the top of the hierarchy downwards. This embodies three of the Principles of Organisation previously mentioned: those of the Scalar Principle, Principle of Unity of Command and the Principle of Span of Control. The line structure is really relevant only for small organisations because, if adopted by an organisation with departments, it would mean that each department would be responsible for all activities such as staffing, purchasing and accounting. If this were so, the advantages of having separate specialist functions would be lost.

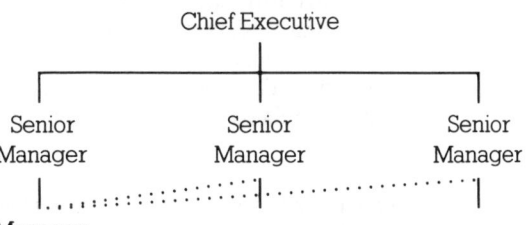

Figure 4

Functional structure

The functional structure was the first design to differ from the traditional line structure. It follows the idea of Taylor who recommended that a factory operative should report not to one, but to many foremen, each of whom would have specialist duties. The formal functional relationship is in effect a specialist role where there is responsibility for a particular activity. This occurs in many organisations today,

The historical development of organisation theory

but in the developed form of a line and staff structure which is shown in Figure 5. The problem with a pure functional design is that it leads to one person having many superiors of equal status and consequently a difficulty in allocating work priorities.

A modern example of the functional structure is evident in a commercial bank where a district manager reports to area directors. The directors are not only direct line managers *per se*, but also have authority over particular banking activities for all the districts in their areas. Sometimes, to avoid confusion, these functional relationships are represented by a dotted line as in Figure 4.

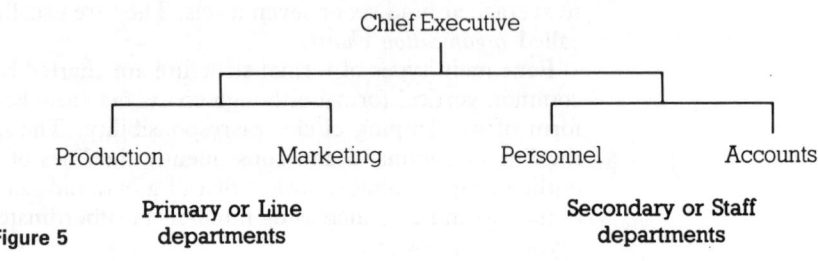

Figure 5

Line and staff

The words 'line' and 'staff' in this context are both used slightly unusually. The two departments of Production and Marketing are deemed directly responsible for meeting corporate objectives and they are consequently termed primary or line departments. The other departments are seen as advisory and assisting departments to the line ones and are called secondary or staff departments. Their authority is similar to that of the functional structure in that, for example, the Personnel Manager would deal with recruitment for all the organisation's departments. This distinction between a line and a staff department is still used, but the status differential implied in the titles is not very meaningful today, because of the interdependence of all departments.

It should be stressed that the word 'staff' is *not* used here to refer to all employees or only to non-manual workers in the organisation. Nor is it used as in 'staff relationship'. It has already been explained that a line relationship is the authority relationship between superior and subordinates. A staff relationship, the third use of the word 'staff', relates to specialist individuals, who service and advise line managers but who have no personal authority themselves. These advisers are sometimes called Personal Assistants although this term has been lately misused to overinflate the role of a secretary to a senior manager. Many organisations fail to recognise the fact that staff relationships often involve functional authority, and this inevitably causes problems of communication and control. For example, a Marketing Assistant to a Marketing Manager might take a vicarious decision in his absence concerning a customer credit problem that the Accounts section is querying. This further complicates the issue and underlines the fact that all non-line relationships are ambiguous.

Matrix structure

The matrix structure was imported from America in the 1960s and was very popular with consumer goods marketing firms. The job of Product Brand Manager was created for someone who was to be responsible for only one particular product (or product range). This person had to liaise with the conventional line and staff departments for all matters concerning that product. The chart overleaf (Figure 6) shows why the word 'matrix' is used, because the structure resembles a mathematical matrix of rows and columns. The title Project Manager or Small Project Group is more commonly used today, and this structure is typical of

Figure 6

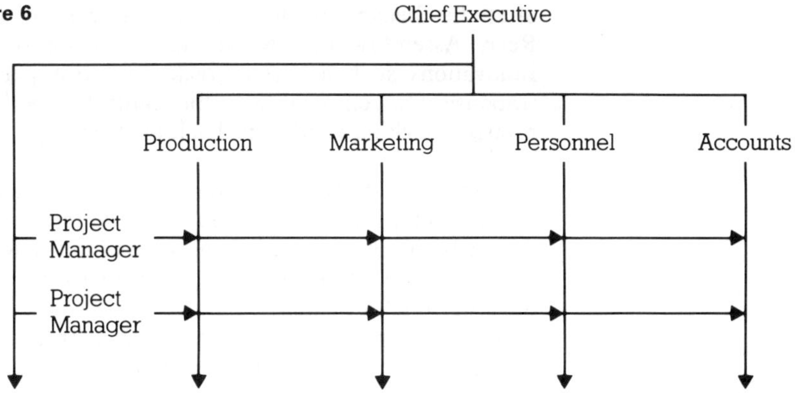

```
                           Chief Executive
         ┌─────────────┬──────────┬──────────┬──────────┐
                   Production  Marketing  Personnel  Accounts
  Project
  Manager ────────────▶─────────▶─────────▶─────────▶
  Project
  Manager ────────────▶─────────▶─────────▶─────────▶
                       ▼          ▼          ▼          ▼
```

engineering and Research and Development organisations. There is an organisational problem of co-ordinating Project Managers and ensuring that each co-operates with the conventional departments.

Evaluation

Organisation charts can be useful for reference and training within the organisation. The construction of the chart is in itself a useful exercise to clarify existing structures and perhaps to question the status quo. However, an undue emphasis on such charts in the day-to-day running of the organisation can cause problems. The charts do not show all levels of authority, the complete content of job descriptions or the informal relationships which might exist. They are edited, static and often out of date. Constant reference to them may create inflexible attitudes towards the operation of the organisation.

2.2 The Human Relations approach

The organisation as viewed by the Classical writers consists of a formal structure of job positions controlled by a management hierarchy, forming what is known as a pyramid of power. This pyramid of power is basically what the organisation chart represents. A modern reviewer of organisation theory, Perrow, has characterised the features of this type of organisation as having centralised authority, clear lines of authority, high degrees of specialisation, clear distinctions between line and staff departments, and rules and regulations. But what these Classical writers failed to take into account was that organisations consist of people who are not always rational and rule-abiding perfectionists.

In the 1920s a movement in the UK led by J. Myers looked at two aspects of manual factory work; the fatigue caused by repetition and the boredom caused by monotony. The approach subsequently developed, called 'Human factor industrial psychology', suggested that the worker was a far more complex individual than the Classical writers had assumed.

This view was supported by a series of studies at the Hawthorne plant of the Western Electric Company.

The Hawthorne studies

In 1924 company engineers conducting some Taylor-inspired efficiency studies found an anomaly in workers' behaviour: output increased when lighting levels were increased *and* when they were reduced back to their original level.

Social scientists from Harvard University were called in and a three-phase series of studies began. In the first phase a group of female operatives working in the Relay Assembly Test Room had their physical working conditions changed. Innovations such as meal breaks and rest periods led to higher output. The response was comparable to the lighting experiments: when the twelfth change brought working conditions back to their original state output reached its highest level.

In the second phase an extensive interviewing programme covering over twenty thousand employees was conducted. The interviewers were trained to listen rather than ask specific structured questions, and it was found that many respondents welcomed the opportunity to give vent to their pent-up frustrations concerning their personal situation.

In phase three the research moved away from the clinical counselling atmosphere of the interviewing programme and back to the laboratory methodology of the Test Room research. This time a group of male operatives in the Bank Wiring Observation Room were studied. It was found that these workers had formed informal sub-groups and more importantly, they informally acknowledged and worked towards their concept of what constituted a fair day's work. This level of efficiency was at variance with the formal targets set by their management.

These puzzling results prompted a fundamental questioning of Classical organisation theory. The conclusions drawn have had a strong influence on the understanding of work behaviour, despite subsequent criticisms of the original research methods used.

One significant finding became known as the 'Hawthorne effect'. In the words of Elton Mayo, the most famous writer associated with the studies: 'Sometimes the mere presence of investigators and the interest they have shown in employees' work has caused increases in output.' This explains the odd results obtained in the original lighting experiments.

What was of more relevance to organisation theory was the published ideas of two of the researchers, Roethlisberger and Dickson, which were at variance with the views of the Classical writers and especially those of Taylor. They suggested that the production workers' behaviour was not affected by incentive wage rates, the physical conditions or the type of supervision, but by workers' relationships with their work colleagues. The role each worker had in his or her informal friendship groups was seen by the researchers as a source of social need-fulfilment, a compensating factor for the inadequate lifestyles the workers led outside work. It seemed that the main motivator was social need, and consequently interpersonal relationships were the main determinant of behaviour. Thus the significance of the informal structure which exists in every organisation was isolated and underlined.

Recommendations of the early Human Relations writers

If it was true that an employee was most influenced by the people he or she worked with, this could be translated into better organisational practices. Advice was given to managers that they should adopt a 'Human Relations' style of supervision. Managers were trained in social skills and it was hoped that conflict would disappear in the harmonious context of participation. It was suggested that if the informal group could be as important as, or more important, than formal authority, then why not try and combine the two? The more involved the worker could be, greater the motivation could be to work harder. Communication was the key element, and writers urged the adoption of more open channels of communication up the hierarchy. In practical terms this led to more suggestion schemes, the introduction of joint consultative committees and the use of house magazines and works journals. An attempt was made to create a happy family atmosphere through the increase of welfare schemes and sports and recreational facilities. A democratic style of leadership was recommended to go along with this new package.

The Human Relations approach

The Neo-Human Relations approach

The ideas of these early writers led to an increasing awareness of the need to understand the psychological make-up of employees, and in the 1950s and 1960s several American writers published work which developed this theme. Their ideas centred around 'the individual at work', and are explored in greater depth in Part B. Major names include McGregor, whose classifications of management attitudes are discussed on page 28; Likert, who recommended a more open, less bureaucratic organisation structure based on linked workgroups; Argyris, who used the idea of assimilating the employee's personality into organisational goal-setting and achieving; Herzberg, who constructed a 'two factor' theory of motivation (see p. 29); and Maslow, who offered a model of ascending human motivating factors which he called a 'hierarchy of needs'.

The impact of these later Human Relations writers on organisations was the introduction of schemes for job enlargement, job rotation and general attempts to enrich the workload of individuals. Managers were given training in the necessity to be sensitive to the needs of others. Emphasis had switched from centring on the behaviour of the work group to that of the individual.

Evaluation of the Human Relations approach

The Human Relations approach offered a refreshing alternative to the existing orthodoxy, and made an important contribution in pointing out the complexities of the work situation and the importance of people and their motivation within it. However, in some way it was an over-reaction to the simple specifications of Taylorism. Mayo, for example, tended to overstate his case in his enthusiasm for discovering the informal organisation and in asserting that the 'logic of sentiment' is more important than the 'logic of cost'.

One fundamental assumption of the Human Relations approach has been particularly criticised, and that is that individuals' needs can be identified and satisfied at work. The organisation is not a substitute for the community and cannot accommodate all the factors influencing the external environment. There was also an underlying pro-management bias in the new approach; ideas were put forward on how to 'manipulate' the worker to work harder. If the increased openness between managers and managed was real and not token, it was welcome, but it would never eliminate all conflict.

However, later writers were sensitive to further variables and were perhaps less pro-management in their bias. The Human Relations approach had had a profound and lasting influence on organisation theory and management theory and practice.

Self-test questions

1 Would you like to be paid on a piece-rate system? Would your feelings differ if you were part of a work team?

2 Can you think of occasions where simple repetitive work is enjoyable?

3 Fayol's terminology for organisational activities is not all used today: can you identify the modern departmental names given for each of his six areas?

4 Draw an organisation chart for your own organisation i.e. school, college, company, or club. If there is a chart already, make comparisons and note any differences. If no such chart exists what conclusions can be drawn?

5 Can you identify any staff relationships in your organisation which also carry functional authority?

6 Which of the Principles of Management do you think are essential prerequisites to business efficiency? Why are they?

7 How important is the Hawthorne effect when conducting social research?

8 What external factors can influence an employee's work efficiency?

3 More recent contributions to organisation theory

- More recent developments in organisation theory view the organisation as a system with integrative parts that process inputs into outputs.
- The Systems approach has been criticised for its lack of detailed analysis of employee behaviour which is covered by an alternative perspective called the Action approach.
- There are more minor theories including the Decision-Making approach and Contingency theory.

Chapter 2 considered two broad approaches that still have a considerable influence on organisation theory: the Classical and Human Relations approaches which gave importance to formal and informal organisational structure respectively. However, the study area is constantly evolving and several new perspectives have been put forward, the most significant alternative approaches being the Systems approach and the Action approach.

3.1 The Systems approach

The origins of the Systems approach can be traced to two sources. The first is a sociological idea that society makes man (rather than man makes society). This is called Structural-Functionalism; it takes organisations as systems and attempts to explain their structure in terms of their contribution, i.e. the functions they fulfill, in maintaining society.

The second source has been termed the Socio-Technical System approach. It can best be represented by research done by two English researchers, Woodward and Trist.

Woodward

Woodward studied over 100 manufacturing firms in Essex. She categorised them by their production processes – unit, batch/mass and process technologies (see Chapter 18 on Production). She concluded that any of the successful firms in each category tended to show the same structural characteristics. For example, in unit and process technologies it appeared that there was more participative management and less stress on formal procedures whereas in mass production the ideas of the Classical approach writers were found.

This research suggested that the factor that determined an organisation's structure, and therefore employee behaviour, was its technical system.

The Systems approach

Trist

Trist's work is a stronger influence on the Systems approach. He studied the results of mechanisation in the Durham coalfields. The Coal Board had brought in mechanical coal-cutting equipment and had rearranged the miners into large shift gangs, thereby breaking up the previous small groups of workers. The new method, called 'Conventional Longwall Method' after the fact that a long stretch of coal seam was cut, relied on three independent shifts. In theory, the new method should have brought significant increases in productivity, but in practice, the miners were dissatisfied; absenteesim rose and production levels fell. Trist recommended that the sharp division between work shifts should be dropped and the level of supervision reduced. This replacement 'Composite Longwall Method' led to greater productivity.

Trist argued that it was wrong to consider technical efficiency in isolation, but behavioural factors should be included too. He coined the phrase 'a socio-technical system' to stress the interdependence of the two areas in organisations.

The systems concept

Both writers had identified the important interplay between people's behaviour and work processes and recognised that it was a mistake to consider either alone. This led to the idea that the organisation should be seen as a system made up of interrelated, interdependent component parts or sub-systems. Expressed in model terms, there are several basic components to the system:

A The primary task system

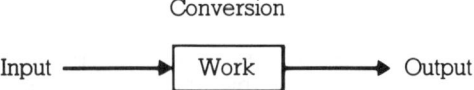

which converts resources from and to the external environment.

B The secondary system

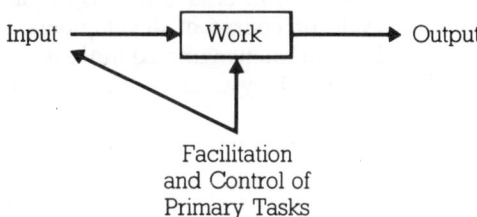

which adds to **A** the provision and control of resources.

C The managing system

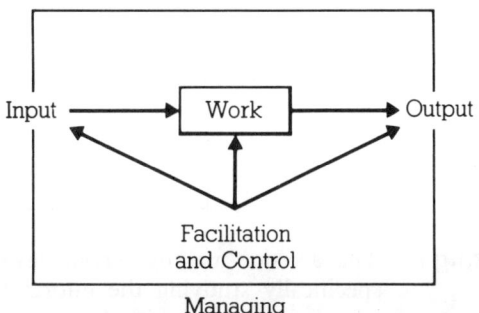

which determines and co-ordinates the primary and secondary systems.

19

More recent contributions to organisation theory

Each system has its own sub-system. For example, the 'Work' box above could be broken down into sub-systems, sub-sub-systems and so on to the ultimate stages of a work process such as having an in-tray and an out-tray. Each sub-system has its own inputs from and outputs to other sub-systems. To view the organisation in the traditional departmental way is seen as inadequate. The key to successful organisation is to identify the intersystem relationships and to try to provide adequate information flows. Rather than use an organisation chart, the Systems approach would show a network of systems, within each of which the following variables interact:

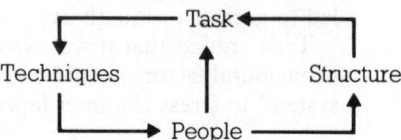

The employee has a task to perform, using various work methods (technology can refer to procedures as well as equipment) within a formal structure. This constitutes the organisation's internal environment. It is referred to as a socio-technical system. When a business organisation is studied it is a socio-*economic*-technical system. When just the organisation's internal environment is considered it constitutes a *closed* system. When, however, account is also taken of the influence of external factors over which the organisation has no direct control, then it constitutes an *open* system.

The overriding emphasis of the Systems approach is the idea that any system is more than the sum of its parts (or sub-systems). Applied to organisations it was suggested that they have a kind of systematic unity characteristic of what are literally biological organisms. As an organism is different from a mechanism or a simple aggregate, its parts or sub-systems are dependent for their nature and existence on the whole. This implies that organisations have sub-systems that are unified by internal relationships and that the whole system has a characteristic life cycle or course of development that attempts to maintain a homeostatic equilibrium in changing conditions. This disposition applies within a sub-system, between sub-systems and, more importantly, between the system and its boundary with its external environment. Each sub-system operates to maintain this state of homeostasis within its socio-technical and economic parameters.

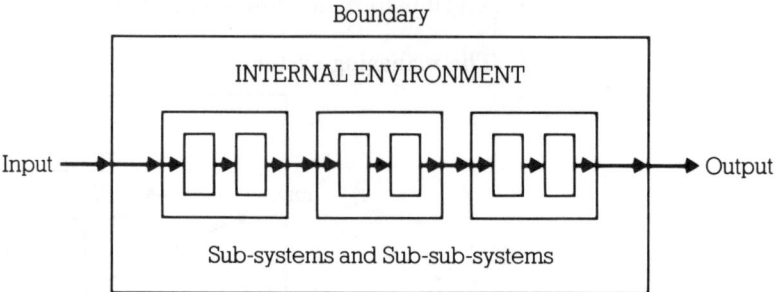

The decision-making school

The decision-making school developed one aspect of the Systems approach by specifically studying the information flows between the sub-systems. This approach, associated with American writers such as Cyert and March, concentrates on the inputs and outputs to decision-making centres in the organisation. Many of the ideas are similar to the work of a computer systems analyst, who considers work processes and information flows, disregarding conventional departmental boundaries. The importance of people's behaviour at work is not ignored, but the emphasis moves towards a more mathematical analysis.

This has led to a set of business problem-solving techniques collectively referred to as Operations Research or the Management Sciences – the latter term an ironic echo of Taylor's Scientific Management.

3.2 The Action approach – an alternative view

The Action or Social Action approach rejects the Systems concept, and concentrates much more on the individuality of the employee. Gouldner suggested that the background of the individual was the strongest determinant of his behaviour at work. This was extended by the work of Silverman who, in an approach known as Phenomenological Actionalism, suggested that any event which occurs in an organisation is uniquely defined by the individual through his personal perception. How the individual defines the situation, and gives a meaning to it, will be particular and based on experiences both prior to and during work. This approach gives a note of caution to management: it is dangerous and perhaps impossible to make any generalised predictive comments about workplace behaviour. It rejects as irrelevant any conventional demarcation between the formal and informal structures of the organisation. It implies that the employee is not a passive individual, but one who will interpret the work environment in the context of a wider social environment in his or her own terms. Research evidence produced by Goldthorpe and Lockwood among carworkers in Luton supported this view and gave warning that Taylor's idea should not be easily discounted. A production worker could 'use' work purely as an instrument to earn money and may not consciously seek any further fulfillment from work. The Action approaches, therefore, put the emphasis more on the individual than the organisation as such.

3.3 The Contingency approach

The Contingency writers hold a view that is more closely linked to the Systems view. They accept that in all organisations there will be inevitable conflict over goals arising from internal and external factors. This school of thought suggests that few specific recommendations can be made as to how an organisation can best be designed and its activities co-ordinated because this depends on the circumstances. One possibility is to compare organisations and to draw conclusions as to how they cope with specific situations. Burns and Stalker modelled two types of organisation for comparison: the mechanistic and organistic. The mechanistic type features the characteristics of Weber's bureaucratic model. It is best suited to specialised tasks in stable market conditions which lend themselves to routine operations. Its opposite, the organistic or organic model, is run by people more conscious of the systems nature of activities. There is a continual modification of tasks and associated job roles. Information and advice is exchanged rather than the usual giving and receiving of orders. This type adapts to change because it is more flexible and can cope with unstable market conditions.

Similar work was done by Lawrence and Lorsch who suggested that the successful organisation is the type which adapts its structure to the situation. They suggest that where there are more stable economic environments, the more classicial structure is appropriate.

More recent contributions to organisation theory

Evaluation

Chapters 2 and 3 have traced the ideas of some of the more famous writers in organisational theory. The Classical approach concentrated on how best to manage the formal activities in a hierarchy designed for specialisation. The Human Relations approach reacted to this and introduced the concept of the informal organisation. Employees were treated less as a resource than as thinking and feeling individuals. Job enlargement rather than job specialisation, consultation rather than control, were the resulting recommendations. Recent theories, seeing the organisation as a system, have yet to receive as wide a support as the other approaches have done (and still do to a significant extent). The early Systems writers, like Trist and Woodward, have been criticised for dwelling too much on the closed system, and for being preoccupied with the influence of technology. Their lack of recognition of important outside factors such as the local community, class background and trade union activity led others to concentrate more on the individual's concept of reality. This had the effect of moving away from the tendency to see things only from the managers' point of view.

The Systems approach models organisations as having inputs and outputs which are basically commercial, such as products and services: the Action approach adopts a different paradigm and suggests that inputs and outputs can be analysed at the level of individual meanings. The former is predictive in that it suggests the likely effect on organisations which may be associated with changes in technology or in the market. The latter does not guarantee any uniform response to organisational structure, management style etc. and therefore describes the process, and not necessarily the content, of any activity.

The Systems approach and the Action approach are not therefore mutually exclusive. The former, despite the limitations highlighted by the latter, is still a core perspective in organisation theory. Although it plays down political and status issues and glosses over individual differences, it is still a valid and useful social construct. Just as there is no single ideal structure for all organisations, so there is no single ideal approach to organisation theory. The influence of each idea in these various approaches has had its effect on management practice, as many people at work can appreciate. As a basis for trying to understand why and how people in organisations behave as they do, they offer no easy answers but at least they offer some clues.

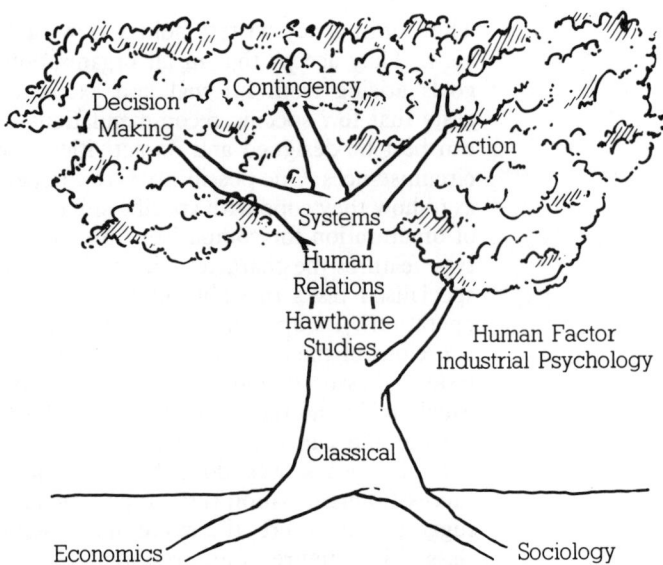

Figure 7
Tree of Knowledge of organisation studies

The Contingency approach

Self-test questions

1 In your own organisation what are the main factors that have influenced the pattern of work?

2 What are the inputs and outputs of the following?
   a a commercial bank
   b a polytechnic
   c a car factory
   d a night club

3 How valid is it to make a distinction between the formal and informal structures of organisations?

4 Why do individuals not share the same interpretations of their working environments?

5 Is your organisation mechanistic or organic? What evidence is there to support your choice?

6 If you had to advise management trainees, what areas of management theory would you strongly recommend them to study?

Chronological bibliography of the main writers on organisation theory

Classical
1916 Fayol: *Administration Industrielle et Générale* (translated 1947)
1947 Urwick: *The Elements of Administration*. Pitman
1947 Taylor: *Scientific Management*. Harper and Row (collected works)
1957 Brech: *Organization: the Framework of Management*. Longman

Human Relations
1938 Barnard: *The Functions of the Executive*. Harvard University Press
1939 Lewin, Lippitt and White: 'Patterns of Aggressive Behaviour in Experimentally Created Social Climates'. *Journal of Social Psychology*.
1948 Argyris: *Personality and Organisation*. Chapman and Hall
1949 Mayo: *The Social Problems of an Industrial Civilization*. Routledge
1949 Roethlisberger and Dickson: *Management and the Worker*. Harvard University Press
1954 Maslow: *Motivation and Personality*. Harper and Row
1960 Argyris: *The Impact of the Formal Organisation upon the Individual*. Tavistock
1960 McGregor: *The Human Side of Enterprise*. McGraw-Hill
1961 Likert: *The Principle of Supportive Relationships*. McGraw-Hill
1966 Herzberg: *Work and the Nature of Man*. World Publishing Co.

Systems
1951 Trist and Bamforth: *Some Social and Psychological consequences of the Longwall Method of coal getting*. Human Relations No 4
1954 Gouldner: *Patterns of Industrial Bureaucracy*. Free Press
1958 Woodward: *Management and Technology*. HMSO
1961 Burns and Stalker: *The Management of Innovation*. Tavistock
1963 Cyert and March: *A Behavioural Theory of the Firm*. Prentice-Hall
1967 Lawrence and Lorsch: *Organisation and Environment*. Harvard University Press
1970 Silverman: *The Theory of Organisations*. Heinemann

General texts
1978 Rose: *Industrial Behaviour: theoretical developments since Taylor*. Penguin
1980 Watson: *Sociology, Work and Industry*. Routledge & Kegan Paul

PART B

Why do people work? What determines how much energy, effort and time they are prepared to invest in their working lives? Do they work for money alone or is there something more which working people value as outputs or rewards for their work?

If we can establish answers to these questions, and explore people's motives and priorities; if we can say what the effect, if any, the nature of the work itself, the way it is organised, payment systems, working conditions, styles of management and other factors may have, then we are some way to developing practical answers to problems of employee dissatisfaction. We are also further forward in improving productivity and workplace efficiency.

In this Part, we begin with an evaluation of major, early contributions to motivation theory, most of which link closely to early organisation theories, and move on to consider more recent ideas. We look at motivation and the problems of motivation theory, and we look at groups – an important aspect of work organisation in virtually all organisations. Building effective groups requires an understanding of many factors, such as principles of task and work organisation, and an understanding of motivation theory and its different applications. A third, key, variable in group effectiveness is leadership. We look at leadership, the different approaches to the difficult task of leadership in modern organisations and their apparent effects on levels of motivation, involvement, and productivity.

Finally, we look at role theory, exploring the formal and informal expectations that others have of people occupying social or organisational positions. Much stress and conflict at work can be avoided by a proper understanding of role theory, and by dealing with the potential problems inherent in the allocation of specific and unspecific responsibilities to individuals in an organisation hierarchy, role theory allows us to integrate our ideas on job and work structuring, groups, leadership and motivation.

4 Motivation and behaviour at work

- Taylor's ideas on motivation tended to be based on the extrinsic motivating force of money, but this was questioned by the Human Relations writers who considered social pressure to be important.
- Many writers on motivation over-generalise about factors that act as motivators and forget that individuals are uniquely different.

When considering people's motives at work, it is usual to begin with an analysis and evaluation of the main theoretical contributions to the subject area. This chapter and the one which follows will also adopt this approach. It will not however, be with the aim of deciding which is 'right' or best, but in an attempt to discover what can be learned from each. What is sought is an insight into what makes people invest their time and energies in particular ways, and what reasons lie behind their choices. What this chapter does *not* offer is any simple, 'magic key' which will unleash people's energies at work in pursuit of established organisational goals. If there were one, there is no question that it would have been used!

4.1 Why study motivation?

Our reasons here are several. Firstly, when people's motives and the 'origins' of those motives are understood, their behaviour, which may often puzzle the casual observer, is itself more easily understood. This understanding may have several applications. It may be used in an attempt to increase the commitment which people have to performing certain tasks and to completing them successfully – though as we have cautioned there is no simple solution here; what may have an effect on one person may have none on another, or may be ineffective in a different situation or at a different time. Nonetheless, any achievements in this direction will profit, at least potentially, all of the organisation's 'interest groups', including the employees themselves.

Secondly, if the factors and conditions which promote increased motivation can be identified, it may be possible to design jobs and to structure organisations in such a way that people can derive greater satisfaction from their experience of work.

Finally, the management and control of people at work may generate less conflict, and prove more rewarding for all concerned, where those in leadership positions are sensitive to the expectations and aspirations of the individuals and groups they manage, and where steps are taken to accommodate these. These, however, are only possible benefits. They are by no means the guaranteed outcome of any planned organisational changes. As we have said, changes that appear to be effective in one situation may be less effective or even damaging in another, or may be beneficial only to some of the individuals or groups they are aimed at.

4.2 Taylor and the concept of 'economic man'

> It is impossible, through any long period of time, to get workmen to work much harder than the average men around them, unless they are assured a large and permanent increase in their pay.

So wrote F. W. Taylor whose approach to the design and organisation of work we have already considered (see p. 10). For Taylor, money was the prime motivator. It was his conviction that when financial rewards are made dependent upon work output the result will be maximum performance from each individual. This assumption remains the basis of piece-rate payments systems today.

Taylor believed in the basic economic rationality of man: that people would assess the potential economic benefit to themselves of particular courses of action and adopt the most favourable. This, he argued, was the logic underlying workers' desire to unionise, and their workgroup restrictions on output. Both, he suggested, arise out of a desire to ensure job and/or financial security.

The Scientific Management package prescribes techniques both for the design and management of work and for the design of payment systems. Adherence to the 'laws' of Scientific Management would result first in increased efficiency and profitability for the firm. This in turn would allow the payment of higher than average wages. At the same time, job redesign, because of a 'scientifically' derived pace and method of working, would permit more prolonged and consistent effort from the workers. This would benefit them in the form of increased earnings, and would contribute too to the success of the firm.

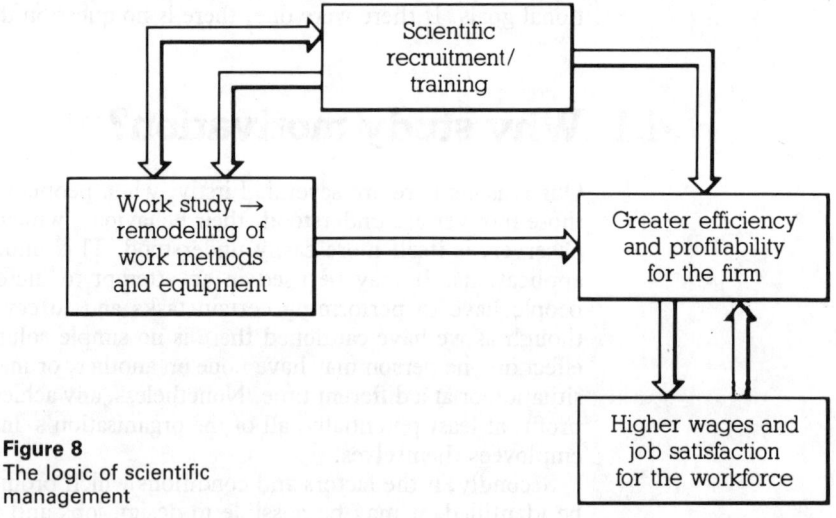

Figure 8
The logic of scientific management

The following extract from his writing gives the flavour of Taylor's approach:

> The development of a science ... involves the establishment of many rules, laws and formulae which replace the judgement of the individual workman....
>
> The work of every workman is planned out fully by the management at least one day in advance, and each man receives in most cases complete written instructions, describing in detail the task which he is to accomplish, as well as the means to be used in doing the work. This task specifies not only what is to be done but how it is to be done and the exact time allowed for doing it....

The science is developed through a comparatively simple analysis and time study of the movements required by the workman to do some small part of his work, and this study is usually made by a man equipped merely with a stop-watch and a properly ruled notebook. Hundreds of these time study men are now engaged in developing elementary scientific knowledge where before existed only rule of thumb.

The general steps ... are as follows;

Find say ten to fifteen different men (preferably in as many separate establishments and different parts of the country) who are especially skilful in doing the particular work to be analysed.

Study the exact series of elementary operations or motions which each of these men uses in doing the work as well as the implements each man uses.

Study with a stop-watch the time required to make each of these elementary movements and then select the quickest way of doing each element of the work.

Eliminate all false movements, slow movements and useless movements.

After doing away with all unnecessary movements collect into one series the quickest and best movements as well as the best implements.

This best method becomes standard, to be taught first to the teachers (or functional foremen) and by them to every workman in the establishment until it is superseded by a quicker or better series of movements.

(In D. S. Pugh (ed.) *Organisation Theory*, Penguin 1971.)

Taylor was genuinely seeking an industrial partnership between management and workers. He was concerned that their preoccupation should change from arguing over the relative distribution of profits to one of mutual commitment to increasing them. In fact he was so convinced of the mutual benefits to be gained from the adoption of Scientific Management principles that he predicted the withering away of trade unionism and of workers' restrictive practices when they realised its superiority in safeguarding and enhancing their economic situation.

The main criticism of Taylor's ideas is that they constitute a 'single factor' explanation which takes no account of other influences on behaviour, or of variance between people and situations. He had a simplistic and generalised view of 'the worker', and he assumed a totally instrumental orientation towards work. He did not consider it germane that the average worker may derive some satisfaction from the act of work itself, or from association with others at the workplace.

In fact, Scientific Management may be a largely self-fulfilling package. If many people appear to be preoccupied with money rewards for work, it may well be partly because the design of jobs and structuring of work (especially where the principles of Scientific Management have been adopted) have made work processes so standardised and restrictive that money represents the only reward or satisfaction possible. There remain few opportunities, under such a system, for non-financial satisfactions to be experienced or pursued. This was a criticism developed by later writers.

4.3 Economic man becomes social man

Taylor's assumptions were undermined by the Hawthorne studies, which showed that the rational, economic man stereotype did not exist. Two important conclusions were reached; that physical influences and economic rewards were not as significant as was previously assumed, and that peoples' social needs, especially in relation to the informal workgroup, were a main determinant of their behaviour. 'Social man' had taken over from 'economic man'.

The Human Relations approach was developed especially by Elton Mayo. Mayo agreed with Taylor that conflict at work was unnecessary, but for a different reason. He argued that if managers would no longer treat their employees as insensitive factors of production and if they would encourage co-operation and consultation, albeit from a management point of view, all would be well. Taylor had suggested that an efficient organisation would create happy employees; Mayo suggested that happy employees would create an efficient organisation. Both approaches, however, assumed that employee satisfaction was correlated to efficiency.

Maslow and self-actualising man

Later writers refined and developed Mayo's Human Relations approach. In 1943 Maslow, an organisational psychologist, offered a universal formula to describe the motivating factors that influence behaviour, a 'hierarchy of relative prepotency'. This suggests that everyone has various areas of need. These needs exist on an ascending scale, with each level assuming importance and motivating the individual once the need below has been satisfied. A satisfied need is not, therefore, a motivator.

The plausibility of the hierarchy is immediately apparent: at the base are physiological needs such as hunger, thirst and sex. These then progress to safety needs relating to one's reaction to the threat of danger. Above the safety needs is the need for love in the sense of affection and the need to 'belong'. These in turn, once met, are replaced by another level – that of the need for esteem such as the desire for self-respect and prestige. At the top of the hierarchy is the ultimate motivator – the need for the individual to fulfil his/her potential. This was termed 'self-actualisation'.

Maslow acknowledged the shortcomings of the hierarchy (such as the neglect of the consideration of habit, cultural influences and interpersonal relationships) but the point he emphasised was that once a need was satisfied, it was no longer a motivator.

Whilst accepting its value as a model, critics have argued that the hierarchy is intuitive and cannot be satisfactorily applied or measured in any work context. For example how would a Personnel Manager use the hierarchy to sort out a problem of mass absenteeism in a factory every Monday morning?

McGregor and 'The task of management'

McGregor reworked the hierarchy and used it to highlight what was wrong with the traditional management theorists' assumptions.

> The fact that management has provided for ... physiological and safety needs has shifted the motivational emphasis to the egoistic needs. Unless there are opportunities *at work* to satisfy these higher level needs, people will be deprived; and their behaviour will reflect this deprivation. Under such conditions, if management continues to focus its attention on physiological needs, its efforts are bound to be ineffective.

The traditional management view emphasises the need for strict managerial direction and control of employees. McGregor labelled it Theory X. It assumes that people naturally dislike work and because of this must be constantly coerced and threatened in order to carry out their tasks. At the same time, people desire only security, are not ambitious and will avoid responsibility. Theory X was the expression of Taylorism; treat employees as irresponsible children needing constant supervision and employ the 'carrot and stick approach' in dealing with them.

The alternative which McGregor offered was termed Theory Y. It was designed to lead to an integration of individual and organisational goals. Theory Y suggests that work itself is as natural as rest or play. People will exercise self-direction in meeting any objectives to which they are committed. They are capable of high levels of creativity, and will accept and even seek responsibility. Under traditional management systems however, the opportunity does not exist for these to be exercised. The result of this frustration is often a preoccupation with money rewards. McGregor's message was clear. It was an 'invitation to innovation'. Managers should discover and develop the potential in all their employees.

> The essential task of management is to arrange organisational conditions and methods of operation so that people can achieve their own objectives best by directing their own efforts toward organisational objectives.

Job enlargement, participatory leadership styles and Management by Objectives schemes should ensure that the individual's needs and the organisation's needs were constructively integrated.

Argyris: Individual development and organisation design

In similar vein to McGregor, Argyris's concern was the conflict which he saw as arising between the demands of formal, efficiency-seeking organisations and the needs of the individuals working within them.

He reasoned that in developing from childhood to adulthood we gradually become less passive, and at the same time, more responsible and independent. We develop more serious interests and are encouraged to pursue an improvement in our social position.

The typical, formal organisation, suggests Argyris, frustrates this progression – most especially at the lowest levels of organisational hierarchies where individual autonomy and responsibility are least. In such positions, where the nature of the work and work situation prevent self-actualisation, people become frustrated, and high labour turnover, absenteeism and a preoccupation with financial rewards result. The managerial response to this situation is likely to be that they become more autocratic and impose stricter controls than before, thus perpetuating feelings of psychological failure amongst their subordinates.

To remedy this situation, Argyris suggests.

1 The enlargement of jobs, horizontally and vertically, thereby increasing individual responsibility and control. Horizontal loading of jobs would involve building on a greater variety of tasks at the same level of complexity whilst vertical loading would build in work of a more complex and responsible nature.
2 An emphasis on more honest and open interpersonal relationships on the part of managers.
3 Increased participation in the decision-making process and an abandonment of unthinking adherence to the principles of formal, 'rational' organisation.

Herzberg's 'Two factor' theory of motivation

Comparable in many respects to the work of McGregor and Argyris and linking closely with Maslow's ideas is the 'Two factor' theory of motivation developed by Herzberg. The initial evidence for his theory came from interviews with two hundred white Pittsburgh engineers and accountants. He asked them to recall times when they felt particularly good or exceptionally bad about their jobs. The results were examined and the factors which subjects believed to be responsible for these feelings were recorded. What emerged is interesting for one main reason.

In the past it had always been assumed that the factor(s) causing job satisfaction would, by their absence, lead to job dissatisfaction. In other words for Taylor, when the money wage paid was relatively high, workers would necessarily be satisfied. When money rewards for work were felt to be low then dissatisfaction would result. Similarly, from a Human Relations point of view, when social and personal development needs were met, job satisfaction would result. When these were frustrated, then individuals would experience job dissatisfaction.

Herzberg's results suggested, however, that a different relationship exists between job satisfaction and job dissatisfaction. From the results of his interviews, he concluded that each state is caused by an entirely separate set of factors.

The first set, which were apparently major determinants of job satisfaction, Herzberg called 'motivators'. They were:

Achievement
Recognition
Work itself
Responsibility
Advancement

The second set, determinant of job dissatisfaction, were termed 'hygiene factors'. They were found principally to be:

Working conditions
Company policy and administration
Interpersonal relations
Supervision
Salary

On the basis of these results Herzberg concluded that job satisfaction and dissatisfaction were separate dimensions of the human condition. Absence of 'motivators' would not cause job dissatisfaction, nor would improvements in 'hygiene factors' result in job satisfaction. Instead, each state is caused by its own set of factors.

The management task, argued Herzberg, is to remedy and prevent job dissatisfaction through improvements in the 'hygiene factors', usefully referred to as affecting the *context* of the job (i.e. the environment) and to manipulate the 'motivators', relating to the job *content*, in order to increase job satisfaction. Thus to allow the 'motivator' to be at all effective a state of 'minimum hygiene', i.e. a reasonable standard of context factors, must exist in an organisation.

Evaluation

In general terms, the work of Argyris, although rather more cautious, is subject to many of the same criticisms as McGregor's. Like McGregor, Argyris's is to an extent a generalised view of man. People at work are seen as responding in the same ways to the same set of stimuli. Even Herzberg's apparently more flexible explanation of what motivates people is deficient in the same way. Implicit in each theory is the assumption of a basic homogeneity or 'sameness' of individuals. As a result, each is quite clearly, like its predecessors, inadequate when it comes to explaining why different individuals in the same jobs and work context will respond differently in terms of the energy they invest in their work and why they may derive different satisfaction from it.

A look at more specific criticisms of Herzberg's theory highlights the dangers of generalising about people and of predicting how they will respond in any given set of circumstances. The way in which 'motivators' and 'hygiene factors' are generally presented, in short outline reviews, suggests that the results were more clear-cut than they in fact were. In Herzberg's original study, there was merely a *tendency* for 'motivators' to be associated with job satisfaction and for 'hygiene factors' to be linked with job dissatisfaction. Certainly, there was not the clear polarisation of factors suggested by so many diagrammatic representations of the findings.

Furthermore the methodology used by Herzberg is suspect in several respects. First, the sample originally chosen is scarely a representative cross-section of working people. In generalising from his results, it is argued that Herzberg ignored possible occupational, class and cultural variations in people's motivation at work and in factors contributing to their satisfaction or dissatisfaction with their work situations.

Secondly, it has been suggested that, given the nature of Herzberg's two sets of determinant factors, it is only natural for people to 'blame' factors largely beyond their control (the 'hygiene factors') for their dissatisfactions and to accredit the times they have felt particularly good to their own efforts on the job.

Thirdly, it has been argued that, given the nature of the research sample, interviewees felt that in their particular occupations and social position they were *expected* to be more concerned with job interest, advancement and responsibility than with material and extrinsic rewards to work. In consequence, it seems likely that, to some extent, the sample conformed to these expectations in the interview situation, by responding in the way they thought they *should*.

Subsequent studies suggest that these criticisms may have some validity. Those which used a methodology similar to Herzberg's have been broadly supportive of his findings whilst those which are methodologically different yield different or contradictory results.

Despite the obvious shortcomings of the post-Hawthorne theories dealt with here, each has had a significant impact on practising managers (to whom they have an obvious appeal). This should serve as a reminder that apparently straightforward and easily implemented 'packages' for use by management everywhere can never be the panacea they are sometimes claimed to be.

If there is one lesson to be learned from this chapter it is that, as Blackler and Williams suggest,

> ...we should abandon the search for overall theories about the nature of men's motives and intentions....We know relatively little about what people do find important, and we should not draw a blind over our ignorance by becoming advocates of simple generalisations and easy prescriptions.

A more realistic approach to the study of motivation is considered in the following chapter.

Self-test questions

1 Is money in the end the only motivator?

2 What factors would make you stay in a job if you liked the work but felt underpaid?

3 Can any form of employment offer self-actualisation?

4 Are individuals trusted more at work than at school?

5 If someone asked you why you did something would you be able to give a complete answer?

5 Motivation: the importance of individual differences

- Money, social satisfaction, achievement, recognition and intrinsically satisfying work can all be key motivators for certain people in certain situations.
- It is important to recognise individual differences in analysing what motivates people at work. Any theory which fails to take account of this is seriously deficient however 'logical' it appears.

5.1 External influences

By the beginning of the 1960s, partly as a result of a number of industrial studies and partly because of growing general criticism of Human Relations theories, two important developments in thinking occurred concerning the nature and origins of workplace attitudes and behaviour. They are clearly related, but are nonetheless worthy of separate treatment.

The first important recognition was that attitudes to work and responses to the work situation are not *determined* by 'in-plant' factors such as technology, job and workplace design, payment systems, or supervisory/management styles, as had been argued for so long. Whilst these could be influential, evidence had begun to accumulate that their effect is modified by other factors. First, the nature and character of the community *outside* work – its culture, traditions and norms, as well as friendship groups – appeared to shape aspirations and individual and collective attitudes to work and supervision.

A second, closely related influence on the individual emerged from studies which indicated a variation in work priorities according to 'personal circumstances,' e.g. age, marital status, financial commitments and skill level. All of these, except the last, are unconnected with specific features of people's work situation, yet each was shown to influence workplace behaviour.

In some instances, an individual worker might be positively drawn perhaps because of high financial rewards, into repetitive, machine-paced jobs; be unconcerned with lack of 'social' satisfactions at work; show no signs of a frustrated desire to self-actualise; be critical of 'human relations' styles of management and supervision; and often indicate no general desire to seek other, more intrinsically satisfying work elsewhere, even when this was freely available. The reason, it was suggested is that an individual's orientations to work are shaped by a wide variety of factors external to the workplace. In the example above, the individual, for a combination of social, personal and circumstantial reasons, may have attached the highest priority at work to his or her level of earnings, presumably preferring to satisfy social and other needs *outside* the work situation. Work, therefore, for that individual, is seen as being largely instrumental to external satisfactions.

The implications of these findings are wide-ranging. Goldthorpe, for example, concludes that, where there is a choice of employment possibilities, an individual

External influences

will select the job which offers the set of satisfactions best suited to meet the personal priorities he/she currently holds. Some, therefore, will seek work with high intrinsic (job-centred) satisfactions, and/or possibilities for developing social relations at work. Others will locate these low on their list of priorities, perhaps substituting high wages as the most important reward from their work. Some people, then, will be prepared to sacrifice extrinsic, economic rewards for greater intrinsic rewards, whilst others will do the reverse.

This state of affairs is readily recognised at a simple level when people refer to some jobs as being vocational, e.g. nursing, teaching. The usual implication is that such occupations are filled by those who are more interested in the intrinsic rewards the job offers than in any high salary. (A further refinement on such a view might also add however that employers can get away with paying a low salary because the demand for, and commitment to, such jobs is above average).

In short, people *bring to* the workplace sets of goals and preferences shaped by external factors which must be acknowledged and examined if their workplace behaviour is to be fully understood. At the same time the inappropriateness of universal prescriptions for enhanced worker motivation which take no account of external cultural, situational, and workplace variations can be finally established.

McClelland's theory of achievement motivation

Evidence supporting these themes was provided by McClelland (1953, 1961) who argued that there is an identifiable personality dimension in us all – the need to 'achieve'. Some have a high measure of this need and will invest substantial effort to achieve successes, whilst others have a low need for achievement and appear largely unconcerned with goal-attainment.

In attempting to establish the causes of differential 'achievement motivation', McClelland suggests that the strength of one's need for achievement is not an inherited personality feature but is determined at a relatively early age by *environmental* influences. Notably, these include cultural environment, education and parental attitudes to goal achievement. For example, supportive, encouraging and non-authoritarian parents who set relatively high achievement goals are likely to produce children who themselves have a high need for achievement.

Those with high achievement needs, suggests McClelland, will set themselves goals which are moderately high – but not so high that there is only a slight probability of attainment, nor so low that the satisfaction gained from achievement is only small. Similarly, because of a high need for *personal* achievements, the individual prefers situations where there is a high measure of autonomy, responsibility and control over tasks. If this is not the case, the achievement is less directly attributable to that individual and is therefore less satisfying. Finally, in order to derive satisfaction from achievements, the individual requires clear and immediate *feedback* on performance.

McClelland's ideas seem to support the view that the goals and priorities an individual has at work may be very largely *imported* by him/her when taking up employment. They confirm that, if we are to understand behaviour within the place of work, we may have to begin our analyses outside it.

A cautionary note

Just as we have argued that it would be wrong to assert that technology, workplace design, reward systems and other features within the firm are determinants of workplace attitudes and behaviour, so it would be wrong to suggest that community ties and influences, family and life-cycle situations, and other external variables, will similarly determine responses to, and actions at, work.

The point was made earlier that these influences should be seen as modifying the effects or influence of workplace characteristics. For example, an instrumental

Motivation: the importance of individual differences

orientation to work, possibly generated by factors outside the plant, might account for less observable frustration and resentment in situations where work design and technology limit intrinsic satisfactions and social affiliation than would be the case for individuals attaching higher priority to social and/or intrinsic satisfactions required to work under the same conditions.

Importantly though, it should be noted that even within groups of employees whose community and domestic circumstances are parallel, each individual may interpret that situation and the workplace situation differently, and therefore be influenced differently. It would be a mistake to suggest that individuals are helplessly buffeted and directed in their lives and life goals by the twin deterministic forces of their workplace and outside work situations. Any two individuals may formulate their own goals and priorities differently and therefore direct their energies differently even though each is faced with the same or similar situation and influences. It is how each perceives that situation which is of most significance. Consider for example what happens to a group of schoolchildren in the same stream at school who take up a variety of career opportunities on leaving school.

5.2 Individuals' perceptions of their situation

It has been argued in this chapter, that whilst people at work may be influenced by a wide variety of workplace and non-work factors, they are likely to be affected differently by them.

The remainder of this chapter shifts its attention away from the factors which may or may not be influential in shaping actions at work, and considers a number of theories which outline the process(es) by which individuals decide on their own work priorities. Each stresses the importance of the individual's *own perceptions* of his/her situation in making these choices.

Equity theory

The first theory to be considered under this heading is that formulated by Jacques (1961). He asserts that there are agreed 'norms' as to what rewards should be given for different jobs or levels of work, and suggests that each individual worker is 'intuitively aware' of the 'equitable' payment level for his/her job, and that each seeks a state of balance between what he/she puts into a job and the rewards that come from it.

Two factors contribute to what Jacques calls 'psycho-economic equilibrium'. They are

1 A level of work which corresponds to the worker's perception of his/her own work 'capacity'.
2 Equitable payment for that work.

If either condition is not met, then disequilibrium results. The disequilibrium, e.g. over- or under-payment and/or an inappropriate level of work in terms of the individual's capacity, will lead, it is suggested, to different and progressively less desirable outcomes. For example, with increasing disequilibrium employees move from expressions of mild dissatisfaction with their lot, to depression and reduced efficiency and to considering and seeking alternative employment where this is possible. If the disequilibrium is positive and the employees feel they are getting 'more than a fair deal', they may experience guilt and anxiety.

Individuals' perceptions of their situation

Adams's equity theory

In similar vein to Jacques, Adams (1962; 1963; 1964; 1965) suggests that people compare and try to equate job inputs and outputs. Where the ratios are not equal, the individual takes measures to achieve or restore a balance between them. Adams however, emphasises outputs other than payment (e.g. fringe benefits, status) and includes in his range of inputs such things as effort, ability, training and age.

In a number of studies, individual responses to perceived disequilibrium between inputs and outputs were examined. By and large, the results supported Adams's assertions. In situations where subjects felt overpaid, they tended to increase their performance. When they were overpaid on a piece-rate system, instead of working harder to increase the quantity produced, which would have raised their payment still further, subjects improved the *quality* of their work in order to establish equilibrium.

Expectancy theory

A number of writers have researched and contributed to this area of theory. Possibly the most influential formulation has been Vroom's (1964).

Vroom argues that an individual's motivation is determined by two variables. The first variable relates to the order of preference an individual has for different possible outcomes of behaviour. For example, prestige among colleagues might be felt to be more important than a higher salary. This ordering, or strength of preference is termed *valence* (literally: that which stands out), and may be positive or negative. It would be negative valence if the individual would rather an event did not occur.

The second variable relates to how likely the individual feels a certain outcome will follow from certain behaviour. For example, if the individual works unpaid overtime will this create a good impression with the boss? This degree of prediction is known as *expectancy*. This expectation may range from zero – in which case the individual believes that there is *no* possibility of the outcome resulting from his/her course of action to a complete belief in the inevitability of the outcome.

Vroom suggests that the strength of an individual's motivation to perform in any context is a function of these two variables in interaction.

Expectancy theory at its most basic sees the individual as asking two questions:

'What am I most likely to get out of this if I do it?' (Expectancy)

and

'How much do I want what I am likely to get out of it?' (Valence)

In each case, the answer to these questions is based solely on the individuals *own perceptions* of (*a*) a range of potential outcomes and the likelihood of each occurring, and (*b*) their anticipated value to him/her.

Since Vroom's formulation, expectancy theory has been extended and refined. For example, the distinction has been made between two types of expectancy:

(*a*) the expectancy that a reward will in fact follow the achievement of a task (e.g. that promotion will follow greater effort at work).
(*b*) the expectancy that the expenditure of effort by the individual will actually lead to the successful attainment of the task. Certainly, the distinction appears to be a logical one as there is often no guarantee that a reward *will* be given on the completion of a task (even though there may still be intrinsic rewards in achieving it) nor is there any guarantee, perhaps because of personal limitations or situational barriers, that the expenditure of effort will lead to goal achievement (e.g. promotion might be difficult because of job cuts).

Motivation: the importance of individual differences

Given this distinction between two types of expectancy, the individual is seen now as asking the following questions;

(a) 'What chance is there that I will get what I want through effective performance?'
(b) 'What chance is there that by attempting the task, I will be able to achieve it?'

In this rather more complicated formulation of the theory, it is the two types of expectancy with the valence of the reward which determine the strength of the force on the individual to act in any context.

Clearly, from the point of view of the expectancy theorists, the individual makes choices based on a multiplicity of perceptions. These will include:

- perceptions of the potential rewards (extrinsic and intrinsic) in any situation and the likelihood of their resulting from a course of action taken by the individual and successfully completed.
- the likelihood that the expenditure of effort will lead to successful goal accomplishment. (This in turn will depend on perceptions of the situational barriers to goal accomplishment and the individual's perceptions of his/her own abilities.)

Though perhaps quite complex, expectancy theory draws attention to the factors which seem to account for the variability in peoples' motivation, and, like equity theory, offers a potentially fruitful direction for future research. By their very nature however, these theories must be seen as having a limited *predictive* potential: different individuals, even supposing they act rationally in terms of the model by surveying probabilities and assigning to them a valence, are likely to perceive and value any reward or set of rewards differently and to be differently motivated to pursue them. The theory's real practical value may simply lie in its recognition that it may be better to carefully and rigorously select and place the right personnel for different jobs or work situations rather than implementing large-scale job design changes for all employees or attempting to fit jobs to people.

Evaluation

The theories considered in Chapter 4 each, implicitly or explicitly, made *universal* prescriptions to enable managers everywhere to increase the energy and commitment with which their employees pursue their formal work objectives.

They failed to take into account that:

- there may be significant variation in the factors which will motivate any two individuals in the same context.
- any work context may have unique characteristics and features which influence employee motivation.
- there may be changes in an individual's priorities at work over time and with changing circumstances.

This chapter has explored some of the causes of individual differences in attitudes and motivation at work. It has confirmed the influence of factors at work and introduced a range of external variables as being influential on work motivation. In each case, however, it has been stressed that neither of these categories of influence determines workplace behaviour. The extent to which they will be significant will depend on the individual's own interpretation of his/her circumstances both at work and outside work.

We may bring to the work situation a variety of preconceptions about what satisfactions are possible from it, with an already ordered list of priorities shaped by our background and upbringing, our circumstances and our membership of groups outside work. All of these will colour our perceptions and influence our actions, but may themselves be revised in the light of our actual work experience. This may suggest to us which of our original aspirations are attainable and which are not and are therefore unrealistic. Some original goals will therefore be abandoned, or will be relegated down our ranking of priorities, making way for others which are more likely, in our experience, to be attainable. Alternatively, in most major respects, experience of work may confirm, or conform to, the expectations which we held prior to beginning it. This was the case with the workers studied by Goldthorpe *et al.*, whose *choice* of job reflected a desire for a particular set of rewards which that job was thought to offer. Fox (1971) makes a significant point when he suggests that 'From the earliest age, children from manual wage-earning families are likely to be absorbing from parents, relatives and older siblings a multitude of hints and clues as to the expectations that it is appropriate to entertain about work. By the time they themselves enter work their level of aspirations may already be suitably adjusted downwards.' In fact, many sons and daughters follow the occupational footsteps of their parents.

At work, then, a whole range of factors might differently influence or confirm an individual's aspirations. Job design and technology, supervisory and managerial styles, group membership at work and many others may be influential. Whether they are, and if so to what extent, will depend on the individual in question.

Equity and expectancy theories help us to understand the processes which seem to be central in deciding individual priorities and actions. Whilst both have their critics who question their practical and predictive value as well as their implication that individuals are consistently rational in their thinking, each has, in an enormously complex field, suggested which variables may be influential and in what ways, when we are considering the nature and origins of people's motives at work.

In spite of the questions they leave unanswered these theories represent an attempt to make progress in our understanding of motivation. Their main concern is 'how' we are motivated – the *process* of motivation – rather than what particular factor may motivate people to do particular things. They leave us with the conclusion that 'what' will motivate individuals and groups must be ascertained for each specific organisational context. Rewards that may be available in one organisation may be unobtainable in another. Similarly, different rewards and costs of working in the same organisation may be perceived and valued differently by different individuals.

Constructive staff appraisal systems (see Chapter 19) and surveys of staff are among the techniques that may be used. Of course for everyone, to a degree, good working conditions, pay, job interest and social relations will be factors in their own personal equation; but to what extent individuals differ in their aspirations and priorities at work can only be reliably established *with* them in the context of specific work situations.

Finally, it should be said again that there are few easy answers in this field of study and that, whilst it is daunting and sometimes depressing to be reminded of how much we are unsure of in such a central area of study as this, it is surely better to have partial theories which offer genuine insights into the processes of motivation than neatly packaged and oversimplified organisational remedies.

Motivation: the importance of individual differences

Self-test questions

1. Why might an individual's priorities at work change over time?
2. List some of the factors that might shape our expectations of work before we ever take a job.
3. Who has influenced you in your choice of career or job?
4. The theories of Jacques and Adams both employ the concept of 'equilibrium'. In each case, explain how this equilibrium is achieved.
5. Rank the inputs to and outputs from your job or routine as a student. Now, if possible, compare your rankings with others engaged in the same work.
6. How do you think theories of motivation which recognise the importance of the individual's own perceptions of work situations can have any practical value for managers?
7. What motivates people at work?

6 The nature and significance of groups

- The study of people's behaviour in groups is fundamental to the study of organisations because it gives insights into what makes certain groups effective and others not.
- Individuals belong to various types of group in and outside work and are influenced by them for several reasons in several ways.
- Measuring group effectiveness is the aim of most research into groups and can be related to productivity or group member satisfaction.

The previous chapter examined the factors that might motivate the individual outside and inside work. As a rule, however, people do not work alone and therefore it is equally important to consider the individual in a group context.

This chapter will describe the types of group within an organisation and identify certain features of group behaviour. An understanding of groups is one of the most significant ways of developing an understanding of people's work behaviour.

6.1 Defining a group

Everybody belongs to a variety of groups. Certain groups are more influential than others: the family group or a circle of close friends may generate a feeling of commitment whereas other groups, such as a school class or a department at work, may be more psychologically distant. The former type of group is called a primary group and the latter a secondary group. Whoever the other members of any particular group are, two things are inevitable.

- They will influence the behaviour of individuals in the group.
- They will themselves be influenced by the behaviour of other members of the group.

This process is called group activity and the interaction that goes on is referred to as group dynamics.

So far the word 'group' has been used as a common collective noun. Specific criteria that can help to define a group for the social scientist are as follows:

1 A group consists of more than one person (apparently self-evident, but then there are "committees" of one).
2 It is a collection of people who share a common purpose or interest.
3 The members communicate and interact in various ways.
4 The members are psychologically aware of each other.

These four criteria are appropriate but insufficient. They might well refer to a

The nature and significance of groups

cinema queue or any random collection of individuals. To define a group properly a fifth criterion is necessary.

5 The group members must see themselves as part of the group; they must have some conscious perception of belonging and be sensitive of each other's feelings.

6.2 Formal and informal groups

Just as there are primary and secondary groups, so at the workplace different types of groups can be distinguished. Ever since the factory system started grouping people together on one site, employees have been given a formal group identity. The organisation chart as outlined in Chapter 2 is a pictoral representation of these formal groups. The group is deliberately and officially organised, membership is prescribed and there is usually a hierarchical structure with explicit regulations and procedural rules.

In any organisation, however, people will spontaneously form their own voluntary groups. These informal groups are usually 'created' for friendship reasons. They will not necessarily match the structures of the formal groups although they will develop within them. It would be difficult to draw an organisation chart to show their distribution or hierarchy but their significance to an individual (and their effect on the organisation) can be as important as that of the formal group. An example of a formal group would be a factory night shift, and of an informal group, the people who regularly eat together in a canteen. Both formal and informal groups will have particular characteristics which will be shaped by the initial reason for the existence of the group and the stage of the development life cycle of the group.

The formal group consists of carefully selected individuals chosen by the organisation for their particular skills and aptitude for meeting pre-established official goals. Its structure will be clearly seen by an observer – the formal leader, the subordinates, the location where the group operates and the task the group has to do.

The informal group is different because it is self-generating. Its origins will depend on what factors attracted the individuals to come together: compatibility might come from sex, age, socio-economic class, status, race, occupation or some other common attribute seen as significant. The informal group will develop through various stages of formalisation. The more similar the individuals are, the more homogenous the group and, at least in the short term, the more effective the group is in meeting its unofficial goals.

6.3 The characteristics of groups

All groups have their own ways of meeting their aims, forming membership roles and developing styles of behaviour. After a time, a particular pattern of behaviour can be identified as unique and acceptable to any one group – the group norm. Most fully-developed groups will have elements of the following characteristics:

- A special language: words or 'in' phrases unique to that group's range of activities, sometimes called jargon. (Consider the jargon that is appearing in this book – words only relevant to this study area.)

- Special ways of doing things, sometimes trivial, sometimes dramatic. Take for example, the once-common initiation 'rites' for craft apprentices, or the Christmas office party where the boss is expected to dance with all the secretaries
- Certain shared attitudes, beliefs and reactions to outside events that reinforce the group's cohesion, like those in the Accounts department who distrust those who work in Marketing.

These characteristics are not necessarily stable or obvious but they will be implicitly understood and followed to a certain degree by the group members.

6.4 Group membership

To the individual group member the influence of the group will depend on how significant he sees it within his or her lifestyle. The individual accepts prescribed membership of the formal group at work because, traditionally, organisations are structured on the basis of specialisation and the formal division of labour. This is readily accepted as a way of allocating work and letting the individual employee know what his duties are, thereby helping him to understand his formal role in the organisation.

Within the informal groups to which the individual might belong the benefits tend to fall into two broad areas:

- in meeting social needs, such as the need for stimulation, affiliation and the shaping of an identity.
- in meeting task-orientated needs, whereby people use groups to meet their own personal objectives, such as pursuing a hobby interest in a club or society.

The more an individual complies and identifies with the group's outlook, the more he will adopt and internalise, i.e. presume as natural, the accepted features of his membership role.

An influence on individual behaviour

The needs the individual has for the group will affect the group's influence on the individual. Many people will model their behaviour on the group norm and may even attempt to conform to groups of which they are not members—reference groups such as the jet-set image used by advertisers. Whatever the influence, the collective psychological pressure of a group can have a tremendous effect on the individual. Many experiments have shown that an individual often feels obliged to share in and agree with a group's decision or attitude to some external factor even though he or she would react differently if making a personal judgement. This point has considerable implications for the individual and for the organisation, as will be seen. The group is not only a socially disciplining unit, it can sway people's opinions and create an identity that is stronger than that of the individual members.

6.5 The uses of groups in organisations

The general point that organisations use groups to distribute work has already been made. Although it cannot be overstressed that the prime management reason for group work is to complete tasks more easily and efficiently, there are other justifications for forming groups. As well as task allocation, the formal group structure is obviously very suitable for locating areas of responsibility, for co-ordinating and controlling people, and for giving and receiving information (although there are problems here, as will be seen in Chapter 12). The justification for groups is that participation as a whole will improve performance in decision making, problem solving and task achievement. Group work can be seen in various forms in the organisation:

1. in routine decision making, such as standing committees and boards of directors;
2. in creative decision-making, such as spontaneous discussion, brainstorming, 'think tanks' and research and development teams;
3. in negotiated decision-making, such as joint consultative committees and that whole area of management and managed participation known as Industrial Democracy;
4. in production technology, such as the semi-autonomous working groups used in the production methods developed in the Swedish car industry;
5. in training, such as 'T' group exercises where people are obliged to accept personal criticism from others to increase their awareness of interpersonal relationships.

In all these areas the benefits of group work should be evident in resource economies, constructive team spirit and greater efficiency.

6.6 Formal group effectiveness

The effectiveness of these formal groupings will depend on the commitment of the individuals to achieving the particular group goals, assuming of course that such goals exist and are not in conflict with the goals of any informal group. The process known as synergy, by which the outputs are greater than the inputs, $(2 + 2 = 5)$ should evolve, but much will depend on the personal values of the individual group members, the compatibility of the group and, not least, the size of the group. It is thought that approximately six members is the optimum number to allow full interaction and commitment, and although this figure is not kept to in a typical hierarchy, especially at its lower levels, it is significant to note that most team games do not have sides greater than double that number.

Other factors, such as the particular job to be done, the organisational setting, the technology and the formal organisational structure can be strong influences. It is assumed that by group effectiveness, task output and productivity are referred to, but it might equally refer to individual member satisfaction and the attainment of discrete personal goals. Where these two elements do not match up, there is bound to be a certain amount of confusion and possibly conflict. This point is a reminder that a happy worker is not necessarily a good worker and vice versa.

6.7 Group cohesion

It is clear from research and from most people's experience that an effective group is, in essence, a cohesive group. Factors such as size, compatibility, supervision etc. are all really helping to shape degrees of unity and therefore conformity in the group.

The level of group cohesion shows itself when the group members enjoy their group identity, participate in work sharing and hold favourable relationships with each other. This may lead to greater productivity, although this will depend on the group's adopted norms as the Hawthorne studies showed. What is certain is that if cohesion is not there, tensions will exist which will manifest themselves in various forms of conflict such as low productivity, absenteeism and higher labour turnover (see Chapter 10). The power of group cohesion can, however, sometimes work against formal goals. Taylor, for example, was always anxious to break up groups and rotate workers between groups to avoid any discontent being collectively generated against his theories on ideal work practices.

6.8 Group involvement

Advantages

That old aphorism 'two heads are better than one' might well summarise the advantages to organisations of using groups. Groups should offer a greater sum total of knowledge and experience to decision making and give more approaches to problem solving. They should allow for less individual bias and a group-made choice should offer a better chance of understanding and acceptance.

Successful group membership is not limited to the achievement of mental tasks but obviously also applies to the performance of physical work. In both areas, co-operation is encouraged and a sense of team spirit can be developed that may be directed towards the achievement of the organisation's objectives. Whatever type of work is involved, the group is an invaluable method of allocating duties to a specialist team.

Disadvantages

'Too many cooks spoil the broth.' In any task-solving situation the use of groups will present several problems. A desire by individuals to conform to the group norm might well favour consensus and stifle potentially constructive disagreement. Groups often come out with a compromise solution, often the first offered (although, through a process known as 'risky shift', groups can present radical answers to problems because the individual members can hide themselves behind the anonymity of the group). Group involvement as a whole can take more time than individual decision making – committees take 'minutes' but waste hours. Lastly, although as a whole the advantages of group work will outweigh the disadvantages, the fact that the informal group will not always fit in with the objectives of the formal group means that there is often a 'hidden agenda' in group work that can lead to apparently unwarranted obstinacy. It is widely recognised as 'office politics' or workshop bloody-mindedness.

Evaluation

This chapter has attempted to outline those features of groups which have a bearing on the organisation. Like other chapters in this section, it should have shown that understanding human behaviour is a complex matter. Group dynamics is the basis of much of social psychology. Although formal groups are easily

The nature and significance of groups

identifiable, the equally important but less readily seen informal groupings in an organisation should not be ignored. An effective workplace is one where the needs of the individual employee are satisfied within the attainment of organisational goals; where ideally the formal and informal groups coincide. A high proportion of a manager's time is spent leading official formal groups and much of the rest of the time is spent with informal group activities. Because of the complexities of human behaviour the study of groups should not be treated in isolation. The fact that at work people do things *with* others and, in a socio-psychological sense, *to* each other should encourage people to study groups more, and organisers should try to design work methods and procedures in line with recognisable patterns of group behaviour, however idiosyncratic they may be.

Self-test questions

1 Identify six groups to which you belong. Classify them as either formal or informal.
2 What are the group norms of each of these groups?
3 Suggest three reference groups for a teenager.
4 Can you identify the jargon used in Chapter 6?
5 Would you rather work alone or in a group? Can you explain your preference and relate it to the type of work involved?
6 Which is more important in group effectiveness, the achievement of the task or membership satisfaction? Does your answer depend on whose point of view you adopted?
7 Which aphorism is fairer, 'Too many cooks spoil the broth' or 'Two heads are better than one'?

7 Leadership

- Different approaches to and styles of leadership should be matched to specific features of the situation within which it will be practised. There are no simple formulae which can be applied in every context.
- Effective leadership alone will not guarantee effective working – it is an intervening variable which complements other areas of sound organisational practice.

This chapter aims to present various ideas on what constitutes leadership and to trace, largely in chronological order, the main leadership theories. An understanding of what is or what makes an effective leader is very important in understanding the organisation and, as the previous chapter indicated, a key variable to group effectiveness is the position of leader.

Defining leadership

Analysing leadership has proved to be an enigma for both businessmen and academics. It is recognised that leadership consists of an ability to influence others to meet defined objectives. It is thus part of a group activity process. The traditional structuring of the organisation into a hierarchy inevitably means that some employees will lead and others will be led. However, it is important to distinguish between two types of leader; in any group of people one or more members will eventually emerge to lead. Informal, *de facto*, leadership might arise spontaneously, but the positions of control in a hierarchy are staffed by formal, *de jure*, leaders who are appointed to direct the activities of their subordinates. These leaders are readily identified by their job titles such as manager, supervisor or head of department. Most leadership theory considers the effectiveness of the formal leader, but both the formal and the informal leader are important.

7.1 Early approaches to leadership theory

Many attempts have been made to explain what makes a good leader, and for many years two approaches offered a ready answer. They are commonly referred to as the Qualities and the Situational theories.

The Qualities approach

This was based on the idea that leaders are born and not made: that certain people have certain innate skills and qualities that precondition them for a leadership role. Such people would not need any training in leadership.

However, formal 'leaders of men' do not automatically emerge. There is no consensus in fact on what the qualities or character traits of leadership are. All the

Leadership

research findings are inconclusive, and studies of past and present acknowledged effective leaders have found no common variable. Likely significant variables such as intelligence, extraversion, health, and unlikely ones such as sex, height and wealth all offered no correlation. This is not only true of business but of any field of organisational activity. It has been suggested that there might exist one quality, the 'helicopter factor', an ability to identify major issues from a mass of minor problems. This is really only a use of the old adage of 'not being able to see the wood for the trees', and even this factor has been retitled by cynics as the 'glider factor', the ability to rise up the hierarchy by chasing round in circles on a mass of hot air.

Despite these criticisms many of the underlying assumptions of the Qualities approach are widespread. Many personnel managers, for example, still feel that certain qualities are necessary for leadership, even though they might find it difficult to articulate them, and such feelings almost certainly influence them when interviewing, for example.

The Situational approach

In essence this approach says that different group situations call for different skills. The person with the greatest degree of expertise relevant to a particular situation would be the best leader in that situation. For example, if a group is stuck in a lift the person who knows how to free the lift would be the most suitable leader.

The premise that the leadership role is based on someone's expertise is questionable, however. It is widely recognised for example, that qualifications do not guarantee success in leadership. On a more mundane level, it would be administratively inconvenient to change formal leaders at work every time a group's task changed.

It is now generally recognised that someone does not have to be an authority to be in authority. Nevertheless the basis of much internal promotion is a person's competence in a particular field. The 'Peter Principle' even goes so far as to claim that people are promoted until they reach their level of incompetence. It should also not be forgotten that Weber assumed that staff selection would be based largely on examination success, which is seen today as a legitimate measure of expertise, despite misgivings as to its accuracy. The main criticisms of both the Qualities and Situational approaches to analysing leadership are that they are too simplistic. They tend to concentrate on one particular leadership variable. When the later human relations writers started to examine what a leader does rather than what a leader is, a more complete understanding of leadership was developed.

7.2 More recent approaches to leadership theory

The Functional approach

A popular analysis of leadership, used in many management training courses in this country, is the action-centred model of an Englishman, Adair. This stems from the ideas of McGregor (see p. 28), and is a functional approach in that it identifies the functions of a leader in relation to the basic needs common to all leadership situations. These needs are threefold: those of the group, the individual, and the task.

The model shows that any one area of need exerts an influence on the other two. The function of the leader is to decide on the priorities of each need and to try to satisfy them in varying circumstances. An effective leader will ensure that all the

More recent approaches to leadership theory

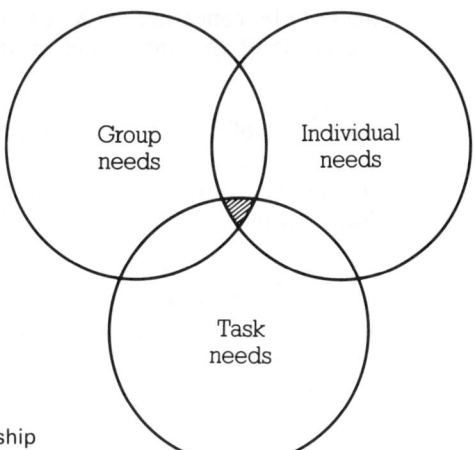

Figure 9
The basis of the action-centred leadership model of J. Adair

interacting needs harmonise. His or her functions or activities will include defining objectives, planning, communicating, supporting, controlling and evaluating.

Adair's approach claims that the skills of leadership can be recognised, practised and developed to be sensitive to the key variabilities of leadership. However his checklist of functions is reminiscent of Fayol's on management and lends itself to the criticism of being mechanistic. The problem remains of how, in practice, the needs of any particular group can be met. Leadership and the management of staff cannot be simply read about in a training manual; they are just as much an art as a science.

Leadership styles

In addition to concentrating on what makes a good leader or what functions he or she performs, many approaches have looked at a suggested key determinant of effective group supervision, that of the leader's role behaviour – in particular, style. The origins of the study of leadership style are found in the research work of Lewin in America in the late 1930s. He observed the behaviour of young adolescents in four youth clubs where the club leaders assumed different styles of control. These styles were termed autocratic, democratic and *laissez-faire* (abstention from interference). On analysis it was claimed that, under the authoritarian style, the boys were leader-dependent but their task achievement was highest. Under the democratic style, the subjects had the greatest group member satisfaction and, although performance was slightly worse than under the authoritarian style of leadership, they would continue working unsupervised. Scores for task achievement and satisfaction were lowest with the *laissez-faire* style of supervision.

The research was criticised for not clearly differentiating between the teaching (leadership) styles and the teaching method of organising the children's activities and for using what are clearly fairly emotive adjectives for the styles. Despite these objections, the labels used by Lewin have strongly influenced theorists when considering styles of leader. Other names have been used, such as task-centred, people-centred, directive and non-directive, structuring and supportive, dominative and integrative, but Lewin's terminology has tended to stick. It is therefore useful to examine in more detail what he meant.

Authoritarian

The authoritarian leader is one who centralises power and decision-making. He or she tends to have a personality which is preoccupied with power and status and identifies with conventional and conservative values. This type of leader is more

Leadership

likely to be concerned with achieving the group's task than with worrying about the needs of the individuals in the group.

Democratic

This type of leader decentralises power and shares authority by encouraging participation. Concern for subordinates is more important than concern for productivity directly. This style is akin to McGregor's Theory Y set of attitudes. Most people would claim that they would prefer this style of leadership.

Laissez-faire

This 'leader' avoids power and lets the subordinate take any decisions. The leadership role is only a nominal one.

The problem with these descriptions is that they offer instant stereotypes. Many business leaders do not fall easily into any of the three categories. This is partly because the categories are over-simplifications, and partly because any leader will

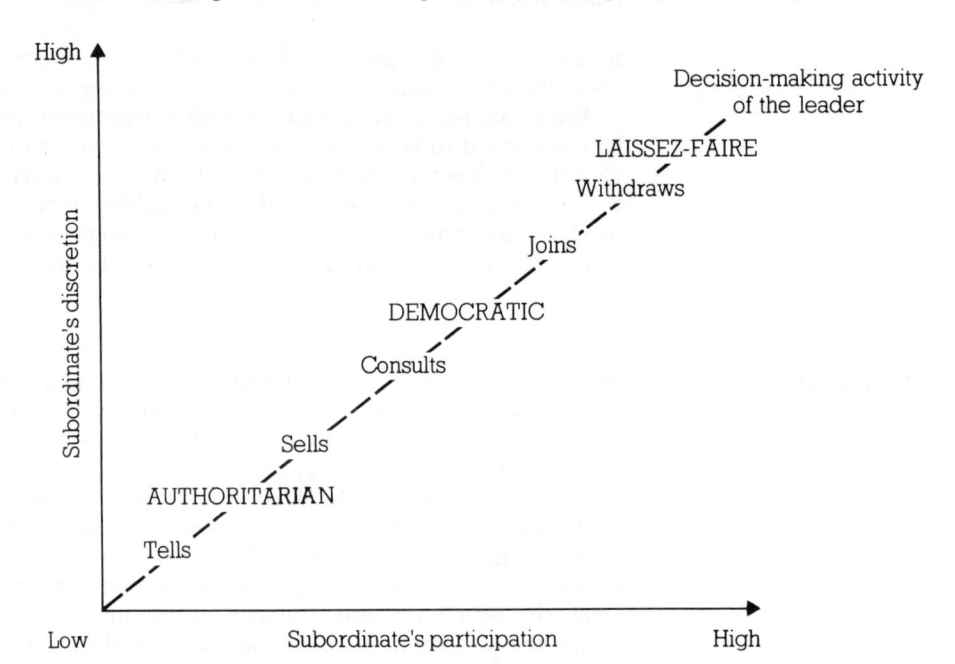

Figure 10
Leadership styles – loosely based on the ideas of Tannenbaum and Schmidt

vary his style according to the circumstances. This latter fact is drawn out by the Contingency theorists discussed below.

A useful summary of various leadership styles is shown in Figure 10.

The Contingency approach

The Contingency approach was first put forward by the American, Fiedler. His idea was that a leader's ability to influence subordinates effectively will rest ultimately on the style he adopts. To establish which style is appropriate in particular circumstances, Fiedler suggested that two main types of leader could be identified. The two types related to how friendly the leader was to the individual member of his subordinate group whom he liked the least. This individual was called the Least Preferred Co-worker (LPC). The theory states that the more the LPC is liked, the more democratic is the leader and the more permissive the leader is in consideration of the whole group. Conversely, if the LPC is strongly disliked, then the leader is more authoritarian and possibly more hostile to the whole group.

More recent approaches to leadership theory

Although the approach identified a potentially useful correlation between leadership style and leader/led relationships, it did not end there, but went on to suggest other influencing variables. Fiedler described a range of situations that would suit each style. The key variables to each situation would be:

a the quality of the leader-subordinate relationships;
b the extent to which the group's task was clearly set out, structured and routine;
c the degree of ambiguity between the leader's formal status and respect and his access to higher management backing, i.e. how powerful was his position in the hierarchy.

If these variables are set out in a matrix, it can be seen that certain combinations result in a situation conducive to group effectiveness. At either extreme of the favourable to unfavourable scale, i.e. combinations 1, 2 and 7, 8, Fiedler suggested that the task-centred style of leader is appropriate; the person-centred style adopted by a democratic leader is suitable in between these combinations.

Variables	Combinations							
	1	2	3	4	5	6	7	8
A. Relationships	good	good	good	good	bad	bad	bad	bad
B. Tasks	structured	structured	unstructured	unstructured	structured	structured	unstructured	unstructured
C. leader's status	high	low	high	low	high	low	high	low
Resulting Group Performance	Favourable ←――――――――――――――――――――――――→ Unfavourable							

Figure 11

Fiedler makes the important point that leadership all depends on the prevailing circumstances. To illustrate this consider an emergency situation such as on a battlefront, or a large committee without an agenda; in these circumstances the task-orientated authoritarian style is probably the best to adopt. In everyday work situations the more people-centred approach is better. In the former case a stronger, more forceful leader is needed, whereas in the latter, a more considerate style is required.

This idea that there is no one style of leader suitable for all occasions has been developed and adapted by a second contingency theorist, an Englishman, Handy. Handy maintains that an effective leader is one who 'best fits' into the requirements of the situation. His essential situation variables are:

- the leader's style (which is not, of course, necessarily constant);
- the subordinates' expectations of the leader's behaviour;
- the objectives of the group;
- the environment of the organisation.

These variables are measured by Handy on a range of tight to flexible and the best combination, or best fit, is where each matches up on the dimension scale.

Evaluation

Organisational leaders manage people. They do this usually through supervising groups and thus carry the responsibility to ensure that organisational objectives are reached. Each manager has different problems because he or she is dealing with

Leadership

different individuals in different groups within different organisational settings. How can leadership theory help?

A review of the main approaches to leadership theory can only stress that, as with other areas in the social sciences, there are no simple conclusions. The early approaches to leadership did not offer conclusive evidence for an understanding; the functional approach set a useful base for analysis but it is unable to offer more than a descriptive checklist (rather like the prescriptions of Classical writers); the Contingency approaches identify many important factors in the complexities of group dynamics, but offer little more than an 'it all depends' conclusion. Perhaps this latter is sufficient.

The criteria for measuring leadership effectiveness are, traditionally, high productivity and low labour turnover. These two factors can in turn be paraphrased, in task achievement and individual satisfaction respectively. However, there is no proof that high morale in a group causes high productivity, as the Hawthorne studies showed. Leadership theories give insights into why this is an enigmatic area of study, but in practical terms they can fall short in suggesting ways an organisation can best select, train and develop potential or even existing managers. In an ideal world, the placement of individuals into formal leadership roles would take into account all the variables that have been discussed. It could be therefore concluded that there are no good or bad leaders as such, just suitable or unsuitable individuals for given circumstances. Sometimes these circumstances might allow an informal leader to play a compensating and complementary role to the official leader, thereby creating, incidentally, a productive leader-led relationship.

A checklist for the effective leader

There are many published checklists offered as simple summaries of effective leadership. The list below was compiled by an American, Likert, and is given here to see whether its components in any way match the expectations and experience people have of effective leaders.

A good supervisor:

- spends time in supervisory skills rather than in personally working on the group's task;
- is person-centered and considerate;
- encourages people to speak their minds freely;
- reacts supportively, rather than punitively, to mistakes;
- supervises more discreetly than others and enlarges the area of responsibility left to subordinates, whilst retaining ultimate accountability.

Clearly this checklist is not a perfect model to follow: leadership is not an easy study area. Nevertheless it is vital to the efficiency of organisations that good leaders are employed. Checklists of factors in effective leadership are worth considering and using, but no one list can be anything more than a generalisation.

The role of leadership is complex. In many instances an informal leader can have more influence over a group than the formal leader, although leadership theory naturally concentrates on the latter because that person, to use Weber's term, is the 'legal-rational' leader. The only advice to intending or practising managers is to appreciate the message of the Contingency theorists with their caveat that 'it all depends'. There are no easy routes to an understanding of the complexities of leader/led relationships in an organisation.

More recent approaches to leadership theory

Self-test questions

1 Identify the *de facto* leader of each of three groups to which you belong. Does this role position vary according to the group's activity?

2 What are the most important qualities of good leaders you have come across? Are these qualities innate or have they been shaped by the person's background and position?

3 How important for effective leadership is expertise in the group's task?

4 In Adair's model is there any one variable which is more important than any other?

5 Is the *laissez-faire* style of leader ever appropriate in achieving either task effectiveness or group member satisfaction?

6 In the Contingency approach what is meant by the phrase 'the subordinates' expectations of the leader's behaviour?

8 Do you prefer a manager who is concerned with getting the work done or one who is concerned with keeping you happy?

9 Would you select a leader for a group or a group for a leader?

10 What points would you include on a checklist for an effective supervisor?

11 Is management an art or a science?

8 Roles and role theory

- An important influence on people's behaviour is the formal and informal expectations of others, which can be analysed through role theory.
- Role-related problems can be affected by job design, job placement and organisation structure.
- Different people will perceive the expectations of others differently, and as a result individuals are likely to respond in unique ways to situations which confront them.

In any social situation, at home, at work, or out with friends, we are the subject of others' expectations. Role theory is about these expectations, and the term 'role' is used to describe the behaviour expected of anyone occupying a given social position.

Role theory can provide a great many insights in the study of organisations. It allows us to study the influence that rules, norms and expectations associated with formal and informal positions have on individual actions and behaviour.

In simple terms role theory can help us put together our ideas on organisation on the one hand and theories of motivation on the other. It helps us to establish the effects of both formal and informal expectations on individuals and individual performance, and can suggest what aspects of motivation theory should be incorporated into theories of work organisation.

Throughout this chapter we shall be seeking to establish:

1 What effect(s) playing a role can have on individual performance and motivation.
2 What effect(s) individual personality can have on the way someone performs a particular role.

8.1 Basic role concepts

We all try to fulfill many roles in our lives. For example, a sales manager is only a 'sales manager' for some time at work; at home this role will be left behind and another role, say that of 'parent', will come to the fore. Simultaneously, the parent may be playing the role of husband or wife, and may, later in the evening, be required to attend a meeting of a residents' association in the role of treasurer.

In each of these situations, our role player, whom we shall call the focal person, will be the subject of the expectations of a different set of people. The group of people holding expectations of someone playing any particular role is called a role set (see Fig. 12). In fact, its members need not know each other – their link is the focal person of whom they expect a certain pattern of behaviour. Each of our roles then carries with it its own role set of people, each expecting us to act in particular ways.

The focal person and the role set are the basic structural components of role theory.

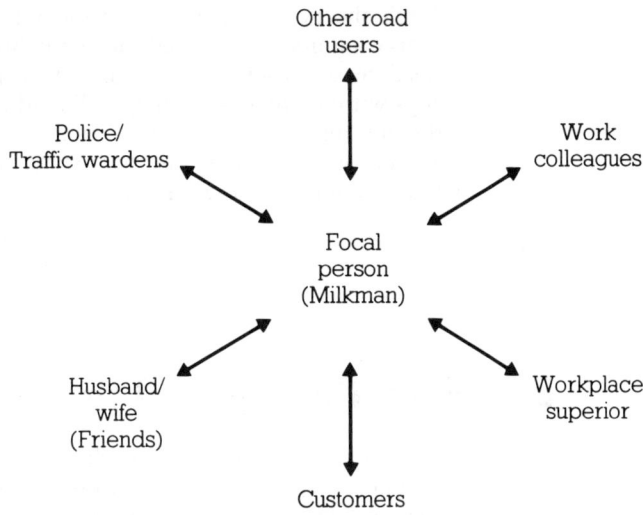

Figure 12
Model showing typical members of a role set

Role set members around Focal person (Milkman): Other road users, Work colleagues, Workplace superior, Customers, Husband/wife (Friends), Police/Traffic wardens.

8.2 Defining different roles

Any focal person is subject to more than the casual or informal expectations of the role set. Additionally, in any organisation, many of the expectations held of someone will have been formalised, perhaps in writing, in the form of rules, procedures and so on. A job description, defining the duties of members of the organisation, is a good example of this.

Sometimes too, expectations may derive from the particular culture within which the role is being played. The role of women, for example, is extremely varied from culture to culture. What might be expected of women in one culture would label them as deviant or abnormal in another. The women's movement is an example of a pressure group demanding that 'society' revises its expectations of women as housewives and childrearers, and that women themselves do the same.

Sometimes the law defines the duties and responsibilities of those holding positions within society. Magistrates, doctors, policemen and many others have certain duties defined and limited by law. So the expectations held of us when playing any role may be a combination of the formal and the informal, the explicit and implicit. This is one reason why we should not be surprised that no two parents, managers, students or policemen carry out their roles exactly the same way. Expectations of them may vary – depending on their situation and role set, they may interpret rules, norms and expectations differently, may attach different priorities to them, or may not even be equally aware of them.

This leads us to an important point. One way of trying to define any role would be to list and combine the total expectations that people in the role set have of the focal person. Establishing this role definition is, however, problematic. Apart from the difficulties already discussed, what would happen when it was discovered, as it almost certainly would be, that two individuals or groups within a role set hold different, perhaps conflicting, expectations of the focal person? Whose expectations will we take for our role definition? A shop steward, for example, might be expected to carry out his/her role in different ways by his/her constituents, by management, and by the trade union officialdom. Which set of expectations can be said to define the role of the shop steward?

If role theory is really to be of value, it is crucial that we do not assume that there are large numbers of agreed and straightforward roles or patterns of behaviour defined by a consensus of norms and expectations. Different members of, and groups within, any role set may well hold different expectations of the focal person and therefore subject him/her to conflicting or incompatible pressures. It would be a mistake to look for or assume a static consensus of expectations, and to try to define any role in these terms.

8.3 Role theory and problem diagnosis

It has been suggested that role theory can help us to appreciate the nature and causes of a range of problems evident in most organisations.

Let us begin by looking at quite a common problem. Imagine that after a number of years working for a firm you are called to see your departmental manager. She compliments you on the way you have worked whilst with the company, commends your ability to establish friendly relations with your workmates and, mainly because of this, offers you promotion to a supervisory position with your present workgroup. Just imagine for a moment all the changed expectations that promotion might bring. What expectations, for example, are management now likely to have? They will certainly expect you to supervise effectively. That may demand quite a shift in your attitudes and behaviour towards your workmates. You may even have to reprimand them occasionally. Consider, too, how their expectations might have changed. Will they expect you to act now as any other supervisor might, or differently because for so long you were one of them and they feel entitled to expect a few 'favours'? In what ways will the behaviour you expect of management and the workgroup change as a result of the promotion? Will you expect management to treat you differently, to support you in your new position, to socialise with you more? Will you expect your workmates to socialise with you exactly as before, or want them to keep rather more 'at a distance' because of your new responsibilities?

You may well find yourself in a position in which different members of your role set – in this case management and long-standing workmates – hold incompatible expectations of you, the focal person.

In our example, your workmates may expect that you will continue very much as before in dealings with them and you will overlook minor indiscretions and misdemeanours on their part. At the same time, management will clearly be expecting you to make an effective job of supervision. This may mean disciplining members of the workgroup, some of whom will be old friends. The pressures which these situations of role incompatibility can create are both distressing and destructive. Fortunately, there are ways to alleviate or avoid them, and these will be discussed later in this chapter.

Closely related to role incompatibility is another 'role related' problem termed role conflict. Again, it arises in situations where expectations are in conflict. Here, though, it is two or more roles which conflict, rather than different expectations of someone playing one role. The ambitious young executive, taking on more work and staying late at the office to accomplish it, finds his marriage and family life suffering because he is so rarely at home with his wife and children. These tensions at home begin, in turn, to affect his ability to work. In this case, the husband/father role is in conflict with his perception of the executive role. To give priority to either will mean that the other suffers. This will cause stress and frustration unless something is done.

This problem is familiar to women, who are often forced to choose between career commitments and home and family. Compromises in either direction can lead to feelings of guilt, anxiety or resentment. These kinds of fundamental role conflict can be very difficult to resolve successfully: we shall be examining some possibilities later. Role conflicts which are contained within the work context, where it is two 'work roles' which are in conflict, may be easier to resolve but this still generally involves a measure of compromise.

It was stressed earlier that different people may be more or less aware of the expectations held of them in any situation. We may be oblivious to some, unclear about others. Most frequently this occurs when we find ourselves playing a new role or when our role set changes. For example, on moving to a new job, we may be fairly clear (perhaps after interviews and induction training) about what actual duties we are required to perform. We are much less likely to be certain of the informal expectations held of us by members of our new role set. What kind of relationship did our predecessor have with our superiors and subordinates, what informal practices and 'taken for granteds' have evolved in those relationships? What style of management or leadership was practised before us? What degree of participation was exercised and in which areas? How rigidly were the formal rules of the organisation over, say, time off work applied?

All these uncertainties may confront the new job-holder. As with any new social situation, there will be unwritten norms and expectations which we will be initially unaware of. Where this uncertainty over expectations exists, it is called role ambiguity. It occurs whenever uncertainty of expectations exists, in either direction, between the focal person and his/her role set. Like other role related problems, role ambiguity may manifest itself as lack of confidence and/or anxiety and usually leads to ineffective performance. If long-standing, informal expectations are violated, this can cause resentment and may even provoke industrial action in defence of 'custom and practice'.

Role theory most clearly provides a link between theories of motivation and those of work organisation when we consider the likely effects of an individual being faced with either too many, or too few, roles to perform. The first situation is perhaps most common at the higher levels of the organisation hierarchy. The individual is besieged by expectations on all fronts. His or her responsibilities are usually wide-ranging, in a number of different areas and in dealing with different groups. The sheer volume of expectations, of competing priority and from different sources, can result in what has been called role overload. Individuals will have different strategies for dealing with it, but its likely effects in the long term can be severe. Periodic role overload is almost impossible to avoid at these higher levels of the organisation, but as we shall see, measures can be taken to prevent its becoming a normal feature of the executive's life.

Role overload can be contrasted with role underload, where an individual feels him/herself to be playing too *few* roles. This occurs when the individual feels that the expectations of him/her from different sources are too few or too trivial. (This should not be confused with feelings of too little *work* to do – it is quite possible to be working continuously and still suffer from role underload.) It may arise, for example, when someone feels they have too few responsibilities or too little autonomy in their work. Those doing repetitive machine-paced tasks frequently suffer role underload at work.

Clearly, the extent and severity of both role overload and role underload will be determined largely by the ways in which work and responsibilities are allocated and organised. As we shall see, there are strategies, which depend on the reorganisation of responsibilities, to ease or eliminate these two varieties of role problems.

8.4 Applications of role theory

Faced with the problem situations described above, individuals will nearly always adopt strategies of their own to make their situation at work more tolerable. In the final resort, they may even decide to leave the organisation to escape the stresses to which they are being subjected. This withdrawal, though, is clearly a drastic course, wasteful of skills, expertise and experience. Even the less drastic strategies which the individual might pursue are unlikely to prove entirely satisfactory. Stress and a low level of performance are likely to endure unless the problems are tackled at their root. Strategies which may prove effective range from those which involve structural change and are based on job design to those which simply involve more open communications between individuals and groups. They may be used in an attempt to avoid, as far as possible, the incidence of role problems, but also to remedy them, if and when they arise. In other words, they may be used as either prevention or cure.

Role incompatibility

It is important to try to anticipate where problems are likely to arise. The formal and informal expectations likely to be held of the focal person (or job holder) need to be established. If the job holder is able to have discussions with his/her predecessor, or someone else close to the job, these various demands can be considered, and, with assistance, potential conflicts and ways of coping with them can be outlined.

Of course some of the expectations will be impossible to predict – no situation is static, and competing or conflicting expectations within the role set will be constantly changing. Nevertheless the majority of these expectations will be known and the strain on the individual will be reduced where some counselling has prepared the ground beforehand.

Role incompatibility will manifest itself less frequently where the focal person makes it quite clear how he or she sees the role in question, and what expectations are appropriate. Tactfully done, this will discourage members of the role set from harbouring expectations of the focal person which are unlikely to be gratified or fulfilled. Of course, in those positions where role incompatibility often seems to be inherent and where it is accepted that some conflicting expectations will be generated within the role set, it is important that – in addition to the measures outlined above – people assigned to these positions have a relatively high tolerance for stress and are therefore less likely than others to be adversely affected by their situation.

Role conflict

The strategies which can be adopted here are basically similar to those described above. Sympathetic discussion, clear job descriptions and demarcation of duties will allow the individual to establish in his/her own mind a picture and ranking of the expectations which will be held of him or her and from where they will come. Where two work roles do come into conflict the individual will then be better placed to determine priorities.

In the main, though, role conflict at work is better prevented than cured. It should be possible (with only a few exceptions), through skilled and thoughtful job design, to avoid grouping roles which may be fundamentally in conflict within the same job. Where role conflict is experienced, either because of a failure to eliminate it through job design or perhaps because of the way an individual interprets and carries out work roles, the possibilities of removing or excluding one of the roles should be considered.

This strategy, however can only be practised where the roles in conflict are not interdependent. In those few positions where role conflict cannot be prevented, two roles being interdependent and clearly in potential conflict, the selection and training of people in these positions should attempt to ensure their resilience to the emotional stress which such conflicts may cause.

Role ambiguity

Role ambiguity occurs when either members of the role set, or the focal person, are uncertain of the expectations held by the other(s). One or both of the parties is unclear about what is expected of them. Once more, clear, detailed job descriptions will assist in avoiding role ambiguity. Open discussion with members of the role set will also help the focal person establish these different expectations. As we suggested in our discussion of role incompatibility, where the focal person makes it quite clear what he or she expects of the members of the role set and is consistent in those expectations, role ambiguity will be minimised for them. As situations change, regular discussion with both superiors and subordinates will help to prevent uncertainties in both formal and informal expectations arising.

Role ambiguity tends to be more prevalent at the higher levels of an organisation's hierarchy because job duties and responsibilities are less closely prescribed and autonomy is greater, than at lower levels. Much more is left unsaid about *how* a role should be performed, the standards that are expected and so on. The scope for ambiguities in these instances is clearly greater than for the closely supervised employee with a much smaller discretionary element involved in the work.

Role overload and role underload

We suggested earlier that the most fruitful avenue to explore in dealing with role overload and underload would be that of job design and organisation.

Role overload, it will be recalled, occurs when a person is attempting to play too many roles. Obviously different people will have different capacities in this respect, but where role overload is occurring or seems likely to occur there is no reason why the job or position should not be redefined or restructured to exclude one or more roles or sets of expectations. Where this is not possible, it may sometimes be as effective to encourage the delegation of areas of work to subordinates. Certainly this strategy will often be more protective of the individual's self-esteem, it being less likely to be seen as evidence of his or her inability to cope with the stresses of the job. Interestingly, role overload is frequently aggravated by a superior being reluctant or unable to delegate work sensibly, and for subordinates to suffer a measure of role underload in consequence!

Role underload, more common at lower levels of the organisation, is therefore also alleviated by effective delegation by superiors. Greater participation by and involvement of subordinates in relevant areas of decision making will help also, as will the implementation of well-established principles of job design. In this context, job enrichment, job rotation and increased autonomy for individuals and groups at lower levels of the hierarchy are examples of the measures that might be agreed upon and implemented.

Evaluation

To avoid or contain the role problems outlined above, a range of strategies has been discussed.

The first set of strategies is based on job design and work reorganisation: increasing or reducing the volume of different expectations, or screening out some which may conflict with others. This is often best done in co-operation with those experienced in, or very close to, the job in question. A second set of strategies simply employs improved and more open communications: preparing people through discussions for the formal and informal expectations to which they are likely to be exposed, and encouraging them to make their own expectations explicit. Conflicts and incompatibilities may even be negotiated out. These measures, whilst they are a most useful preliminary step for someone taking on a new position, should, of course, be ongoing.

Finally, when it is acknowledged that people in certain positions cannot be protected from conflicting or competing expectations, a sensible strategy to adopt is the careful selection of individuals with a high tolerance for the stresses these may create.

Before leaving the subject of role, it is worth looking briefly at some of the difficulties with role theory and the concepts it incorporates. A major difficulty is that many role concepts, including those dealt with here, are rarely described and used consistently. Even the term 'role' is itself variously defined and is employed in an inconsistent way. Sometimes it is used to mean the position or 'status' held by someone, sometimes the behaviour they display whilst occupying a given position, and at other times the expected behaviour of someone in a particular position. Similar discrepancies are evident in connection with many of the role concepts we have discussed – perhaps most notably in role conflict. Obviously, in view of these differences in interpretation, it is important that in using the terminology of role theory, we define and use our terms carefully and consistently.

A second difficulty is that the value and validity of role theory in total is sometimes questioned. It is said that role theory depicts individuals responding predictably to externally generated expectations, that it is a deterministic theory presenting people as being no more than puppets manipulated by events and circumstances and incapable of original or unpredictable action.

If role theory did present this picture, it would indeed be dangerously misleading. Not only must we accept that roles will influence the individual, but just as important, individuals will influence and modify their roles. External expectations will be perceived and interpreted differently by different people. Individuals will attach different priorities to different expectations and will adopt different strategies in responding to them. Some may be discounted by a role-player as being inconsistent with his or her own perceptions or beliefs about what that role involves or should involve. As a consequence, each individual is likely to respond in a unique way to the same 'objective' set of pressures and circumstances, and this unique response will, in turn, stimulate the modification and evolution of the expectations of members of the role set.

These cautionary notes do not undermine role theory itself, merely the more simplistic formulations of it. In role theory we have a useful framework for linking organisational structure with individual motivation and performance and one which provides many practical lessons and clues to more effective organisational functioning.

Self-test questions

1 List as many of your own roles as you can think of.

2 Recall any situations where you have experienced role incompatibilities and/or conflicts. How do you usually resolve such problems yourself?

3 From what you know of role theory, why might it not be sensible to recruit the best qualified/most experienced applicant for every job which falls vacant?

4 A job holder experiences role conflict, but the two roles are interdependent and need to be performed by the same person. What strategy or strategies can eliminate or reduce the effects of such conflict?

5 Distinguish between formal and informal expectations.

6 Why can defining a role be problematic?

7 What are the links between organisation theory and role theory?

Case studies on Part B

A

Before joining the company, employees at a factory were asked to rank in order of importance to them various aspects of work – money, interest in the work itself, social contacts and so on.

At this stage, most people rated interest in the work higher than money on their list. Two years later, employees were questioned about how they felt about their jobs, and the following information emerged.

Production unit. In this unit, the work had been broken down into small, repetitive tasks on 'Taylor' principles. Supervision kept a close check on workers on the basis that this was the way to maintain high output and efficiency. A piece-work system gave the opportunity of high earnings. There was very little employee turnover, although absenteeism was comparatively high.

Employees reported on their jobs as follows: They were very satisfied with their jobs but would not choose the same job if starting over again. The money was good but they would like more. They were indifferent to the views and activities of senior managers and were also indifferent to social activities and socialising at work. They did not like the way supervision was so close. They had liked previous jobs better.

Drawing office. Apprentice-trained draughtsmen were employed in adapting standard equipment to suit customer requirements within a prescribed system. After a recent rationalisation of the work system it now resembled the production line mentioned above. It was deskilled and repetitive. It involved much clerical work rather than designing, although it was not easy to detect this from conversation with the draughtsmen. Turnover and absenteeism were low, except in one section where the supervisor adopted a dictatorial attitude and where turnover was high.

Employees reported as follows: Low satisfaction with jobs and disappointment with their careers. They would not choose the same jobs if they were starting again. In so far as contact with supervision was necessary, they liked it to be supportive and civilised, but were indifferent to senior management. They valued the close friendly relations they had with their colleagues, and the social activities which they had organised, such as the darts teams. They also liked the area in which the factory was situated – 'Couldn't live anywhere else after here' was one comment.

Quality production group. These were skilled workers, apprentice-trained, operating machine tools. Each was expected to exercise discretion over tasks allocated and would have resented any attempt to tell them how to deal with tasks. 'You take it for granted a craftsman knows how to do the job' was one supervisor's comment. In discussing their work they used a good deal of technical jargon, largely incomprehensible to others. They were friendly to each other, but not a close-knit social group. There was little absenteeism or employee turnover.

Employees reported: Low job satisfaction both in terms of pay and interest. They would however choose the same job again. They were not particularly concerned about the style of supervision they received, and although they liked a friendly atmosphere, they were not especially concerned about socialising with colleagues. They had some views about what senior management should be doing.

Analyse the situations above. Try to determine why these people responded to their work situations in the ways they did.

(Adapted from Biddle and Hutton: *Towards a Tolerance Theory of Worker Adaptation*)

Case studies on Part B

B

You are the nominal leader of a commune formed in the West Country to operate as a craft workshop. The members of the commune value their independence and have at least as much knowledge as you do; they respect your views and have given you informal sanctions as their leader.

The commune is just beginning and little is known about which products would sell best. The tourist season peaks in three months' time and a decision has to be made about which products to concentrate on and how to organise the commune.

All members are interested in the commune becoming self-sufficient.

What information have you learned from studying organisations which can be used to practical benefit?

PART C

What are the different sources of power, authority and influence in the workplace, and what are their differing effects and implications? Why does conflict occur? Is it inevitable? Is it destructive? When and how should it be prevented or resolved? Can conflict, for example, be managed best by a redistribution of power and authority such as might occur under a formal system of employee participation?

Authority is a resource enabling one person to act in particular ways, and to require others to do so too. In the organisation it derives largely from the organisation's structure and the individual's position within it, but it is not the only means of influencing people. In this section we look at the different forms and sources of power, authority and influence and the conflicts that may arise from their use. We also look at the many and varying suggested remedies to these inbuilt problems of organisation which come under the general heading of participation, a complex area of study concerning individual aspirations, expectations, organisation structure, authority, conflict, groups, roles and leadership.

Finally, in this section we look at communications within the organisation. Many problems faced by the organisation arise because communications are lacking or inappropriate. Awareness of the complexities and importance of communications is essential for organisational effectiveness. Does information flow up, down and across the organisation structure as it should? Is the communication system tailored to its structure? Does the style of communication, its degree of openness and formality, help to motivate and involve employees?

Communication between the organisation and its environment is equally important, and the need for the organisation to devise strategies in the context of a changing external environment is also highlighted.

9 Power and authority in organisations

- There are different sources of power, including the legitimated power called authority.
- Recourse to any source of power is likely to provoke different kinds of response in those over whom it is exercised.
- Power is a resource used as a method of influencing others.
- Particular kinds of power depend for their effectiveness on certain preconditions being set.

One of the features of organisational roles discussed in the previous chapter is that each of them confronts the individual with certain formal rights and duties. These may include the right to issue certain orders, the right to organise work in a particular way, the duty to enforce standards of work and performance, and so on.

The distribution of these rights and duties is a fundamental aspect of any organisational role system, and therefore of an organisation's structure. To ensure that formal organisational goals are achieved, an individual manager must be able to exercise some control over the behaviour of his or her subordinates. How this control is exercised, and the consequences of exercising it in particular ways, are the subject matter of this chapter.

9.1 Authority and power

Authority is most simply described as the formal right to exercise control, that right being conferred by virtue of position. The fact that authority has been formally bestowed, however, does not necessarily enable effective control in practice. Claiming that we have the right to do something does not always mean that we will be able or permitted to do it. Thus, if one is to exercise control by virtue of authority, those over whom it will be exercised must also, in general, accept one's right to do so. In other words, the right to control must be 'legitimate' not only in the eyes of those who bestow it and those on whom it is bestowed, but also in the eyes of those subject to it. Thus, an authority relationship is one within which the superordinate is seen by the subordinates as having the right to exercise control over them, and within which the subordinates places themselves under the direction or command of the superior.

Because of the relationship between *position* and authority, systems of authority are described by an organisation's hierarchy. These systems of authority are clearly central to the control of work and the subsequent accomplishment of organisational objectives, not least because when people accept the authority of their superior they are likely to accept too (though they may not agree with) the directions and sanctions which emanate from him or her. For example, suppose we are stopped by a policeman for speeding and we are subsequently fined by a magistrate. We are likely to accept their right to have acted as they did as well as the sanctions they impose on us. However, if someone else, say another motorist, had stopped and attempted to fine us in the same situation, we would question their right to do so, and would certainly not pay any fine they attempted to impose.

Despite the need for authority systems in controlling work, there will be times when authority is challenged and thus when it will not elicit or provoke desired behaviour. In these circumstances, power may be used instead to achieve the compliance of subordinates. Here authority can be contrasted with power. Although power is another resource for the exercise of control, it differs from authority, the *right* to exercise control, in that it is instead, the *ability* or capacity to exercise control. There is an obvious and important difference. To exercise control through power, one need have no legitimation at all. One is simply *able* to do so by virtue of a power source. No one else needs to agree that one has a right to direct or control, which is why the use of power is often resented and will sometimes provoke the retaliatory use of power by subordinates to resist that of the superior.

Influence

We have differentiated already between power and authority. Power, we said, was an ability or capacity to exercise control over others, and authority a formal right to do so. At the risk of creating confusion, another concept now needs to be introduced. It is that of influence. Whilst power may be seen as a resource or something one *has*, influence is something one *does*. Thus the different sources of power, which we shall now review, give their holder access to different *methods* of influence, each relying for its effectiveness on the power source which underlies it.

9.2 Sources of power

As with so many other areas in the study of organisations, a lack of consistency in definitions can cause confusion. The problem lies in different terms which may be employed for different power sources. It is important that we distinguish them carefully, not least because recourse to different kinds of power will usually elicit different kinds of response – some of which will be more damaging than others. In the same way, different uses of power tend to engender different kinds of involvement in the organisation on the part of those over whom the power is exercised.

For the purpose of distinguishing between different bases or sources of power, we shall be using the five categories suggested by French and Raven: reward power, coercive power, legitimate power, referent power, and expert power.

Reward power

Sometimes called 'resource' or 'remunerative' power, this exists when one person is able to offer rewards to another in return for desired behaviour. The reward need not be financial or even material – praise, promotion, increased status and many other 'rewards' can be equally successful in achieving results.

Reward power, however, will not prove effective unless the individual or group being offered the reward actually desires it. Different rewards will have a different attraction for the individual and will therefore differ in their effectiveness as a basis of control. Reward power as a basis for influence or control should be considered in the light of expectancy and other theories of motivation dealt with in Chapters 4 and 5.

Power and authority in organisations

Coercive power

Coercive power is the power to control by threat or acts of 'punishment'. The punishment, at its most basic, may be physical, or it may involve penalties of different kinds. These may be financial or non-financial – such as withdrawal of privileges – or, in the last resort, dismissal. At its most blatant, coercive power will be found in prisons, some mental hospitals and other such institutions, but 'punishment' of different kinds, or the threat of it, is a common enough basis of power in all organisations and even in informal groups, where, for example, members may be ostracised or 'punished' in other ways for violating group 'norms' or expectations.

Legitimate power

This is sometimes called 'position' power because it usually derives from position. It depends on a belief that the person exercising control has the right to do so. As such, this form of power or ability to control can be equated with authority when that authority has been acknowledged by those over whom it is exercised.

Referent power

Sometimes called 'personal' power or charisma, referent power is the ability to control, not by rewards and punishment or by virtue of position, but by force of personality – a degree of charisma. Whilst it is most clearly a very useful resource, usually being resented much less than other forms of power, it can be very unstable. It 'leaves' the organisation with those who possess it, and therefore it may have to be replaced with other, more readily available but more resented, forms of power. People will usually submit willingly and voluntarily to another's referent power. In other words, it tends to have a high 'legitimacy'. Indeed, it will be recalled from Chapter 1 that Weber cited charisma as one of three 'pure types of legitimate authority'.

Expert power

Expert power, as a basis for control, derives from an individual's actual or claimed expertise or knowledge in a given field. To be used as a power source, one's expertise must, however, be acknowledged by those over whom it is exercised.

Once again, expert power is rarely resented strongly. We all have to rely on experts such as doctors, lawyers and teachers from time to time, and most of us recognise that in certain situations this is the logical and sensible thing to do. In fact, because of this, expert power is a form of authority or legitimate power, especially when it is linked to occupation or position.

A sixth basis of power

These, then, are the five principal sources or bases of power suggested by French and Raven. Their framework, very useful as it stands, has however been supplemented and modified. For example, if one could create, by various means, a commitment to the formal goals of the organisation on the part of its members, one would clearly have an effective way of ensuring control. People would be self-motivated towards organisational goals. This commitment on the part of an organisation's members has been suggested as a sixth basis of power. Its creation depends on the ability of those in group management positions to create groups whose purposes and objectives are acknowledged and approved by their members and are salient to them. It is usually suggested that achieving this will depend upon such things as leadership skills, delegation, and extensive participation in decision making from the top to the bottom of the organisation.

9.3 Responses to different power sources

We have already suggested that different power sources and the ways in which they are employed can have different effects. One type of power is likely to be more or less resented than another, and so generate different attitudes and a different kind of involvement in the organisation.

A study by Etzioni clarifies this relationship between power used and membership involvement with the organisation. He uses different labels for types of power than those we have used here, but the point he is making is still clear. Etzioni describes three different kinds of involvement in organisations on the part of their members. The first is what he calls 'calculative' involvement and is typical amongst most members of conventional work organisations. An individual involved in this way is participating voluntarily in an organisation for the benefits, usually material, which membership brings him or her. Membership is the result of a rational decision, made after consideration of the rewards and costs of belonging to that organisation. Basically, an exchange relationship is operating, with the 'organisation' exchanging resources for the time and effort of the individual.

'Moral' involvement is Etzioni's second type, and whilst calculative involvement is a fairly neutral, instrumental involvement, this is an intense, committed and strongly favourable form of involvement with the organisation and its goals. It is perhaps commonest amongst members of religious and political groups, but can be found in business organisations. Appeals for loyalty to the organisation may be designed to create or maintain such an involvement as, to some extent, might programmes of downward communication, job enrichment and worker participation.

The third kind of involvement Etzioni describes is what he calls 'alienative' involvement. This describes a state of non-identification with the organisation and its goals. It is a negative form of involvement, often intensely so, where the member is dissociated from the organisation and is often a member of it against his or her will. A prison is an example of an organisation where such a form of involvement would be typical.

Together with these three kinds of involvement, Etzioni describes three kinds of power. He labels these 'remunerative', 'normative' and 'coercive' power. Each of these kinds of power tends to be found paired with a different kind of involvement. One kind of power tends to induce a certain kind of involvement and vice versa. Reliance on remunerative power will tend to generate calculative involvement and in turn, calculative involvement provokes the use of, and reliance on, remunerative power. In the same way, coercive power can be linked with alienative involvement, and normative power, the allocation or withholding of 'symbolic' rewards such as prestige, acceptance or esteem, links with moral involvement. Where the three kinds of power and involvement are found differently paired, these other pairings, suggests Etzioni, will be both less stable and less effective than those we have described.

Essentially, then, employing any particular power source is likely to provoke a different response and a different form of involvement than would another. At the same time, any particular form of individual or collective involvement is likely to render some forms of power less effective than others.

Thus, whilst we began by suggesting that organisations depend on at least a measure of compliance from their members, what we are now saying is that this compliance will be more or less productive, in terms of the organisation's goals, and more or less freely given, depending on the power source which is used to gain it. To revert to our labels of the different power sources, and to generalise, *coercive* power, manifested as threats, punishment and the like, is likely to generate alienation or hostility. Reliance on *reward* power, on the other hand, is likely to generate fairly neutral, instrumental involvement with the organisation and its goals. In just the same way, it seems probable that over-reliance on *legitimate* power in a generally authoritarian climate will lead to fairly rigid, bureaucratic forms of organisation where open communications and flexible, participative leadership cannot flourish. Compliance and control will normally be achieved, but only because people are responding to directions from someone they see as having the formal right to issue them. There is no guarantee that the recipient of the directions will identify with them or the goals they are designed to achieve. Indeed, subordinates might be completely unaware of what goals their efforts are being directed towards.

Where control is exercised through referent or expert power, and these are employed sensibly, much greater identification with the goals being pursued by a group is likely. For example, it has been suggested that where the 'superior' sees himself or herself as a working member of a group, in the full sense, rather than as something 'above' it, where people have open access to his or her expertise when they require it, and where through open and participative leadership group members are involved throughout in policy and decision-making processes, they will recognise for themselves what needs to be done from their own assessment of the work situation. They will have been persuaded by the logic of their situation to follow a course of action, rather than having been instructed to follow it. In this vein it has been argued that one *person* should not give orders to another *person* but both should agree to take their orders from the situation. If this can be achieved, the sixth power source, that of a common commitment to agreed goals, will be established and will operate as self-generating control mechanism. On the other hand both referent and expert power can be employed in the pursuit of less worthy ends than group identification with task objectives. They can each, for example, be used by a superior to retain individual and personal control by mystifying the decision-making process or by a refusal to delegate and consult with subordinates.

Evaluation

In general terms, we have established possible responses to the exercise of different kinds of power. They range from grudging or enforced obedience to genuine personal commitment on the part of those over whom it is exercised. The latter, if it can be established, is likely to be the most enduring, but might take months or years to achieve. Of course the very nature of certain organisations, prisons, for example, precludes this kind of involvement. So, the different sources of power have their own applications, situations where one will prove more effective than another. Choosing the power source which should be used in any situation will depend on many factors. General considerations include the nature and character of the organisation, the nature of its members' involvement (to the extent that this can be generalised), and whether it is felt that this can be modified. More specifically it will depend on the aspirations and priorities of each individual over whom it is to be exercised. Reward power for example, will depend for its effectiveness on the desirability to the recipient of the reward being offered. (See Chapter 5 on expectancy theory.)

Once again, it is clear that there are no easy answers to problems of gaining commitment or of establishing effective control. The manager of a group may well try first to join with that group, combine his knowledge with theirs, and encourage joint responsibility for performance. Sometimes this can be achieved; when it cannot, or before it has been, he may have to resort to legitimate, reward or coercive power to achieve results. In these cases, commitment is likely to be reduced or even non-existent – with the possibility of tension and hostility taking

Responses to different power sources

Source of power
(French and Raven)

[Diagram: boxes for Reward, Coercive, Legitimate (authority), Referent, Expert across the top; Calculative, Alienative, Normative across the bottom; Commitment box on the right. Arrows connect sources to involvement levels.]

Level of involvement
(Etzioni)

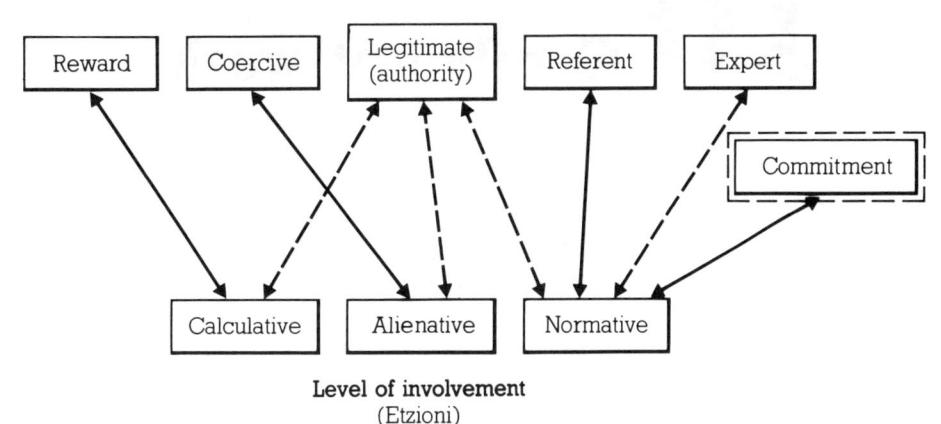

Figure 13
Model showing power/involvement interrelationships

its place. In Chapter 11 we shall examine the dimensions of employee participation in decision making and, amongst other things, offer views on its efficacy in achieving employee commitment and personal involvement with the formal goals of organisations and work groups. The following chapter however, examines situations where authority is challenged, where agreement cannot be reached, and where applications of power are resisted. We shall consider the tensions which typically arise within and between groups and suggest what might be their causes.

Self-test questions

1 Distinguish between power, authority and influence – what methods of influence do you think each source of power permits its holder?
2 Why does it matter which power source is used in organisations provided that control is maintained?
3 What connection is there between this chapter and what you know about leadership and leadership styles from Chapter 7?
4 What conditions must apply before reward power will be effective?
5 Etzioni gives three different types of power and three types of involvement. What are these and why does it matter how they are paired?
6 How best can the sixth basis of power discussed in this chapter be mobilised?

10 Conflict at work

- Assumptions about the nature and causes of conflict determine approaches to its resolution.
- The perception of conflict, including the unitary and pluralistic views, can lead to the adoption of more or less appropriate strategies for its avoidance and resolution.
- Conflict is multi-dimensional and can therefore be categorised in several ways.

We established in the previous chapter that systems of authority aim to provide for the formal control of workplace activities. However, where individuals or groups 'withdraw legitimacy' from those above them in the organisation's hierarchy, various forms of power may be drawn on in order to gain compliance from those individuals and groups, by threat or coercion for example. The possible result of situations of this kind is open conflict, with each side attempting to impose its will on the other and recruiting various forms of power to this end.

In addition to conflicts arising out of authority relationships, conflicts occur just as commonly between two individuals or groups at the same level of the organisation's hierarchy. Thus conflict in organisations is multi-dimensional, it has many causes and many effects. It can be destructive or it can lead to positive and beneficial change.

Before we examine specific types and causes of conflict, it will be useful first to consider briefly some of the different assumptions which are made about conflicts and work. The reason for this is that it will be a person's assumptions about the nature and causes of conflict which will lead him or her to adopt particular strategies for dealing with it. If their assumptions are misguided or mistaken, their strategies almost certainly will be too.

10.1 Unitary and pluralistic views of organisations

A classic and most useful distinction between different sets of assumptions and beliefs about organisational conflict is described by the 'unitary' and 'pluralistic' frames of reference outlined by Fox (1966). Each describes very different perceptions of conflict which have important implications for the ways in which it is managed.

Unitary and pluralistic views of organisations

The unitary perspective

Firstly, and fundamentally, the unitary view asserts that the interests of all the participants in, or interest groups of, an organisation are essentially the same. This assumption of shared interests leads to the organisation being seen as something of a team with management playing the role of team captain. In evidence to the Donovan Commission, the chairman of one company stated: 'We reject the idea that amongst the employees of a company there are "two sides" meaning the executive directors and managers on the one hand and the weekly paid employees on the other. Executive directors are just as much employees as anyone else. We are all on the same side, members of the same team.'

This is a view characteristic of the unitary perspective. Out of this assumption or belief, another logically follows. It is that conflict has no legitimate place within the organisation. Whilst its existence is not usually denied, it is seen as being both wrong and unnecessary. Further, management is seen as having the inalienable right to manage – the managerial prerogative. When this legitimacy is challenged, the challenge itself – being necessarily misguided – must be eliminated. These challenges to management and subsequent conflicts, are seen as arising because individuals and groups: (a) fail to see where their 'true' interests lie or (b) have been misled and manipulated by agitators.

To avoid or remedy conflicts arising for what are seen as these reasons, the management tries to improve communications in order to demonstrate better that management has the employees' true interests at heart, and that the goals they define and are pursuing will be mutually beneficial. At the same time, the importance of trust in the actions of management and loyalty to the organisation is stressed. Employees, it is hoped, will be less inclined to join trade unions – which amongst other things serve as power vehicles for the 'disruptors' – if the organisation is better able to provide the employees with a feeling of 'belongingness' and a conviction that their interests are being cared for. It is because this conviction is lacking that employees are seen as being drawn into unions in the first place. Their loyalty must be won back. Better communication and consultation must be achieved and better leadership practised.

The unions themselves are seen, from a unitary perspective, as being largely outdated. Whilst they had a function once, the age of more enlightened management has made them less relevant. They mistake the true interests of their membership and no longer have a logical place in the modern business organisation. Whilst a small number of their activities, complementary to management, may be 'legitimate', they are basically seen as representatives of sectional interests, misguided in challenging the goals of the management of the enterprise. Their real failure is in a lack of understanding, or shallow perception, of employees' *real* interests. In cases where unions violate and incite violation of the managerial prerogative, or hinder or obstruct the fulfilment of managerial objectives, they are acting against these interests.

Whilst it still has its adherents, the unitary perspective is increasingly being rejected by managers faced with the realities of modern industrial life. Its assumption of shared interests identified and articulated by management, and pursued to everyone's benefit, is notably difficult to equate with those industrial realities. To dismiss major conflicts as always being due to poor communication and misunderstanding, to the work of a handful of troublemakers, or to a simple failure on the part of employees to recognise what is good for them, is as naive as it is convenient in absolving managers from accusations of mismanagement. Of course, many conflict situations *are* due to faulty or untimely communication, and employers do share with their employees a wide range of interests.

However, the unitary view precludes examination of any conflict which arises from real divergence of interests between the parties and is thus limited in terms of its value as a model and tool of analysis. As Fox notes, to the extent that employees

Conflict at work

and others are persuaded by the unitary view and accept its assumptions, management and the actions of management gain in legitimacy and their authority is reinforced. To the extent that people who challenge that authority are believed by others to be irresponsible or non-conformist, the challenge will be easier to resist.

The pluralist perspective

The pluralist view, to the extent to which it may be generalised, begins from an entirely different set of assumptions and accordingly carries with it very different implications. It offers a description of the organisation as comprising many group and individual interests. Their aspirations and priorities differ significantly. In essence, the concept of a single, shared set of interests gives way to one of management through negotiated compromise. Management and labour are seen as being but two of the groups competing to achieve their goals within a broadly accepted structure. There will, nonetheless, be shared interests between all the parties to a pluralistic system, as there will be alliances between two or more of them when this is thought likely to further mutual interests. These groups, or 'stake-holders', which might include shareholders, suppliers, consumers, Government and employees, continually present management with their claims and expectations. These must be managed in such a way that each party – at least in the long term – will make some progress towards satisfying its sectional goals.

The pluralist, because of the very nature of the system described, anticipates and even welcomes conflicts arising out of competition between interest groups. The only qualification is that these do not escalate too far and threaten the continued collaboration of the different parties to the system. Where protracted and deep-rooted conflicts do recur, this may be taken as evidence of a failure in the system to accommodate sufficiently the aspirations of one or more groups – that suitable compromises are not being reached. In these instances, to ensure the continued collaboration of disenchanted groups, management, perhaps by adjusting the balance of rewards from the system, must restore stability to it. In absolute contrast to the unitary view, trade unions are seen as being entirely legitimate, competing alongside other interest groups to achieve their own sectional ends. The pressures to which they or their members subject management are therefore legitimate too.

Implications

The manager who subscribes to either of the two views outlined above, or to some approximation of either, will perceive conflicts and their origins differently, and will respond to them differently as a result. One will see challenges to his or her authority as misguided and destructive – something to be eliminated; they will be seen as being either subversive or the result of misunderstanding or a failure by employees to perceive the logic of the management's actions. These convictions will lead the manager to a specific set of strategies aimed at eliminating the conflict. In the same situation, the pluralist will not question the legitimacy of employees' right to challenge or pressurise, but will seek to establish an acceptable and workable compromise within the complex of constraints which currently operate on him.

The crucial point being made here is that perceptions of conflicts and responses to them are conditioned by the set of beliefs and assumptions held by the different parties involved: we shall appreciate differences in managerial responses to conflict only by first understanding their starting point in terms of assumptions made or beliefs held.

10.2 The dimensions and types of organisational conflict

We move now to an examination of some of the different types of conflicts likely to be evident in organisations. It would be easy to gain the impression that organisational conflicts occur almost exclusively between 'the management' and trade unions acting on behalf of groups of employees. In fact, this is only one dimension or variety of organisational conflict. For example, conflicts may be between individuals. In the case of a superior-subordinate conflict, formal rules and procedures will usually be available for its resolution. Where conflict arises between two individuals at the same level of the hierarchy, however, there is much less likely to be any formal procedure such as a disciplinary or appeals procedure through which the conflict may be resolved or channelled. Resolution of such interpersonal conflicts can therefore be difficult and sensitive, especially where the basis of the conflict is emotional. Often, as we shall see later, the only practical course is to attempt to control the conflict and thereby minimise its negative effects.

Conflicts may be neither interpersonal, nor between management and workers. Other forms of intergroup conflicts are quite common. Conflicts between trade unions, between departments or between groupings within management frequently manifest themselves. These may have a wide variety of causes, which will need to be recognised before the conflict(s) can be effectively resolved. We shall shortly examine the different bases of organisational conflicts and consider ways in which they may be prevented, resolved or rendered constructive. Before this, however, one final distinction between varieties of conflict needs to be made.

Organised and unorganised conflicts

Organised conflicts are those where conflicting attitudes or priorities are expressed, usually by some form of planned group action. They include such extreme forms as strikes as well as other expressions such as working to rule, overtime bans and a range of similar formal, collective sanctions.

Unorganised conflict, on the other hand, generally refers to less direct, usually individual, forms. It is not likely to form part of any planned strategy and may in fact be entirely unplanned and spontaneous. It includes lateness, absenteeism,

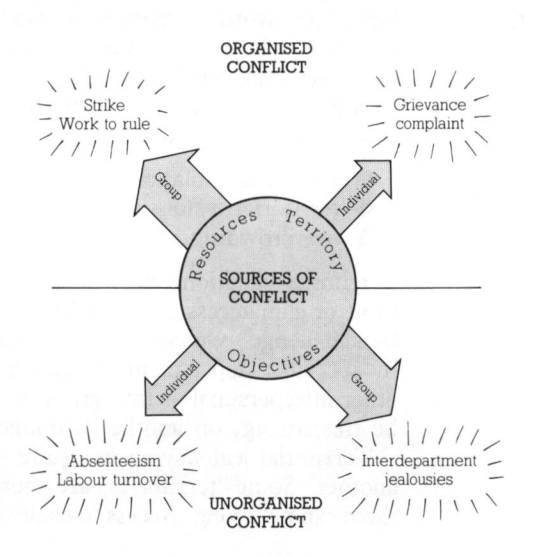

Figure 14
Model showing the parameters of conflict

pilfering, sabotage, and expressions of 'negative' attitudes generally. Of course, an ultimate expression of discontent by the individual is complete withdrawal from the organisation.

This distinction between organised and unorganised conflict is an important one. It serves not only to remind us that we should not gauge the extent of organisational conflict only by such apparent and highly visible phenomena as strikes and other planned, formal actions. A decline in the number of strikes or their duration in an organisation is an unreliable indication of a decline in unrest or conflict. It may simply mean that opposition and discontent are being channelled and expressed in other ways.

10.3 The underlying causes of conflicts

We have stressed already that perceptions of the causes of any episode of conflict will be shaped by assumptions, attitudes and beliefs. From a unitary perspective, conflicts over the goals and actions of management are both wrong and unnecessary and must be eradicated for the good of all. The pluralistic view contends that conflict between groups is the legitimate expression of competition and that as such, competing claims on 'resources', in the widest sense of the term, must be managed in such a way that each group gains something from its continued collaboration with the others. In this section, we discuss three general conditions or situations likely to generate conflict of either an interpersonal or an intergroup nature.

Competition for resources

If we take 'resources' here to include not only money but also power, status and prestige, competition for these resources often forms the basis both of individual and group conflicts. Where one party competes with another for an additional measure of such a resource, then each will exercise power to obtain it. Typically, these kinds of 'distributive' conflict occur between the interest groups within the organisation, e.g. trade unions and management, between functional departments competing for resources, and between individuals vying for personal power and status.

Competition for, or violation of, territory

Here, the word 'territory' is used in a broad sense. It refers to formal job territory – the rights, duties and jurisdiction of any job holder, and also to any privileges and practices which may have evolved over time. Of course certain territories can bring with them different resources or the kind mentioned above.

Territory can be the source of conflict in three ways;

- territorial violation;
- territorial jealousy;
- overcrowding.

Territorial violation refers to situations where one party seeks to exercise control over, or gain access to, something which another party regards as his own. It may be a challenge to 'managerial prerogative' from the shop floor, it may be an attempt by specialist departments to exercise control over line managers, or indeed any other interpersonal or intergroup situation where one party trespasses, or is felt to be trespassing, on another's 'domain'.

Territorial jealousy occurs quite simply where one party envies the territory of another. Some 'territories' are more attractive than others and competition for them can be strong. Access to exclusive groups or the privileges attaching to certain positions are examples of 'territory' which may be prized by those who do not have them and which can therefore generate conflicts.

Over-crowding is where people have, or feel they have, insufficient 'territory' which they can call their own. The likely result is that people spend time and energy competing for, or protecting, territory. It basically occurs in situations where too many people are doing too few jobs. The result of such overcrowding is likely to be conflict.

Goal divergence

Conflicts arising out of goal divergence occur when two parties, who need to co-operate and work together, cannot agree on their objectives or the best means of achieving them. The severity of any conflict will depend on the strength of each party's convictions and the extent or degree to which they must co-operate with the other(s). It is a very common form of interpersonal and intergroup conflict in most organisations.

In summary, competition for resources, threats to autonomy or security, territorial jealousy or overcrowding, and incompatible objectives or ideologies are all conditions of latent or potential conflict. Where individuals perceive themselves to be in any of these situations (whether they actually are or not) then there is conflict potential which may later manifest itself in a variety of actions or behaviour.

10.4 Conflict management

Recurrent conflicts, some would say inevitable conflicts, such as those over the distribution of resources between organisational interest groups, tend to generate formal control mechanisms through which the conflict can be channelled. Collective bargaining is an example of conflict which is regulated by procedure and by 'rules of the game'; disciplinary matters and the treatment of grievances are other issues likely to be settled by agreed procedure.

Where a conflict is not of the recurrent or continual kind, like most interpersonal conflicts, other strategies to resolve or contain it may be employed. One option is arbitration by a third party. This may not eliminate the cause of the conflict but is likely to prevent its escalation and minimise its harmful effects. Where it seems that arbitration would be an unsuitable remedy or option, two other courses may be considered. The first is fairly drastic because it involves a crude separation of the parties to the conflict. This separation may be permanent or only for a temporary 'cooling off' period.

The second option is to allow the parties to the conflict openly to encounter each other to negotiate out their differences. One possibility is for the parties first to articulate their grievance(s) and then to exchange concessions with each other until agreed terms are reached. This option is essentially a negotiation exercise though it is much less formal than collective bargaining. Often, depending on the attitudes of the parties to it, it can result in a mutually satisfactory agreement and the resumption of an effective working relationship. Such confrontations, perhaps most valuable in territorial conflicts, are often to be preferred to resolution through arbitration where the 'solution' can easily alienate one of the parties.

Conflict at work

Evaluation

We began this chapter by looking at some of the assumptions made about conflict and how it can be perceived very differently by different people. These assumptions predispose people to adopt particular strategies for dealing with conflict when it arises. If it is seen as a necessary and natural manifestation of competition between individuals and groups, or even as a necessary agent for change, emphasis will be placed on conflict management and the pursuit of constructive change or resolution. Where conflict is seen as wrong and unnecessary, emphasis will be placed on its prevention and elimination.

We examined the different dimensions of conflict which can involve individuals and groups and drew an important distinction between 'organised' and 'unorganised' conflicts. Lastly, we surveyed the underlying causes of conflicts and suggested some ways in which they may be effectively managed. In conclusion, one additional point needs to be made. It is that conflicts at work are extraordinarily complex phenomena. No given set of conditions will necessarily generate conflict, neither will any third-party intervention or strategy resolve it. In some cases, especially in interpersonal or intergroup conflict, both parties do not explicitly recognise or acknowledge that conflict exists. In such cases formal attempts at conflict management by various methods are likely to fail before they start. Similarly, interventions aimed at resolving or containing conflicts will only be as effective as the accuracy with which those conflicts are perceived by those who attempt to defuse or resolve them. Without attempting to dismay the reader it must be pointed out that there is an extensive range of possible inputs into any conflict situation. They include the economic, political and social context of the conflict, structural considerations such as technology and work organisation, the people involved, their personalities and ideologies as well as their relative organisational status. Taken together, these inputs combine to present us with a formidable phenomenon to understand. It is difficult enough to unravel their relative importance and influence in the context of any one specific episode. It is even more difficult and precarious to generalise.

In spite of this, however, it should be remembered that there are available useful and practical conflict management techniques appropriate to different situations. We have reviewed some of them here, and others were discussed in our treatment of roles in Chapter 8.

Self-test questions

1 Which parties or groups might be included amongst the interest groups of an organisation? To what extent are their interests the same?

2 Can conflict ever be functional or constructive?

3 What is unorganised conflict?

4 Why might strike statistics be a deficient measure of organisational conflict?

5 In what sense is the term 'territory' used in this chapter?

6 How would you define 'conflict'?

7 What determines the severity of conflicts arising out of goal divergence?

8 What are some of the tools and strategies of conflict management?

11 Employee participation in decision making

- A major problem in evaluating the merits of employee participation is defining and categorising systems of participation.
- Different forms of participation involve different individuals and groups, permit or preclude different interactions, and are likely to reinforce particular kinds of involvement in the organisation.

Few people would deny that what is generally, though loosely, termed 'participation' is one of the most important organisational issues confronting a modern industrialised society. British legislative impetus towards the introduction of statutory systems – either along European lines or those outlined by the Bullock Commission in 1977 – has recently waned, but there is still considerable debate and pressure for moves towards forms of industrial participation. Proposals include moves towards greater disclosure of information for employees, co-operative forms of organisational ownership and management, profit sharing and greater employee participation in strategic decision making.

Overall, there is an unusual measure of consensus amongst academics, managers, trade unions, employees, employers' associations and government that participation is both necessary and desirable. A brief look at some of the benefits which have been claimed for participation goes a long way to explaining this broad-based interest in, and commitment to, participation. The following list takes the main points (often quite similar) from a number of studies into its effects.

- increased work satisfaction
- higher productivity
- more positive attitudes to superiors and to the company/organisation
- lower staff turnover and grievance rates
- improved work attendance
- reduced alienation (i.e. the sense of powerlessness, meaningless and isolation that comes with certain repetitive, machine-paced jobs)
- enhanced communication
- better managerial decision making
- greater trust by workers in the motives and actions of management
- a rise in workers' sense of responsibility towards, and identification with, the organisation
- more harmonious interpersonal relations

The list is impressive – at first sight it would seem that participation is a panacea for the many ailments which afflict modern organisations. But if this is so why has progress towards increased employee participation been so slow? If the case for the introduction or extension of participation is as strong and straightforward as it seems, with all parties deriving benefit, why is it that many systems 'fail' or simply fall into disuse?

Employee participation in decision making

The central reason is that 'participation' is usually discussed and considered as though it had one simple, precise and universally endorsed meaning. This misconception accounts for the apparent consensus over the desirability of participation and for much of the confusion surrounding the subject. In fact, as Warr and Wall (1975) observe: '"Participation" has taken on several meanings and herein lies a major difficulty ... since whilst the same word is used by different authors, they are often referring to very different processes.'

The conventionally accepted benefits of participation, including those listed above, are the outcomes of very different forms or systems of participation. Each different form or system rests on different assumptions, permits or precludes different interactions, and affords very different benefits to the parties involved. Everyone may be 'for it' whilst the term participation remains unqualified, but when the precise form of participation which different parties prefer is specified closely, consensus tends to dissolve quickly. It is possible for individuals or interest groups to claim to be wholly in favour of participation yet vigorously to decry or resist a specific scheme in a specific context.

It is worth bearing in mind that, by definition, participation will change the allocation of authority and responsibility in an organisation to a greater or lesser degree, and will have implications for conflict and conflict management, as well as for other topics discussed in earlier chapters. Meaningful discussions must therefore centre on specific systems or forms of participation, and their nature and effects must be distinguished carefully.

11.1 Forms of participation

The task of classifying and defining forms of participation is a difficult one: schemes vary widely and can share few characteristics. For these reasons most attempts at classification tend to confine themselves to making very basic distinctions.

Immediate and distant participation

One way of distinguishing systems of participation is by the criterion of 'distance'. At what sort of level of decision making is the employee permitted influence? 'Immediate' participation involves employees in decisions affecting their own job and everyday work. Medium and distant level decisions are those normally concluded at middle and top management levels respectively. Here the employee is involved in decision areas normally outside the scope of his or her own job and immediate work situation. This 'distance' distinction is a useful one. There is considerable evidence, for example, that there is variation in employee (and management) interest and attitudes in forms of participation in immediate decision areas compared with those in more distant issues or decisions. We shall be looking at examples from each category later in the chapter.

Direct and indirect forms

Another important distinction is that between what are usually termed 'direct' and 'indirect' (or representative) forms of participation. As the labels suggest, the first describes those forms where individual employees participate, or are entitled to participate, directly, in their own right and on their own behalf (e.g. suggestion schemes). Indirect participation occurs where employees' interests are channelled through a representative who is chosen to act on their behalf. Works councils, co-determination, collective bargaining, and joint consultation are all important examples of indirect forms of participation.

Forms of participation

Informal and formal (structural) forms

An alternative or supplementary categorisation of forms of participation is into informal and formal, or structural, types. Participation is informal where it occurs outside structures specifically designed for that purpose – perhaps through an employee's daily interactions with superiors who adopt participative supervision or leadership styles. Formal participation occurs through formal structures or processes within the organisation. Suggestion schemes, works councils, collective bargaining, joint consultation and autonomous group working are all common examples of formal participation.

Individual and collective forms

Styles or types of participation vary between those which can be labelled 'individual' and those which are 'collective'. The distinction is largely evident from these labels; individual forms are those where participation occurs on an individual rather than a group basis, through a suggestion scheme, through the delegation of work by a superior to a subordinate, and through various forms of job extension such as job enlargement and job enrichment. Collective forms are those where groups of employees or their representatives participate in the decision-making process in any of a variety of ways. Again, works councils, collective bargaining and autonomous group working are examples.

Participation in management, government or ownership

This categorisation reminds us that not all forms of workers' participation involve participation in 'management' decision making (or what are traditionally regarded as areas of management decision making). Employees may participate, too, in the ownership of an enterprise by maintaining a shareholding in it. Different forms of profit-sharing schemes provide workers with a stake in the ownership of a company – usually on the assumption that this will increase the employees' identification with, and interest in, the aims of the enterprise.

Participation in the government of an enterprise arises through employees or trade unionists having representatives at board or director level. Different European countries have adopted different systems along these lines. The best known is

		Individual	Collective	
Informal		Participative supervision	Participative supervision (Works social club)	Integrative
Formal	Direct	Suggestion schemes Job extension Share ownership Profit sharing	Autonomous work groups Profit sharing	Integrative
Formal	Indirect		Joint consultation Works councils Co-determination	
Formal	Indirect		Collective bargaining (National level Company level Plant level)	Distinctive

Figure 15
A matrix of types of organisational participation

probably the system of co-determination operating in West Germany. A similar system was proposed for British industry by the Bullock commission in 1977, and European legislation may result in board-level representation where, in a two-tier board system, management would report to a board comprising both worker and shareholder representatives.

These different classifications, summarized in the matrix in Figure 15, highlight the fact that individuals and groups in different organisations may influence the decision-making process in many ways. Different structures and processes have been designed or have evolved to permit different degrees, types, and areas of employee influence. Before discussing the difficulties of designing and evaluating different systems, we should be clear about the detail of those most commonly practised in Britain.

11.2 Some varieties of employee participation

In discussing the different forms of participation in practice, one confronts an immediate difficulty. Forms which may go under the same name, such as suggestion schemes, works councils, or profit sharing, may have evolved differently and may differ somewhat in design. Our examination, therefore, will be limited to the most commonly practised forms as they might typically occur. There are too many variations of each different form of participation to permit discussion of them all here.

Job extension

There is a sizeable, though not entirely consistent, body of evidence which suggests that the majority of employees show a greater desire or willingness to participate *directly* in decisions closely related to their own job and tasks at work than in more distant decisions. This apparent preference for 'immediate' participation might be explained in many ways. It may be that there is a greater interest in these fairly low-level decision areas because they most immediately affect the employees and their work environment. On the other hand, it may be that employees feel a lack of confidence in participating directly in higher level management decisions and would therefore prefer not to participate at all or to do so through a representative.

Two related forms of participation permitting this 'immediate' involvement are job enrichment and autonomous group working. Alternatively, or in addition, thoughtful delegation by superiors can achieve a similar effect to that of these two formal techniques.

The theoretical origins and objects of these techniques were introduced in Chapter 4. Both job enrichment and autonomous group working involve employees in activities and decision making which conventionally or previously would have been the responsibility of those in 'higher' positions. For this reason, job enrichment is sometimes called 'vertical job loading'. In terms of our earlier categorisations, both techniques are direct, formal forms of participation in management. They differ in that job enrichment is usually an individual form of participation whereas autonomous group working is a collective form which has as its aim the transfer to groups of employees of a degree of responsibility for the planning and management of their own work. Usually the group will see the task through from beginning to end, and so their 'psychological ownership' of what is produced is likely to be increased.

Both job enrichment and autonomous group working relate quite closely to delegation practised on a more informal basis. At its best, this will have the same effect of increasing the employee's scope for personal initiative and involvement in his or her work. Usually 'informal' delegation does not involve permanent formal changes in the job content of either delegator or delegatee.

Job design techniques which increase employee autonomy and work variety – whether on an individual or group basis – are often welcomed by employees themselves, but they should not be embraced as a panacea for problems of motivation, alienation, poor productivity, and negative work attitudes. We have already stressed in Chapter 5 the importance of individual differences between people, and how these differences will affect their perceptions, aspirations, and expectations at work. These differences, not unnaturally, lead to a variety of attitudes and responses to the conditions created by these forms of immediate participation. This is most easily demonstrated by the variability of research findings on employee attitudes to job extension. Some describe employees as having a dislike for, or indifference to, a greater discretionary element in their work. Others show no significant improvements in job satisfaction or involvement. A further, more practical difficulty arises where it is difficult or impossible, usually for economic or technological reasons, to redesign jobs so as to 'enrich' them significantly.

A final complicating factor is that these job extension techniques, involving as they do greater responsibility, wider job descriptions and more flexible work roles, can meet with suspicion and resistance from trade unions concerned with the protection of traditional job rights. For this reason, attempts to enrich and extend work roles will usually need to be accompanied by a rethinking and redesign of existing payment systems and agreements with trade unions. Whilst this in itself is not always a bad thing, it can generate its own conflicts and uncertainties and thus reduce the attraction of large-scale job redesign.

Any conclusion here then, must be *in*conclusive. Job extension in its different forms may be both welcomed and enjoyed and different positive benefits can accrue to it. However, it must be recognised that different attempts to redesign jobs, however well intentioned, will meet with different responses from individuals and groups at work. The reaction may not be favourable; instead it may be a neutral one leading to no change in attitudes or performance, or it may be hostility (or disorientation) where employees have a preference for standardised and prescribed work methods or are only instrumentally involved in their work.

Finally, however desirable they may be in theory, these techniques may be difficult to implement successfully. The nature of the task and technology used, economic constraints and industrial relations will, in practice, limit what can be achieved.

Suggestion schemes

Most people are familiar with suggestion schemes of one kind or another. Employees are encouraged to submit their ideas on possible improvements over a range of areas, such as employee facilities, work methods and procedures, and customer services. Usually, when suggestions are taken up by management, the employee(s) who made them will receive a reward or prize which may or may not be related to the value of the suggestion to the organisation.

Advocates of suggestion schemes assert that they encourage employees to consider their work and the way it is performed and that this can increase job involvement and active interest in the organisation. Further, talents not strictly necessary for the job holder to do his job are tapped, and he or she is free to exercise ingenuity whilst doing what is perhaps a routine and otherwise mentally undemanding task.

Although suggestion schemes are relatively widespread, active participation and interest in them by more than a minority of employees has been shown to be rare. The reasons for this seem to include the view that rewards are felt to be too small, that there is poor feedback and delay in considering suggestions made. Finally, and perhaps significantly, many employees seem uncertain of the correct procedure to be followed in making suggestions.

The suggestion scheme then, as it is typically designed and operated, attracts low participation, but does permit all employees to participate in more distant decision areas. Employee criticism of suggestion schemes is widespread and fairly consistent, however, and their survival in many firms is probably attributable to their cosmetic value and/or their value to management rather than to the employees.

Joint consultation

Joint consultation is a representative or indirect, formal type of participation through which individuals or groups can express their interests to the management of an enterprise. Consultation does, of course, occur informally in organisations, for example through participative management styles, but most commonly the term refers to a formal forum for an exchange of views. What are known as joint consultative committees are basically an attempt to integrate, structure, formalise and openly legitimise dialogue between a workforce or its representatives and management.

Many benefits were claimed for joint consultation in its early days. Many, frankly, were extravagant at the time – others have later been shown to be so. Originally seen by many as the vehicle to a new co-operative relationship between management and employees with conflict withering away in its wake, joint consultation has now substantially declined in popularity and effectiveness. This decline can perhaps best be accounted for by two conditions which were originally applied to joint consultation. The first was that there should be no challenge to, or encroachment upon, managerial prerogative. The second was that there should be no discussion of those issues which were the subject of negotiation.

With the growth of workplace collective bargaining and shop stewards' preference for it over consultation, joint consultation has tended to suffer. Reduced jurisdiction has led to more trivial issues being the normal subjects of consultation, and a loss of interest on the part of the work-force has resulted. Indeed one of the most common criticisms of joint consultation by employees concerns the triviality of the issues it gives rise to and resolves. With shop stewards being more interested in negotiation than in consultation (and more effective gains being made through negotiation) most joint consultative committees entered a steady decline. As W. E. J. McCarthy, a former Research Director to the Royal Commission on Trade Unions and Employers Associations, has said, '... plant consultative committees in the strict sense of bodies intended simply to advise management on how to raise efficiency and discuss other matters of assumed "common interest" without reaching binding agreements, cannot survive the development of effective shop floor organisation. Either they must change their character and become essentially negotiating committees ... carrying out functions which are indistinguishable from the formal processes of shop floor bargaining, or they are boycotted by shop stewards and, as the influence of the latter grows, fall into disuse.'

Even where joint consultation has survived the growth and development of workplace bargaining, and where the issues discussed generate sufficient interest to prevent employee apathy, it can suffer from other problems typical of representative forms of participation.

There is the danger that communication between representatives and their constituents will be inadequate. Employees may rarely be contacted by their representatives in order to establish whether they have any issues they want raising in consultative committee meetings. Similarly there is often inadequate feedback, from both representatives and management, on the progress of issues already in hand. Finally, the delay between the raising of an issue and any action being taken

Some varieties of employee participation

on it by management is often excessive and, in that time, interest in the issue on the part of employees has often waned.

Nonetheless, despite these shortcomings, joint consultation remains fairly widespread and can play a useful role. This is especially so where union organisation is weak or non-existent or, alternatively, where management has a 'human relations' orientation and where there is a commitment to a genuine and constructive consultative relationship on both sides.

Collective bargaining

In its analysis of industrial relations in Britain, the Donovan Commission reported in 1968 that collective bargaining was 'most effective way of giving workers the right to representation in decisions affecting their working lives.'

In Britain, collective bargaining operates at different levels:

1 National, where industry-wide negotiations take place between a union or unions and an employers' association or federation of employers' associations to settle such matters as basic wages and conditions of work for the industry in question.
2 At company and plant levels where national agreements on basic wages and conditions are supplemented and extended in agreements between union(s) and management, and shop stewards and plant management, respectively. The issues which may be negotiated at company and plant levels include discipline, work practices, redundancy and recruitment, piece-work prices, overtime, bonuses and other financial incentives. They account for the disparity between actual pay and nationally negotiated rates. At plant level, the interests of union members will be represented by elected shop stewards.

Collective agreements may be of two kinds; 'substantive agreements' which cover issues of substance such as terms and conditions of employment, and 'procedural agreements' which describe the procedure which it is agreed will be followed in, for example, negotiation, grievance handling, disciplinary problems, and redundancy. Clearly, like other forms of representative participation, collective bargaining depends on the effectiveness with which representatives of trade union members ascertain and represent the interests and aspirations of their constituents.

Works councils

The label 'works council' means different things in different industrial contexts. It may be used to refer to either a negotiating or a consultative body. It may be made up exclusively of employees and be independent of management, or it may be a joint management-employee committee. It may be the highest authority in the organisation as for example in Yugoslavia, or it may be very limited in its rights and powers. The term is used to refer to so many very different vehicles for participation that broad generalisations are not possible. We shall concentrate here on works councils in West Germany as being probably the best known and certainly amongst the longest established.

In Germany the works councils form part of a highly structured, legally prescribed framework for the exercise of employee influence as far as board level. The system as a whole is known as co-determination. In many ways, the German works councils play the part of plant-level trade unionism in Britain. They have the right to be consulted specifically over a range of issues and may withold their approval from a range of decisions. The council also negotiates plant-specific agreements supplementary to industry-wide agreements concluded by trade unions.

As a form of participation, works councils are of the indirect or representative type. As such, they are prone to the typical problems and deficiencies of representative participation touched on earlier. Representative systems are really only

Employee participation in decision making

as good as the representatives who work within them. The closeness of their contact with those they represent, the faithfulness and forcefulness within which they represent their constituents' views and the quality of the feedback they provide, are all important ingredients for the success of these systems – as measured not necessarily by their achievements but by the extent to which they further express employees' interests.

The problem of distance between representatives and those they represent tends, naturally perhaps, to be greater the higher up in the organisation the works council operates. One measure of how effective works councils are in allowing meaningful employee participation is employee interest in, and satisfaction with, them. This can be gauged by employee participation in works council elections. Where this is high, and where employees feel that real gains are being made, then clearly the works council, whatever its form and jurisdiction, is an important and valuable body. Where contact between employees and representatives is poor and participation in elections is low, gains and concessions from management may still be made, but it is probably fair to say that more is being done *for* the employees than *with* them and that genuine participation is not being achieved.

Worker directors

Impetus has been given to the debate over the value and effectiveness of employee participation through representatives at board level as a result of both domestic and European proposals for legislation in this area. Probably prompted by the apparent stability and relative success of European systems, there has been much discussion of the merits of introducing such a system in Britain.

In 1977 the Bullock Committee of Inquiry on Industrial Democracy advocated strong worker representation at board level. This was followed by a Labour Government White Paper which endorsed the concept of board-level representation – though within rather a different structure and procedural framework from that proposed by Bullock. The impetus towards mandatory participation of workers on boards of directors diminished sharply with the election of the Conservative Government in 1979. Occasional and somewhat experimental schemes still persist (mainly in the public sector) but there is no mature common model by which the success or potential of worker directors in Britain can be fairly judged. Only a few general observations may be made. It is self-evident that the contributions of worker directors will only be effective when they receive the full and timely information necessary for the proper appreciation of a company's circumstances. Further, the directors need to be skilled in the evaluation of that information. Unless these conditions are met any conclusions would be premature and misleading.

Worker directors, like all representatives, run the risk of failing to ascertain or be informed of their constituents' interests and priorities and this can be compounded if a growing social distance develops. Thus, a crucial risk with such a high-level and exclusive form of representation is that employees may feel no close contact with their representatives, may have insufficient access to them and may receive little or no feedback from them. Regardless of any other problems, those of communication and social distance will need to be resolved if any system is to achieve any real success.

Profit sharing/share ownership schemes

As with other systems, schemes for profit sharing or employee shareholding are extremely diverse in design and operation. They tend to be more popular with both sides of industry in countries other than Britain. In 1977 there were only just over 100 share ownership schemes in the UK, most of which did not cover all employees in the organisation.

Some varieties of employee participation

The case for this form of participation in the ownership of the business is that employees are given a real financial interest in the success of their organisation and are thus encouraged to co-operate in the pursuit of corporate goals and strategies. One way in which schemes differ is in whether shares given or sold to employees carry voting rights or not. Where they do not, schemes differ little from conventional bonus payment schemes except that the rewards given are more remotely linked to the individual's own work efforts.

Criticisms of most schemes are widespread and fairly consistent. Usually rewards are felt to be too small, too distant and too indirect to be a very effective motivator. Further, the shareholding they confer usually brings little or no influence over managerial decision making. It is interesting to note that it is far from uncommon for employees who receive shares under profit-sharing schemes to sell, rather than retain them.

Evaluation

The reader may be frustrated by the lack of any clear advocacy or prescription in this chapter. In fact, the prescriptions are there. In the case of employee participation, it can only be argued that systems must be designed in a way which ensures that they are consistent with the situation and circumstances into which they will be introduced. We began by saying that there is no shortage of comment on participation from different interest groups. There is, however, one crucial paucity of views. It is from employees themselves. Logically, if meaningful participation is a worthwhile and sincerely held goal, it should begin with employee participation in the design and implementation of participative systems, each tailor-made to the needs of a particular workforce in the light of specific organisational and environmental constraints: we cannot claim to be in favour of genuine participation without taking employee views as the starting point for designing specific systems. Initially, certain key questions must be asked: Do the employees concerned aspire to greater influence? If so, how much influence do they want? In which areas? How do they want this influence channelled or expressed?

A participative system designed on the basis of the expressed, rather than the assumed needs, traditions and priorities, of any workforce, stands more chance of real success than the universally applied product of academic or political debate.

Self-test questions

1 What actually is employee participation?

2 What benefits can be expected from the introduction of employee participation?

3 What would you say is the major difficulty with indirect or representative participation?

4 Distinguish between participation in the management, the government, and the ownership of an enterprise.

5 Why is job extension a variant of employee participation?

6 Are suggestion schemes a good idea? Give your reasons.

7 Why has Joint Consultation tended to decline over the years?

8 What might be the best starting point for the design and implementation of a participative system for any specific organisational context?

12 Business communication

- Communication is a two-way process involving different and sometimes complementary methods of transmitting information.
- Communication can be adversely affected if inappropriate methods are used or if communicators are not sensitive to behavioural and structural problem areas.

12.1 The communication process

Communication is the transmitting of information, opinions and ideas through a two-way exchange process. Facts, problems, news, decisions, the expression of feelings – must be transmitted, and received. Unless both parties understand why something is being communicated and what it is, it is arguable whether there is any communication at all. Consider, for example, an American businessman negotiating with a Japanese businessman; unless both use a common language and are sensitive to cultural differences, they will not communicate successfully.

The communicator starts by having an objective, a reason why he or she wants to communicate. Every communication is in a code of some sort, and a decision has to be made as to which message code, such as the written word, speech, visual symbols or non-verbal signals, should be adopted. It must be transmitted by a method of communication such as a memorandum, a talk, a graph or a frown. The receiver of the message needs to translate, or decode, the message. The success of the communication process is revealed by the receiver in some way acknowledging the fact that the message is understood and, if appropriate, responding in the intended manner. This is known as feedback. Generally speaking the more immediate the feedback, the more successful is the complete communication cycle, because the transmitter can instantly evaluate how well the objective has been reached.

The communication process can be modelled simply by the analogy of a radio broadcast (see Figure 16).

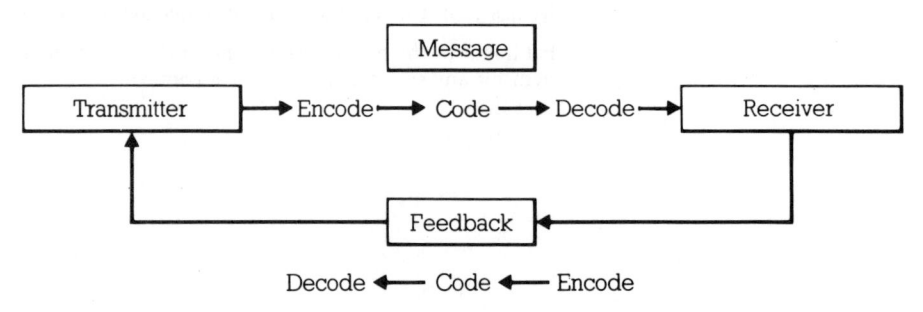

Figure 16
Model of the communication process

The problems of communication

At each stage in the communication process there are potential problems to be overcome. These problems can lead to distortion in the intentions of both the transmitter and the receiver.

The transmitter must have a clear objective. The computer adage of 'garbage in, garbage out' sums up well the point that too often people communicate without having clearly defined intentions. For example it is common to listen to a speaker or read a letter without really knowing what the point of the message is. The choice of code and corresponding medium is critical. For example, a supervisor of a small group of clerical workers might decide to pass instructions on in the form of a notice pinned on the wall whereas it might be more appropriate to call a short meeting and explain directly what the orders were. Choosing the right code has semantic pitfalls: unless people understand the meaning of words communication will suffer. Choosing the right medium brings in technical problems that can distort the message. The reason why business correspondence is usually typed is because of poor handwriting. Technical problems can also arise from interference on telephone lines and such non-mechanical things as the pitch of a speaker's voice.

Finally it must be understood that communication, as an exchange of information, opinions and ideas, is concerned with human relations. There may be psychological barriers to effective communication. If the attitude of the receiver is not attuned to accepting the message the communication process will not work properly. A person may physically receive a message without understanding or indeed making an attempt at understanding. It is common for receivers to nod their heads or make affirmative noises, but it takes a very experienced transmitter to be able to decode feedback and be certain that his original message has been understood. These psychological aspects are particularly relevant when considering the style of leadership to adopt: people can be 'put off' by someone's manner.

In general the problems of communication can be minimised so long as there is an awareness of them on the part of both the transmitter and the receiver. Communication therefore involves more than the clear transmission of information; it has the secondary aspect of behaviour and attitude modification and is thus crucial to all business organisations. We shall therefore discuss its various aspects in more detail.

12.2 The four communication media

Speech

Speech or oral communication is the simplest and one of the most effective media, offering instant feedback. A whole range of organisational communications are best carried out through the spoken word. Giving orders and reporting back are perhaps the commonest: some situations, like the interview, have become so ritualised that they have been given their own names. When events require the sharing of ideas consultation groups like the committee, the briefing group, the conference and the staff meeting are formed to meet on a face-to-face basis.

Oral communication is not, however, necessarily face-to-face. A lot of time and money is spent on the use of oral transmission equipment such as the telephone, public address system, dictaphone, and radio. Their obvious advantage, their ability to cover distances of space and time, makes them an invaluable aid to modern business communications and functioning.

However, precisely because oral communications are 'easy' and common, they can be the source of many basic problems. Speaking and listening are social skills that do not come naturally, and they need to be practised with conscious effort. Oral communication relies on both parties having a sufficient command of language, adequate vocabulary, and an understanding of the logic of discussion to

Business communication

express themselves clearly and concisely. Communicators must be aware of the problems that can be created if one or both parties are lacking in these areas. Slang and jargon can cause further confusion, and if one party is more articulate than the other the message may be distorted, or the recipient may be frustrated or embarrassed.

The loss of face-to-face contact makes machine-aided oral communication less effective and, in some cases, feedback is distorted or far removed. Technical problems can cause further distortion or difficulty in understanding the message.

Communicators therefore need to be fully aware of the potential pitfalls of the various forms of oral communication and should try to avoid or overcome them to ensure their most effective use.

Written communication

To many people written communication is the essence of business communication, and there is little doubt that writing and reading consume a lot of the office worker's time. The reasons for this are twofold. First, the conveyance of information in a written format should, theoretically, prevent any ambiguity in the message. Secondly, a written message is more permanent than an oral message and can therefore be referred to in the future. It also offers an economy of effort – it is easier to communicate to many people at one go with a duplicated written message, hence the proliferation of business letters, memoranda, reports, policy manuals, teleprinter messages, notice boards, house journals, newsletters and sales literature. The spread of electronic transmission will continue this trend.

The problems of the written medium are similar to those of the other media. Many writers will put pen to paper without adequately defining their intentions. Much that is written can be easily shortened. Basic literacy skills, such as a knowledge of grammar, syntax, punctuation and style, are essential, and the misuse of jargon words and phrases, 'commercialese', is common.

The use of electronic aids such as the word processor, Teletext and visual display units is beginning to speed up the transfer of the written word from one location to another. If programmed properly from the start, these should provide fewer excuses for slow communication. Some estimates predict that by 1990 at least 30 per cent of office mail will be transmitted electronically. The use of postal mail and the shorthand typist will be considerably reduced along with the expensive process of writing, filing, sending, receiving, more writing and filing, and so on. Easily accessed tape and disc stores of information should lead to improved communications.

Visual communication

Visual communication uses the sense of sight, and although in one way it refers to all non-aural messages it does not here refer to writing. This medium uses colours, signs and various recognised symbols excluding the letter alphabet (although words are often used to reinforce the message). The common format is that of charts, graphs, and tabulated data that give a quickly digested summary of information. A bar chart for example can convey conveniently what several pages of transcript might take up. Although mainly used by specialists such as statisticians, planners and accountants dealing with quantitative data, there is no reason why more use of visual summaries cannot be made by employees dealing with qualitative, non-numerate data: the use of models in this book supports this idea.

One area of visual communication that is perhaps distinct from the others appears in the area of marketing. Theme, colour and the graphic symbol (logo) are applied to advertise and promote the company itself, its products and services via letter headings, packaging, display and transport fleet liveries, such as the famous red circle with bar of London Transport. Abstract signs, if well designed, can cross

Channels of communication

international boundaries. Road signs are one example and labels on clothing another. Visual media combined with audio channels can be very effective. Films, closed circuit television, sight and sound slide shows are widely used in training and promotion activities.

However, visual communication can have its drawbacks. Too colourful or complicated visual aids can be distracting or confusing. Statistical presentations are notoriously open to bias. The actual use of visual media may be inappropriate – but these are all factors which the skilled communicator will already have considered.

Non-verbal communication

So far it has been suggested that face-to-face oral communication is the most effective medium for getting a message across because of its immediacy of presentation and feedback. An aspect of this personal interaction that has been largely ignored until recently is non-verbal communication, which may substitute for, enhance, or even contradict the verbal message. Face-to-face communication not only involves words and their messages but the way the speakers present themselves and their message.

There are four main areas of non-verbal communication. Firstly, physical appearance will influence the recipients of verbal communication in some way. Dress and hair style signal a projected personality: if a bank employee dyed his or her hair green, his or her promotion prospects would no doubt suffer. When going for a job interview it is accepted that one should present oneself in as smart a way as possible.

A second area of non-verbal communication, paralinguistics, refers to tone and speed of voice. It is widely recognised that some people have a 'confident' voice or, say, an 'insincere' tone. It is important that conference speakers, salesmen, and others in constant face-to-face contact with the public should be properly trained in these areas.

The third area, kinetics, is concerned with movement. Arm and hand gestures may reinforce the speaker's emotions and effect – or they may distract attention from the message. Nodding, facial expression and eye contact are all strong signals. Common sayings such as 'He will never look you in the eye' show that these signals are quickly noticed, however subtle they are.

The fourth area of non-verbal communication is called proxemics and refers to bodily proximity to the listener, body postures and body orientation. Turning away from the speaker can communicate unease or indifference. Getting too close can intimate overfamiliarity or aggression. Too relaxed a posture may be translated as indifference or laziness. Obviously though, all four areas of non-verbal communication can be interpreted in different ways. Many of these signals and counter-signals are unconscious: many are culturally determined and therefore in multi-ethnic groups may be the cause of misunderstanding. Non-verbal communication should not be dismissed as some esoteric spin-off from social anthropology. It needs to be appreciated just as much as the oral, written and visual media. They can all combine into effective ways of communication.

12.3 Channels of communication

Internal channels

Relating the communication process and its associated media to the organisation specifically, it is useful to consider how strong an influence the organisational structure has on the way in which information flows from one party to another. These information flows are often referred to as communication channels. The model in Figure 17 should help to illustrate this idea.

Business communication

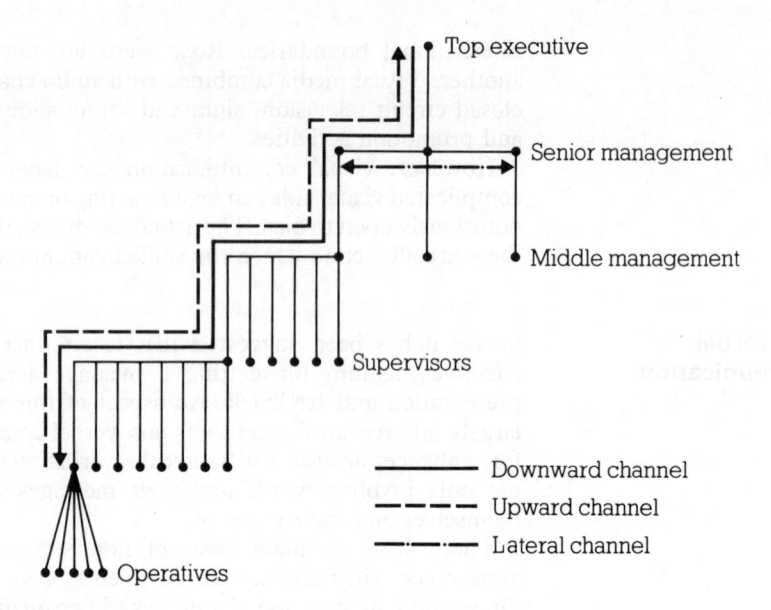

Figure 17

- Top executive
- Senior management
- Middle management
- Supervisors
- Operatives

——— Downward channel
- - - - Upward channel
—-—-— Lateral channel

The downward channel	Messages are passed from the chief executive at the top of the hierarchical pyramid down to the lowest grade of employee at the bottom, usually through a departmental division. Decisions made by senior management are passed down to the operatives usually in the form of orders and instructions. As a rule, the written medium is chosen to prevent ambiguity and to record these items. Policy manuals are issued, targets are minuted and orders are sent down from the hierarchy by means of official memoranda. Oral communication comes into use more often when praise, blame or reprimands are handed out.
The upward channel	The same media are used, as subordinates pass advice, information, progress reports, suggestions and complaints up the hierarchy. The oral or written report is the usual technique. This channel is the organisation's feedback route to those who have the resource and power to create and amend decisions. Without effective feedback brought about by creating, encouraging and allowing the opportunity for upward channels there will be no control in the organisation.
The lateral channel	This consists of inter-departmental information transfer. The communication flows across the hierarchy between employees of similar grade, but working in different sections, and ensures practical liaison of the divided labour force. It should prevent each department going its separate way and working against the others rather than towards common organisational objectives. How often representatives from different departments should meet or in other ways communicate with each other depends on the functional nature of the work. The 'staff' departments such as Accounts and Personnel need constant contact with all sections: Purchasing and Production are closely linked as are, say, the Marketing and Distribution specialists. Progress meetings on a regular basis are necessary to ensure the organisation's plans are on target, and it is usual for the management staff of each department to attend. The lateral channel cuts out the need to take the longer vertical channels and promotes co-operation.

These three channels are called the formal lines of communication. Anyone with experience of working in any type of organisation will appreciate that they are not

Channels of communication

always used properly. Employees, impatient for information, tend to break away from these strict lines. The conversation in the corridor or the quick telephone call offers short-term convenience. In the long term this can be damaging to effective communication. Both supervisor and subordinate can be left ignorant of each other's activities. There is no doubt that confusion and duplication of effort can quickly be the norm if people dismiss the formal communication channels as bureaucratic impediments. The fact that they often are, in reality, dismissed is the fault of the users in not communicating properly.

The grapevine

Rumour and gossip – the grapevine – are inevitable features of any social system and constitute a fourth, informal, channel of communication which has no strict official boundaries. Studies of the grapevine show that at least 90 per cent of the information circulating in this way has a strong element of truth. The grapevine can contribute to morale and a general interest in the workplace and can act as an informal feedback channel, but there is a direct relationship between poorly used formal channels of communication and an increase in rumours. Rumours can cause anxiety or conflict within the organisation and in such circumstances it is the duty of management to use formal channels to intervene.

External channels

Business organisations are not closed systems existing in isolation. They exist mainly to trade with individuals and other organisations. They also have legal and social responsibilities. As will be seen in the next chapter, the business environment necessitates forms of communication to cover these various activities. The model shown in Figure 18 illustrates the various external channels of communication. The output and input channels call for different objectives, media and techniques. A customer will request a technical specification or wish to chase an order. A supplier might have to be told that a contract is terminated. Shareholders have to be informed yearly about the company's progress; the government and its various agencies require a great deal of information. Trade unions and community pressure groups are constantly negotiating with the organisation on what it is doing. On occasions it is necessary to communicate with competitors. All these examples illustrate that there is a constant need for effective external communication.

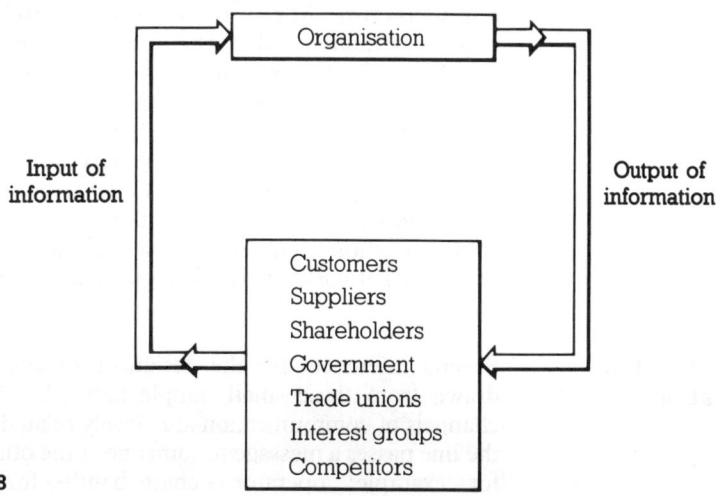

Figure 18

Business communication

Both the importer and exporter of information must choose an appropriate medium to meet their objectives. The written medium is the most common, and business correspondence generates its own mass of paperwork, adding to the records created by the internal communication channels. For speed, if not always greater accuracy, the telephone is used, often supported by written communiqués such as the letter or telex. Many organisations employ a salesforce to represent the company, also acknowledging that face-to-face personal communication with potential buyers can be more cost-effective than money spent on advertising – although usually the one supports the other in practice. Specialist staff, sometimes hired from outside agencies, are employed to do nothing but improve communication. Public relations experts try to establish and maintain a mutual understanding between the organisation and its various publics through building good relationships with journalists and broadcasters, by endorsing and subsidising non-commercial projects and issuing promotional literature and audio-visual packages. This form of image building via corporate advertising is additional to the vast sum of money spent on product and service advertising in the consumer markets.

Choosing the right medium to meet the objectives in each of these external channels of communication is not easy. The success rate is often low. Most people have experienced great annoyance and frustration when dealing with organisations which fail to cope effectively with enquiries. A firm which transfers callers from one telephone extension to another or waits for many weeks before replying to a letter needs to improve its communications. Similarly organisations can waste large amounts of money in advertising without benefiting from an increase in sales. What is at fault in such situations can be identified as a failure to recognise the importance of a good, integrated communication system.

12.4 Designing an effective communication system

There is no simple formula that can be applied to the problem of designing and operating an effective communication system. The organisation is a collection of individuals brought together to have their prescribed activities co-ordinated and controlled to meet some set of explicit objectives. The organising is carried out through the communication process, which in turn is influenced by the organisation's structure. At every level in the hierarchy decisions have to be made on how much information and of what type should be passed on to others. These decisions are shaped by formal objectives and delegated duties, and also by the informal vested interests of the parties concerned.

Studies with small groups have suggested that organisational design has significant implications for the effectiveness of the communication process. These studies centred on how information was passed between five people whose formal relationships were structured like inter- and intra-departmental organisational communication channels. These structures are known as networks, and four principal networks were distinguished (see Figure 19).

Networks in the organisation

Several inferences for the design of an effective communication system can be drawn from these small sample networks. In the typical hierarchy the formal channels of communication are closely related to the chain. Someone at one end of the line passes a message to someone at the other end via several people in between, for example; operator→ chargehand→ foreman→ section head→ department

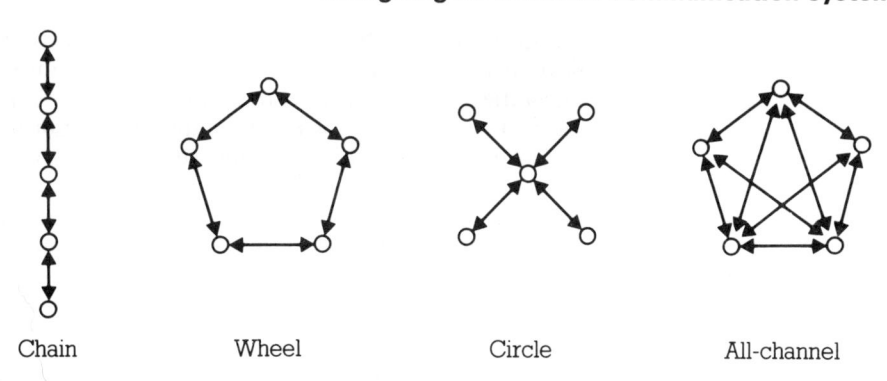

Designing an effective communication system

Figure 19 Chain   Wheel   Circle   All-channel

manager. At each stage in the link a decision is made on how much information to pass on and which medium to choose. The liability to distortion is great even though a written medium may be chosen, which in itself is unlikely at the beginning of the chain. Feedback may be nonexistent. The shorter the chain the fewer the problems. Therefore the flatter the hierarchy is the less problematic the communication process will be.

The circle network is rather like a badly constituted committee, not good at reaching decisions or in passing on ideas. It rather gets people running round in circles not knowing who is responsible for what. Clear job descriptions should prevent this problem occurring, as well as ensuring that any group discussion starts from explicit terms of reference.

The wheel network derives from the chain design. Again it is more typical of the organisation. The managerial role is largely created to act as a central co-ordinator for the information flows in particular sections of a system. All is well so long as the key person can accept and transmit information efficiently. Personal jealousies, or fear of reprimand can lead to the 'gatekeeping' of information, with unfortunate results.

Lastly, the all-channel network, apparently the most effective design, accepts that cross-communication is essential to prevent distortion in the communication process, but it should have one person acting as arbitrator, co-ordinator and controller. In other words this system operates like a well-led committee.

However, it is readily apparent that the organisational hierarchy, when charted, does not consist of a collection of committees. In practice the efficient organisation tries to eliminate the faults of the straight chain and the circle and forms a combination of the wheel and all-channel. Much depends on the size of the organisation, the nature of the tasks and the associated environments and of course, the quality of the employees. With good managers the wheel design is very effective; but if management is weak or the information received is ambiguous, the all-channel system is required. Many firms acknowledge this by having regular staff meetings that act as open forums to clarify any misunderstandings.

However the hierarchy design is just one aspect. Each organisation must set out its communication objectives and communicate them. The policy manual is the acknowledged medium, but unless it is continually updated, it will lead to an inability to cope with non-routine matters where guidelines have not been drawn up. At what point a matter becomes non-routine is the crux of many communication problems. Some companies operate a system of Management by Exception where reporting upwards only occurs when there is a significant deviation from a predetermined set of targets. This is a sound idea because management consultants usually discover that over 80 per cent of all reports in an organisation serve no useful purpose. The wheel design is workable but only if it has been specified how much decision making has been centralised. For a multisite organisation, too much

Business communication

centralised control from head office leads to many problems of delay, lack of local flexibility and lack of feedback, and the failure to delegate only increases difficulties. The all-channel design presupposes a type of centralisation where all relevant parties are involved in the sharing of information. It prevents information overload on one individual, and for this reason the wheel often becomes an all-channel arrangement on occasions that demand group advice in decision making. Individual directors responsible for particular divisions but ultimately reporting to a board committee, exemplify this idea in practice.

Communication training

Whatever design of communication system is adopted there is no doubt that every employee can benefit from training in the skills of communication. This varies from very basic skills such as report and letter writing and telephone answering techniques to more sophisticated interpersonal training such as role negotiation and T-group exercises.

These latter two are recent developments: role negotiation refers to the attempts to get two individuals together to express what irritates them in each other's behaviour and then hopefully to agree on some trade-off of improvements in behaviour for the future. T- (training) group exercises are another form of sensitivity training where a group of employees, secluded away from the organisation's environment and with no formal agenda, are asked to communicate with each other. The result is usually a harrowing group therapy exercise, but it does high-light the complexities of interpersonal relationships. These two forms of training are not common, but that does not mean they are not as useful as training in more basic communication skills such as writing good business letters.

Too much is assumed of the ability of staff to communicate. Pre-employment standards of literacy do not automatically predict competence in an organisational context. Many firms recognise this and run in-service courses but, too often, only for the lower grade of worker. The fact that many organisations seem to operate as if service to the customer is their least important function is a reflection on the lack of good communication systems.

Evaluation

Communication is both an art and a science. However thoroughly an organisation creates an effective communication system, human error will affect its performance. This chapter has tried to point out the significant variables. Without trying to be prescriptive some summary recommendations can be offered. First, any communication must have a purpose. Without an objective there can be no understanding by the transmitter or receiver of information. Secondly, in deciding on the best method of achieving this objective there are various alternative and also supplementary media to choose from. Each must be considered in the light of the particular situation. There is no golden rule to show which offers the best method of transmitting a message. Thirdly, just choosing the right method is not in itself enough, but is paralleled with having an appropriate content. Again this must be tailor-made to the recipient of the message. Fourthly, it should not be assumed that feedback is an automatic process. Without feedback performance cannot be properly maintained.

Communication at whatever level of analysis should be the simplest activity in the organisation. The fact that so many people are left 'in the dark' is because of a failure to appreciate the basic communication process. The one piece of guidance offered in this section is, 'If in doubt, ask'.

Designing an effective communication system

Self-test questions

1 If face-to-face communication is acknowledged as the most effective method of transmitting information, why do organisations generate so much paperwork?

2 Why is an appreciation of non-verbal communication important?

3 By what methods can a manager encourage feedback from subordinates?

4 How far should business correspondence be standardised and how far should it be personalised?

5 Consider each of the following situations and suggest, with reasons, the best action and form of communication that should be adopted.
  a A factory foreman wants to express his concern to an operative, who also happens to be a shop steward, about the latter's consistently poor quality of work.
  b The chairman of a large company wants to advise all the employees of the seriousness of the economic situation and the possibility of redundancies.
  c A marketing manager has received complaints from customers that orders for goods are being delayed in the dispatch section.
  d An internal auditor discovers that many employees regularly make personal telephone calls.

13 The environment of organisations

- Organisations are constrained by the wider environment in which they operate and must therefore anticipate and plan for external change.
- The different interest groups in the different social, legal, economic and political elements of the business environment will, or should, influence managerial decision making.

13.1 The nature of the business environment

The term 'business environment' is usually used very loosely to refer to the set of forces and institutions which constrain or assist the activities of organisations. The business organisation needs to understand the forces, groups and institutions whose existence and behaviour it may, or must anticipate and respond to.

Later in the chapter we shall explore the specific interests and priorities of different groups associated with the organisation, but first let us divide the total environment into

- social
- legal
- economic/technological
- political

environments and consider each in turn.

The social system

Different societies and cultures have their own norms and value patterns. What is and what is not 'socially acceptable' will clearly affect styles of management and operations within an organisation. The conditions of employment for most people which were prevalent a hundred years ago would simply not be tolerated by employees today, neither, one presumes, would they be offered. Similarly, attitudes toward women and work are fairly rigidly defined in most societies and, whilst they may change slowly, they will affect women themselves, employers and those alongside whom women will work.

We have witnessed for some time now pressures for firms to become more socially responsible – that is, to take account of interests and responsibilities other than simply the maximisation of profit by any legal means. These pressures may be to take greater account of the impact of the firm's activities on the community within which it operates, greater care in avoiding damage or detriment to the physical environment through pollution, a greater regard, for example in production and packaging, for the worldwide scarcity of certain resources, the extension of employee participation, and other measures of a similar kind.

People inside and outside the organisation will be influenced to a large degree by wider social and cultural influences and accepted standards of behaviour and conduct. Often, following changes in general social attitudes, legislation will attempt to outlaw those practices which 'society' or 'public opinion' now thinks undesirable. Equal pay and equal opportunity for all employees, protection against arbitrary dismissal, minimum standards of working conditions, consumer protection, and other areas of legal intervention have all followed shifts in general *social* attitudes and expectations.

The legal system

The laws of the land which prescribe or prohibit certain activities are obviously of more precise effect than the social pressures dealt with above. The rights and duties of the different stakeholders in the organisation are defined in law and usually ensure a measure of consistency and equity in business relationships and practice. Trade unions, customers, shareholders, employees, the community in general, suppliers, competitors are all protected to some extent against certain forms of business practice. As a result, the managers of an organisation must ensure compliance with a large number legal obligations.

The economic system

The economic system, the level of business activity, inflation, unemployment, and current monetary and fiscal policies will all affect management's possibilities and the prospects of the organisation. Economic conditions will largely determine the price that must be paid for 'inputs' such as labour, capital, materials and components into the organisation. They will also influence the price which can be obtained for the outputs of goods and/or services produced by the organisation. Advances in technology influence the numbers and types of labour required, productivity and job security. A host of other factors have presented management and employees with new problems to grapple with.

The political system

Pressure may be exerted through the political system in any country on employers, trade unions and others to act in particular ways. The degree of intervention in business and trade, monetary, fiscal and incomes policies, and the scope of commercial and labour law will all vary according to the prevailing political climate and the objectives of the party in power at any particular time.

Thus, environmental conditions at any particular time will influence the nature, scope and success of an organisation's activities. The price and availability of inputs into a business, the motivations and priorities of its stakeholders, and the range and saleability of its outputs all depend to some measure on existing environmental conditions.

We shall see later how an organisation can plan for, and profit from, anticipated environmental change. Before that, though, let us examine briefly the importance and influence of the different interest groups or stakeholders referred to earlier.

13.2 The interest groups of organisations

The survival and success of an organisation depends upon a number of 'internal' and 'external' groups, each of which has an interest in the way the organisation is run, and each of which stands to gain from its success. In some cases, however, these groups' interests may appear to be less than fully compatible, or even in direct conflict with those of other groups. Management needs to retain the support

The environment of organisations

and co-operation of the different groups by seeing to it that their interests are served, in other words, by ensuring that it is profitable (in the widest sense of the word) for them to continue with their support or co-operation. Naturally, each group will exert pressure on management to concede more to them and less to the other stakeholders. The difficulty for management lies in satisfying the aspirations of each group sufficiently to retain their interest without alienating any other group or groups whose commitment to the organisation is equally important.

Shareholders and investors

Whatever kind of business we are discussing, whether it is a sole proprietorship, a partnership, a public or private limited company or a nationalised industry, finance is one of the key inputs without which it cannot even begin to function. In return for their investment, contributors of capital expect a reward. If the firm fails to provide investors with sufficient reward for their money and the risk of loss they have undertaken, then, in the long term, funds will become difficult to acquire and the firm itself will be at risk. What must be decided, though, is just how much the business can afford to pay its investors and how much must be channelled into other areas of recurring commitments.

The local community society

It is obviously difficult to generalise about the interests and expectations of a group such as this one. Within communities and society generally, there are bound to be incompatibilities in terms of what is expected of organisations. The creation of stable and secure employment, good terms and conditions of work, a respect for the community and its environment, are all probably present-day priorities of most local communities and therefore of 'society' at large.

Different political and other pressure groups exhort firms to have due regard to the interests of the communities in which they are situated. It is increasingly common to see demonstrations against factory closures, the consequences of which are often grave for employment in the affected area. In most industrialised countries, people's awareness of environmental issues, pollution, the movement of heavy goods vehicles, conservation and so on is growing. The concern of many firms to preserve goodwill is reflected in the sums they spend in advertising the contributions they are making to environmental protection and reconstruction.

Customers

Quite obviously, unless there are customers for the outputs of an organisation it will not survive. Unless the customer is able to get what he or she wants at a price considered to be fair the custom will be transferred elsewhere. Consumers can exert a major influence over the activities and viability of any producing organisation simply by their patterns of behaviour. There has been much greater awareness and organisation of consumer interests in the last decade: legal definition of what a consumer is entitled to expect from any product has been articulated in consumer protection legislation, and greater competition nationally and internationally has forced companies to survey and provide for the expressed, rather than assumed, needs and wants of consumers. Whilst consumers may lack formal channels of influence over a company and its activities such as those which may be enjoyed by government, employees, shareholders and other groups, their collective influence is no less effective or respected. The extreme importance of a 'consumer orientation' on the part of organisations is explored further in Chapter 16 on marketing.

The interest groups of organisations

Employees

We have talked already about the different ways in which employees may, or may be permitted to, participate in the management, ownership or government of an organisation. We have talked too, in Chapters 5 and 6, about just what employees may expect from the organisation in exchange for their time and effort. The conclusions we can draw from these analyses are that, generally, employees today expect safe and hygienic conditions of work, a reasonable wage relative to others and a measure of autonomy and discretion in their work. Employee interests may be articulated through any of the forms of participation dealt with earlier, that is, informally and individually, or collectively through either consultative or negotiating machinery.

The consequences of neglecting employee interests as they are perceived by the workforce can indeed be severe. Individually, an employee dissatisfied with the returns from work may become disenchanted and less productive; co-operation with, and trust in, management is likely to decrease, change is more likely to be resisted and, as a final resort, the employee may leave the organisation for another. On a collective level morale and productivity are likely to suffer, absenteeism and labour turnover increase, and industrial relations deteriorate. None of this benefits anyone and, whilst management have a duty to protect the interests of all the stakeholders in the organisation, they can only benefit in the long term through the pursuance of a responsible and constructive relationship with their employees and their representatives.

Trade unions and employers' associations

The system of industrial relations in Britain is a complex one which can only be understood by reference to its historical origins and development. Trade union members, approximately half the working population, are represented within their place of work by elected shop stewards who negotiate with management over a range of issues of concern or interest to their members. The shop stewards also act as a link between the union membership and the official trade union structure outside the organisation, which reaches up to national level. The actions and attitudes of trade unions locally and nationally can have far-reaching implications for the organisation.

Employers' associations often help to provide valuable information on trade and technical matters, and also influence the organisation through such issues as trade policy, representations to government and industrial relations.

Government

The influence of government and the State on organisations is clearly substantial. Apart from the general influence of economic and fiscal policy, legislation may be framed to regulate the relations between an organisation and its customers, employees, trade unions and shareholders. The government may pass what may be termed 'promotional' legislation allowing for financial and other aid to the organisation. The State also offers a wide range of statistical and advisory services to help consumers and industry.

Some of the most important government departments are:

- The Treasury
- The Ministry of Agriculture, Fisheries and Food
- The Department of Employment
- The Department of the Environment
- The Department of Energy
- The Department of Trade
- The Department of Industry
- The Department of Prices and Consumer Protection
- The Board of Inland Revenue
- The Board of Customs and Excise

The environment of organisations

Finally, it should be remembered that organisations, as well as operating within an industrial and legal framework managed by the government, are required to furnish it with returns and statistics – an annual company return to Companies House, VAT and National Insurance figures. They must also comply with regulations on importing and exporting, planning permissions and other statutory requirements.

All these interest groups are likely to apply pressure on organisations where they can, to achieve or further their current objectives. The success they each achieve will obviously depend upon their power and the methods of influence they are able to apply to any particular organisation. Each group has a major overall influence on the nature and terms of the employment and business relationship, and generally it is unlikely that specific developments can or would be ignored for long by those firms not unionised, not members of an employers' association, or removed from direct persuasive government influence.

13.3 Anticipating and responding to environmental conditions

So far we have been concerned to establish some of the forces and influences acting on organisations in the modern business environment. What remains to be looked at are the ways in which organisations can minimise the threats to them and their business activities, and identify, and take advantage of, the opportunities created by change.

There are basically two ways in which an organisation can deal with change in its environment. It can wait until changes occur and then react to those changes as it feels most appropriate. The advantage of this is that the nature of the problems and/or opportunities presented by change will be known and can therefore be tackled with some confidence and certainty. Unfortunately, whilst decisions involve less risk when information is relatively complete, this approach has certain dangers. By the time the changes have actually occurred, it may be too late to take the necessary steps either to survive them or to profit from them. Secondly, where a firm reacts to each new set of circumstances on the basis of the short-term problems which they present, there is likely to be a loss of any overall direction or logic to its decisions.

The other approach attempts to anticipate and plan for changes *before* they occur. Of course, the danger here is that judgement, experience and even intuition must be relied on to a significant extent. There is much less certainty when long-term changes have been forecast. The benefits of such an approach, however, more than make up for this difficulty, and new techniques of forecasting, and the development of better and more sophisticated models and decision techniques, have further reduced the risk of serious error. Thus, on the basis of an analysis of probable changes in the environment, a long-term overall plan can be established which will ensure that the necessary resources to profit from new conditions are ready and available, and that the activities of the business are relevant and competitive in the changed environment. Thenceforward all decisions within the firm should be taken in the light of that overall plan which, of course, can be modified in the light of observed differences between expected and actual changes in operating conditions.

Anticipating and responding to environmental conditions

Strategic and tactical planning

The detailed actions to be pursued by different parts of a company should, we have said, be consistent with some wider, longer-term objective or set of objectives. These latter are generally termed strategic objectives, and the means set out to achieve them are called strategic plans. Strategic objectives should be set for all key aspects of a company's operations: its plans for growth and development, its market objectives, its profitability and other such critical facets of performance. Because of their importance and centrality to the success of a business, these strategic objectives will usually be set by top management. It should not be assumed that, because they are long-term statements of intent and are wide in their coverage, strategic objectives can be loosely expressed in the form of some rather vague 'hoped for' result. They cannot. Strategic objectives are, ideally, expressed quantitatively and are specific both in the time scale they refer to as well as the areas of the company they commit. In other words, the objectives should be a 'closed' statement which allows decisions on required resources and their deployment to be made so that the objectives will be achieved in the time given.

Tactical objectives and plans which flow from these strategic considerations are different in nature. They will still be specific in their reference to target results, a particular area of the business and a given time. However, their time scale will tend to be much shorter, probably for periods of up to a year, and they will be formulated by middle management in consultation with the top management team responsible for strategy. Tactical plans specify in detail the action and resources needed to achieve specific results which will be consistent with strategic plans laid down earlier. With strategic planning, the main problem or constraint is uncertainty over the future and the resources that will be needed to safeguard and strengthen the business in the light of forecast developments. With tactical planning, the main constraint is the strategic plan(s), with which tactical plans must be consistent, and the resources currently available. In other words, with tactical planning, the situation or problem is known, as too are the resources at the immediate disposal of the firm. It is the tactical planners' task to combine and deploy these resources in the most effective way possible, bearing in mind the internal and external constraints operating at the time.

The difficulties and challenge faced by the strategic planner have been likened to those confronting a general preparing for a battle. He has some information at his disposal about the military resources which should be available to him on the day the battle is likely to begin. He has less reliable information about the resources of the enemy. He will not know for certain, and must therefore anticipate, how and where those resources are likely to be deployed at the start of the battle. He will be unsure of, and must again anticipate, the strategies which the enemy commander will adopt. He will be unsure of likely weather conditions on the day and must plan around this uncertainty. His problem, it can be seen, is basically one of estimating, forecasting and anticipating the conditions likely to be faced by his army on the day. Having done this to the best of his ability, and having drawn on expert opinion and advice, he can begin to devise a strategy for the battle, the resources he will need to overcome the enemy, and how and where these resources will need to be deployed for maximum effectiveness. This strategy must then be communicated to all the officers involved in it. They will be aware of what contribution they are required to make to the overall goals formulated by the general. However, their planning task is a very different one. They will be aware more precisely of the resources they each have at their disposal, the men, the weapons and where they will be located. When involved in the battle, they will know the precise conditions they must operate under, they will know more exactly the location and strength of enemy forces. Their task is to deploy and utilise their known resources in the most effective way in that known situation. Of course, it would be chaotic if each unit commander operated independently and without knowledge of the overall battle

The environment of organisations

plan. Some might decide to advance, some to retreat and others to entrench. At the end of the day, the forces would be scattered and possibly isolated, and would be unlikely to have achieved anything in overall terms.

Evaluation

In this chapter we have looked in a general way at the environmental pressures likely to influence the nature of an organisation's activities. Social, legal, political and economic pressures influence the actions and behaviour of the managers of any firm. Additional pressures are articulated by different interest groups, each of which has some form of 'stake' in the organisation. Each is necessary to its survival and success, and therefore none can be ignored or alienated if the business is to prosper. It is the difficult task of management to satisfy the aspirations of each of these groups to a satisfactory extent.

Environmental conditions and the expectations of organisational interest groups will constrain the long-term plans of the organisation. Each must be surveyed and anticipated and long-term strategy must be developed on the basis of these results. This should ensure that the organisation is well placed both to safeguard itself against future threats and to take advantage of changed environmental conditions as and when they arise.

This broad strategy, formulated by top management, provides the context for more detailed action plans which will be the responsibility of middle management. The tactical plans aim to make the most effective use of present resources within the constraint of the organisation's strategy. Crucial to the success of this planning approach is the link between strategy and tactics. Where the links are strong, what is achieved is a long-term company plan based on realistic assessment of present and future operating conditions, and detailed action plans committing every area of the company – each devised to profit the organisation in the short term and to shape and equip it for the challenges of the future.

Self-test questions

1 What is meant by the term 'business environment'? Why is it not static?

2 List the interest groups of your own organisation, trying to be as specific as possible. Are they all equally influential? What bases of power underlie their ability to influence the organisation?

3 Distinguish between strategic and tactical planning.

4 What do you understand by the term 'social responsibility'?
In what specific ways might this manifest itself?

Case studies on Part C

THE BUZZ-WORD GENERATOR

This word matrix was originally devised by the Canadian Defence Department to illustrate how easy it is to become an instant 'expert' in any field just by adopting a specialised vocabulary. The method is to choose at random any three numbers and from three associated word lists create a phrase. The result is usually meaningless gobbledegook.

The example below relates to jargon words from management studies.

A	B	C
0. flexible	0. managerial	0. ecology
1. functional	1. scalar	1. approach
2. traditional	2. authoritarian	2. perspective
3. humanistic	3. neo-classical	3. motivator
4. hierarchical	4. autonomous	4. environment
5. planned	5. neutralising	5. role simulation
6. objective	6. rational	6. input
7. psychosometric	7. orientated	7. structure
8. normative	8. delegated	8. culture
9. totalitarian	9. systematic	9. concept
10. classical	10. interactive	10. analysis

EXAMPLE:

Numbers 8 4 4 offer a 'NORMATIVE AUTONOMOUS ENVIRONMENT'.
Numbers 9 3 8 offer a 'TOTALITARIAN NEO-CLASSICAL CULTURE'.

The matrix shows all too clearly how easy it is to generate important sounding phrases which in fact can be meaningless.

A DILEMMA AT SPARKO

Sparko Ltd has three factories each supplying components to local industry, and each aiming to provide a quick delivery service for orders placed at short notice. Sparko Wolverhampton employs some 150 people, 30 of whom are delivery drivers. The organisation chart looks like this:

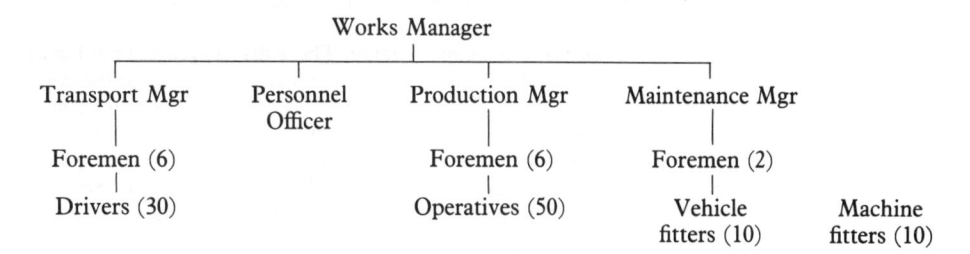

```
                          Works Manager
                               |
     ┌─────────────┬───────────┴──────┬──────────────┐
Transport Mgr   Personnel      Production Mgr    Maintenance Mgr
                 Officer              |                |
     |                                |                |
Foremen (6)                      Foremen (6)      Foremen (2)
     |                                |                |
Drivers (30)                    Operatives (50)    Vehicle       Machine
                                                   fitters (10)  fitters (10)
```

The two other Sparko factories, at Manchester and Sheffield, are of similar structure, but larger, because they have more customers to serve. All Sparko factories operate for 24 hours a day, 7 days a week, so that most people, except managers, work on shifts.

At Sparko Wolverhampton life is uneventful and the atmosphere friendly – or it would be were it not for the drivers, and in particular for their shop steward, David Perks. He is regarded as a militant, anti-management, and always trying to find ways to get more money for his members. He and a few close friends run the drivers' union branch at the factory, and it is said that this group is not above using intimidation to keep union members in line. Perks is regarded by the Transport Manager as outspoken, comparatively articulate and 'no fool', but a constant source of trouble. Everyone at the factory is well paid by local standards, but some people are beginning to feel that the drivers are getting more than their fair share, simply through their aggressive tactics.

Last week, on Sunday, three of the drivers were caught having left the factory in the afternoon without permission and without 'clocking out'. This is an offence for which the company rules clearly specify dismissal, and since one of the offending drivers was David Perks, some people immediately began rejoicing over the prospect of having got rid of him at

Case studies on Part C

last. However, it turned out not to be such a simple matter and the following discussion about the incident is taking place at Wolverhampton. Those present are the Works Manager, the Transport Manager, a Transport Foreman (John), the Personnel Officer (Jenny), and the Production Manager.

Works Manager: Jenny, could you start by telling us what the legal position is? Are we within the law if we dismiss the drivers for this offence?

Personnel Officer: On the face of it, yes. The rule is clearly stated and a copy of it is given to every employee on joining, so we are within our rights, provided the rule has always been applied in the past. This could be a case of unfair dismissal if we have allowed the rule to lapse.

Works Manager: Well, I've not known a case of this nature come up for at least five years if not more, but had there been one I'm sure we would have applied the rule. We can't have people walking off the site whenever they think they will. How can we maintain our service to customers if we don't know how many drivers we've got available? And in any case, they're paid to be here, not to be sitting in their gardens.

Personnel Officer: Yes, but the point is, have the previous cases been reported, or have foremen been turning a blind eye to it? John, perhaps you could throw some light on this?

Transport Foreman: Well, of course I couldn't swear to it. I'd never let those drivers get away with anything, but they're a tricky lot, and you can't be sure that one of the foremen hasn't turned a blind eye to their going off on a Sunday afternoon. Things are always slack on a Sunday, and duty drivers are very often sitting about with nothing to do. I can think of one or two foremen who might – just to try and keep drivers sweet and win a little co-operation!

Production Manager: But does that really matter? Surely we should take a firm stand here and not let the drivers get away with it this time – show them who's boss! I can tell you that some of my people who have always been co-operative and play straight with me are beginning to say that it clearly pays to be difficult and militant, because the management will always give in. If we don't look out, the drivers' attitude will spread to other workers.

Transport Foreman: I agree. Those drivers are just out for what they can get for themselves, and they don't give a damn about what happens to the company. I had one last week who got a so-called 'puncture' outside the factory gate and I'll swear he let the tyre down himself. All he wanted to do was sit in the canteen and get paid for it! And I must admit we foremen are getting fed up with the way our authority is being undermined because management won't back us up in cases like this. I think we must stand firm and sack these men, or the drivers will think they can do as they like.

Personnel Officer: That's all very well, but you know what Perks will say, don't you, that he's been victimised because he criticises management and they are trying to get rid of him. I wouldn't put it past him to take us to court for unfair dismissal – we'll certainly put up a fight if he does!

Works Manager: Not only that, but I wouldn't put it past him to get the drivers at our other factories to support him as a matter of principle – you know how these drivers all stick together. And the Managing Director has said that whatever else we do, we must not at this time put at risk the trading position of the company, and we must think what a strike could do to our profits, not to mention our reputation.

Production Manager: I still think that's a very short-sighted view. We surely owe it to those people here – the majority – who are on our side, to stand firm against a small bunch of reds who are out to ruin Sparko.

Works Manager: Well one thing is certain – a decision must be made. So do we sack the three drivers or don't we?

1 Who is trying to influence whom and in what direction?

2 What types of power are being used as a basis for that influence?

Consider in your answer people who are *not* present at the discussion, as well as those who are.

S.L.E.P.T. LTD.

S.L.E.P.T. Ltd is a medium to large company operating in a very competitive market situation. The last few years have been relatively lean ones in terms of profitability, and management is very concerned to restore the company's market standing.

The Government, concerned about high domestic levels of unemployment and inflation, has indicated, with the agreement of the TUC and the CBI, that wage increases should be held to a norm of 10% unless additional increases are the result of 'self-financing' productivity deals which would be subject to approval and monitoring.

There is a possibility of sanctions against companies which violate the norm, and these, if pursued, would have a seriously adverse effect on the company's trading.

The trade union operating at S.L.E.P.T. has entered an initial claim for a 25% increase in wages for all grades.

The logic of the claim as stated by the union is that 13% is being pursued as a basic increase, with an additional 12% to bring the employees' pay levels into line with equivalent workers in the area. Several local firms have recently settled just outside the pay norm but would be largely unaffected by most anticipated Government sanctions.

Management had originally intended to make an offer of 8% to all grades of employee and feel that payment of 25% claim would, amongst other consequences, undermine the competitiveness of S.L.E.P.T. products in domestic and overseas markets. The claim therefore is considered to be unviable on these grounds alone.

However, the mood of the employees and their representatives is clearly militant. They feel that their claim is a fair one and would only result in their achieving pay parity with other workers doing the same or similar work in other firms in the region. They feel that the initiative now rests with management to make their position clear and to make an offer which will avert the need for the union to contemplate damaging industrial action.

There are no real possibilities for increasing labour productivity without the introduction of new, more efficient technology and work methods. These would lead to a labour surplus of about 10% and redundancies, at a time of high local and national unemployment, would be inevitable.

Few of the workers who would be most likely to go under such circumstances would be qualified for redundancy payments of any substance. They would, additionally, experience great difficulty in finding alternative work in the area.

Informal discussions with shop stewards have indicated to management that the mood of the union membership is serious and determined, and that conformity with the 10% limit, or the possibility of enforced redundancy are, from their point of view totally out of the question.

1 What options are open to management and what are the implications of each?

2 Which option or what package would you present to the union? What are your reasons, and how do you estimate the chances of it being largely accepted?

3 What social, legal, economic, political and technological influences are there on the parties to this case?

PART D

The organisation's resources must be allocated and combined in order to optimise efficiency and productivity. This part looks at the different aspects of managerial control involved in the organisation: management accountancy, budgetary planning, marketing and determining the marketing mix, production planning and control, and the acquisition, development and training of the workforce. It is when the particular tasks associated with each of these functional areas are confronted that the previous chapters of this book become most relevant – and most difficult to apply. Students should bear this in mind throughout the following section.

14 Capital structure and sources of finance

- The different forms of business entity have different means of access to financial capital.
- The problems of access can act as major constraints on any organisational activity, and therefore the role of financial management is of great importance.

Organisations need resources to operate. The simplest way to measure the utility of any resource is through its value in monetary terms. As there is no point in committing an organisation to any activity unless it can provide the appropriate resources, it is clear that finance (or capital) is key to any decision making. It is worth noting with caution that the word 'capital' has various uses. To the layman it refers to a sum of money. Capital can however mean the total tangible resources of an organisation, such as property and equipment as in 'capital assets'. When the word is used in this chapter as in the phrase 'capital structure' it is referring to the various claims of a financial nature made on the organisation's capital assets. This chapter describes in broad terms the possible sources of finance and the capital structures of the main types of organisation in the private and public sectors. The problems facing financial management and in particular the small firm are then reviewed.

14.1 Financing different business entities

The sole trader

As already noted in Chapter 2, the majority of trading organisations are owned and run by private individuals. The advantage of a relatively uncomplicated method of starting such a business is however offset by the major problem of a lack of finance. The initial stake in a one-man business comes from the owner's personal savings. The owner is personally responsible for any bad debts that may arise, a situation known as unlimited liability. The ability to raise more money to finance operations is limited by this risk factor. The owner is unable to seek funds from the general public in the form of shares because the owner is the business. Financial institutions such as the Merchant Banks tend not to lend money in the uncertainty of small-scale investment.

The owner must therefore to a large extent be self-financing from the revenue obtained from selling the products or services although it is possible to find short-term finance. The high street commercial clearing bank may offer overdrafts or short-time loans subject to the discretion of the local bank manager, business premises may be leased or bought under the terms of a mortgage contract, equipment may be hired or bought under a hire-purchase agreement. Occasionally an equipment supplier may offer a loan agreement, but this is usually for expensive goods costing over £1,000 which are not regularly required by the small-scale operator.

All these sources are available but, either through ignorance on the owner's part or through unwillingness on the part of lenders, they are not always fully taken up. The serious problems that face the sole trader are considered further at the end of this chapter.

Capital structure and sources of finance

The partnership

To overcome the problems of the sole trader's lack of finance, many small business organisations either start off or progress to a Partnership agreement. Put simply, the advantage is that more people can supply more capital. Ultimately, however, the problems are the same. Most partnerships are drawn up with the partners subject to unlimited liability. The attractiveness of the limited partnership has lessened because of changes in company law and if people desire this option then nowadays they tend to set up as a private limited company.

The limited company

There are two types of limited company, the private limited company and the public limited company. The financial base of both types is set in their Memorandum of Association as 'nominal capital'. Nominal capital relates to the amount of money that the company may raise from subscriptions from individual members of the public or from other organisations. The advantage of corporate status lies in the limited liability which subscribers gain if they choose to invest in the company. This liability advantage is greater for the public than for the private limited company because the latter is restricted to a maximum of fifty shareholders.

The sources of finance for the limited company can be categorised into two parts: money capital supplied by the owners and money capital supplied by lenders in the form of loans. These are technically external sources of finance but, as with the other types of organisation, it should not be forgotten that very often the most important source for any finance comes from the ploughing back into the business of net undistributed profits.

Owners' finance

The owners of a limited company are those who own shares in it. Shares can be bought and sold like any other commodity. In the private limited company the shares are often owned by the original founder or his relatives but in the public limited company the management who run the company are not necessarily shareholders.

There are two main types of shareholdings. *Preference shares* give the holder a fixed percentage return irrespective of company performance: they have 'preference' over the other type of share when money is paid out in the form of 'dividends'. Some preference shares are 'cumulative', which means that if the company makes a loss one year the year's guaranteed dividend will be paid in another year when the company can afford it. Preference shares, although part of the capital structure of the company, do not usually entitle the possessor to voting rights.

The second type of share, the *ordinary share*, does offer voting rights. In theory, therefore, ordinary shareholders control the company: they can vote directors in or out of office at the Annual General Meeting. The finance provided by ordinary shareholders, equity capital, does not entitle the shareholders to annual fixed percentage dividends. In a year when the company makes a trading loss they do not necessarily receive any dividend but in a good year there is no limit on the amount of dividend that may be paid to them. This particular benefit was, however, curtailed in recent years by dividend restraint demanded of companies as part of restrictions on prices and incomes made by the Government. Certain types of Ordinary shares are known as 'A' shares; these do not carry voting rights and are therefore usually cheaper to buy than normal equity.

Companies make either type of share available to prospective investors on the open market or by offering extra shares to existing holders at preferential rates, in what is known as a Rights Issue. If the whole of one type of share as set out in the company's nominal capital is fully paid up, for administrative convenience they are converted into whole block units. These blocks are known as stock. This is why

Financing different business entities

limited companies are known as joint stock companies. When companies are expanding rapidly they will apply to the Stock Exchange to get their shares publicly quoted and hopefully to attract more investors. Of approximately 16,000 public limited companies, some 3000 are listed on the Stock Exchange.

Lenders' finance

Apart from owners' money capital, finance can also be obtained from loans from individual or organisational creditors. A charge is made for giving these loans in the form of interest. The main type of loan is a Debenture. Debentures are issued, bought and resold rather like shares but they usually have a fixed life before they must be fully repaid by the company. Unlike shares they have no voting rights attached; however, if the company is wound up the debenture holder has a priority claim on the company's assets. This priority for debentures also applies to the distribution of the company's trading gains, because debenture interest is paid out before any profit is allocated to shareholders. Some debentures offer extra security to the holder by being linked to a claim on the company's assets; these are known as mortgage debentures.

The other types of lenders' finance are similar to those considered for the smaller firm, although for the limited company often operating at a higher turnover they are usually more readily available. The commercial banks offer discretionary overdraft and term loan facilities. Mortgage contracts on property, sale and lease back or plain leasing, save the company having to allocate major funds that could be used more favourably in investment projects. The same applies to hire purchase agreements.

Trade credit is an important way of stretching the organisation's cash flow – it is common for invoices to be paid a month after the month of the date of delivery. If there are contractual commitments to suppliers, the latter can offer free advice and service as well as reduced prices for the goods. The availability of these loan sources depends very much on the demand and supply of money at any one time. A comparatively minor source of loan comes in the form of grants from various public bodies. Since the 1930s the government has operated policies for those regions of the country where there is severe structural unemployment. Grants for plant and equipment and tax deferments have been offered to companies to encourage industrial development in these areas. A problem has been that there has never been a consistent system; loans and facilities tend to change with the government of the day. The regional development fund of the EEC may in the long term help to rectify this situation. Various specialist institutions offer loans at commercial rates. The Merchant Banks can offer help to major national and international companies, and agencies such as the Industrial and Commercial Finance Corporation and the European Investment Bank assist in this area.

A growing trend in this country, imported from America, is for some financial institutions to arrange for syndicates of lenders to help the cash flow problems of small but potentially highly successful companies. This is referred to as the raising of venture capital and many of the high street commercial banks have started schemes to provide development capital for small firms.

The public sector

Within the public sector there are many different types of organisation that have to compete with the private sector to finance their operations. Three main categories may be distinguished, central government, local government and the nationalised industries.

Capital structure and sources of finance

Central government

The principal source of finance revenue for the government ministries comes through personal and corporate taxation. In the short term this is supplemented by the issuing of Treasury Bills. These are bills of exchange tendered to discount houses. In the long term low risk loans, called gilt-edged securities, are offered. A significant source of funds also comes from overseas investments.

Overriding these possibilities is the fact that the government is operating in an open and mixed economy. Pressure from other countries through balance of payments deficits and adjustments to the prevailing rates of exchange can all influence how well public expenditure, or as it is otherwise known public investment, is financed.

Local government

The finance for expenditure by local authority for the provision of community services comes from two main sources. Revenue from a variable tax on households called the 'rates' is supplemented by rate support grants from central government. Loans are obtained from the commercial banks, and authorities also offer to the general public competitive fixed interest securities in the form of bonds.

The nationalised industries

The public sector corporations such as British Rail and the utilities such as the Water Boards were originally intended to be self-financing from the charges they made for the services they provided. The costs of their investment programmes however are so high that, at least in the short term, their operations have to be subsidised by central government. At least half of their finance is borrowed in this way and a large proportion from overseas investors. There is a possibility that more direct access to the general public as a loan source will be used and the National Coal Board is particularly interested in this development. The National Enterprise Board is an important, if politically controversial, funding agent for those industries and for commercially unsuccessful private sector corporations that have serious financial problems.

14.2 Financial management

The responsibility of determining the capital structure and sources of finance for any type of organisation is a specialist function. The necessary expertise usually comes from a Financial Manager who will be of board level in the hierarchy. He has to decide on an optimal capital structure based on the availability and cost of the various sources of finance.

Taking the example of the joint stock company, there are two principal considerations: the raising of capital through, for example, the issuing of shares, and decision areas such as the determination of levels of debt loan, dividend policy and the monitoring of alternative investment opportunities. These decisions can be taken in a planned professional manner only if the board has advised on the level of assets the organisation should acquire, maintain and replace and what those assets should consist of. It is usual to consider these variables against different time periods; projections should be made for the present accounting year, the medium term of one to five years and beyond five years in the long term.

For each level of plan the opportunities for finance will be influenced by the cost of capital. As the cost of anything is relative to the cost of something else, the cost of capital must relate to the minimum rate of return it must earn to justify its investment. This is measured as a so-called opportunity cost relating to a comparison with the highest rate of return offered by an alternative investment. To

Financing different business entities

the financial manager this rate of return will be read from the total capital employed; but to any potential investor the rate of return is influenced by *ad hoc* investment opportunities in the money markets. For a limited company the total capital employed will always be greater than the funds supplied from stockholders, and the two rates of return will consequently differ. One target rate set by many companies is that of 15 per cent return on capital employed. The financial manager must therefore decide what proportion of the capital structure should be split between owners (in particular equity) and loans offering fixed interest rates. This problem is known as gearing or financial leverage. A low-geared company is one in which the proportion of equity is higher than other sources of finance. In good trading years the ordinary shareholders will profit more from their riskier but nevertheless unfixed dividend investment. A high-geared company offers a safer risk over the long term but is less attractive to the equity holders, because any gains are absorbed by the fixed interest preference shareholders' and creditors' investments. It is important to appreciate that the track record of the company's trading success and the levels of taxation will be important factors in setting the gearing levels.

To help the financial manager to appraise any capital investment project there are a number of management decision-making techniques that he can use. The most famous are Discounted Cash Flow (DCF) and Net Present Value (NPV). These fairly complex formulas rely on many variables including the company's cash flow, the time period, the cost of capital, the return rate on investment and reinvestment and the levels of taxation. The variety of sources of finance necessitates such quantitative techniques.

Capital structures for limited companies vary considerably because of the complexities of the money markets and the different policies of individual organisations. However some authorities suggest that a proportion of 70, 15 and 15 per cent for retained earnings, shares and loan debt respectively is not untypical. Figure 20 illustrates the relationships of the different types of capital to the various sources of finance that have been described in this chapter.

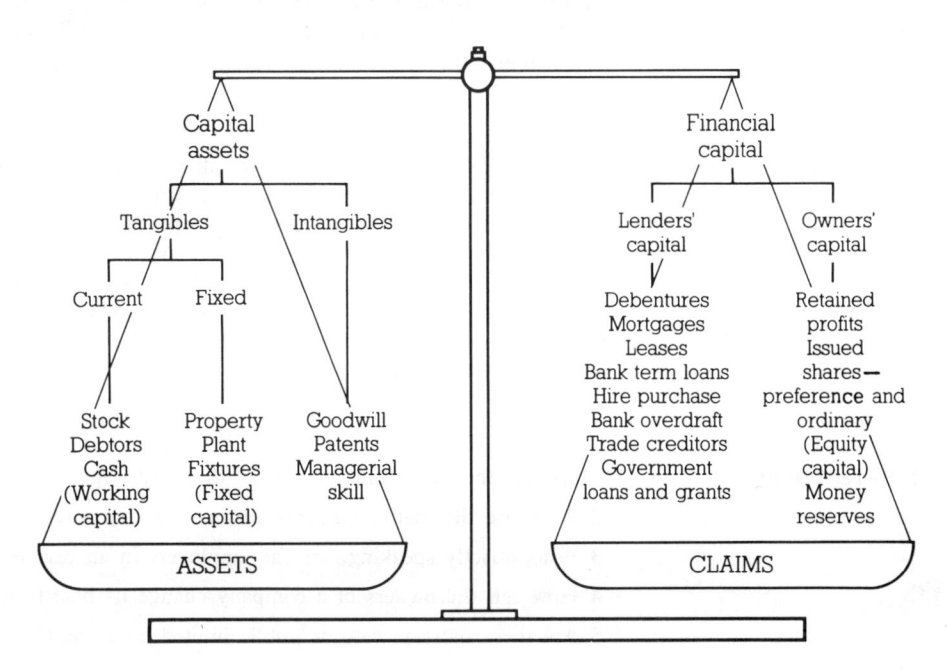

Figure 20
Capital structure of a public limited company

Capital structure and sources of finance

14.3 Finance for the small firm

It is easy to forget that the majority of business organisations in this country are small: there are about $1\frac{1}{2}$ million firms employing under 200 people in the manufacturing sector and they play a very important role in the economy. Raising finance is their major problem: the fact that one in three small firms does not survive its first trading year is largely blamed on inadequate financial provision.

The small firm suffers from the fact that investors are not keen to risk their money in either unproven or fragmented areas. In the short term owners' capital and trade credit supplemented by bank overdrafts are available, but in the medium to long term access to finance for expansion or to cope with temporary trading difficulties becomes restricted. The jump from short-term to long-term sources of finance is very difficult. Small firms either cannot find the investors or have to pay a disproportionately high rate of interest on the money they borrow, endorsed by a requirement for personal guarantees.

This situation is not new. In 1971 the Bolton report on small firms commented that 'small firms have suffered and still suffer a number of genuine disabilities by comparison with larger firms in seeking finance from external sources.' One of its chief recommendations was a change in the taxation system. In 1978 the Chancellor in an attempt to encourage personal investors did allow the right to set business losses against income tax back over three years. The main outcome of the Bolton report was the setting up of the government sponsored Small Firms Counselling Service which, however, does not have any direct lending power. Recently the Wilson Committee reported that the situation had not improved and suggested that two possible methods that could be adopted are firstly, the West German system which allows loans for small businesses to be guaranteed by local government and secondly, to encourage small firm investment companies which would specialize in the problem.

There is no doubt that the potential growth in employment and national wealth from the small firms sector is being neglected because of lack of finance. The lack of share capital in these organisations is a serious drawback. Further initiative is required from the commercial banks, investment companies and both levels of government. The government's Council for Small Industries in Rural Areas is only one of many loan agencies that can offer more help.

Evaluation

In this chapter we have tried to offer an overview of the problems that face organisations in their search for acceptable ways of financing their resources. We have not attempted to go into any great specialist detail. It should be clear, however, that the formation of any capital assets is an immense and recurring problem. To help the financial manager to deal with these difficulties it is essential that the organisation can account for its assets, not least that of money tied up in working capital. In the next chapter we consider this function by looking at the role of the Accountant.

Self-test questions

1 Explain the many different uses of the word 'capital'.
2 What are the main sources of finance for commercial organisations?
3 Who, strictly speaking, are the employers in an organisation?
4 How can the owners of a company change its board level managers?
5 Are there more private or public limited companies?

Financing different business entities

6 What are the main influences on the demand and supply of money available to a company?

7 Identify the sources of finance for British Rail.

8 What does financial leverage refer to?

9 Do you think it is reasonable and practical to measure the value of intangibles such as goodwill?

10 If you were the Chancellor what moves would you make to assist the survival and expansion of small firms?

15 Budgetary planning and control

- The planning and control of any particular resource in the organisation can be done through budgeting.
- Translating forecasts into operating budgets for any activity is a management responsibility beset with behavioural and procedural problems.

In Chapter 13 we examined the environment of organisations and considered how management can plan for environmental change. They do this by establishing a strategy designed to safeguard the organisation from future threats to its operations and to allow it to take advantage of the new opportunities which environmental change may create. Within the context of the long-term strategies laid down by top management, more detailed, shorter-term tactical and day-to-day operating plans will need to be devised, implemented and controlled. All of these plans will have financial implications and will, to a large degree, be judged according to financial criteria. In this chapter we look at the role of the management accountant in the processes of planning and control and at his or her general contribution to the process of management decision making.

15.1 Budgets as a basis for planning and control

Once a strategy framework for an organisation has been established and finance has been acquired, shorter-term tactical plans need to be developed. It will be recalled that the essence of good tactical planning is to make the most effective and economic use of largely known resources in a given situation. The major constraints on what can be done are therefore the resources available and the strategies chosen by top management. Virtually all plans made by management have resource and financial implications. Each will generate its own costs and revenues, and these will therefore be key criteria in the decision whether they are chosen and implemented or rejected.

When the plans of a company are expressed in financial or quantitative form, they are known as budgets. Co-ordinated within the context of long-term strategy, budgets form an overall, quantified master plan for the budget period. These budgets also provide an ideal basis for control, the process of ensuring that planned results are actually achieved and that deviations from plans are recorded and reported in order that corrective action can be taken. Through budgeting, organisations are able to plan costs and revenues for a given period for each functional area. These budgets can then be taken together and the profit for that budget period projected. Quite clearly, the precise targets contained in a budgetary control system are invaluable as a guide to managerial decisions and control across the organisation.

15.2 Budgetary planning

The basic idea underlying budgetary planning is that each functional area or department within the organisation should submit its estimated budget, given a specified level of activity or production. These will then usually be co-ordinated into a master budget by a budget committee. The committee will continue to be responsible for the control function mentioned earlier and will therefore need to establish and report on significant variances from planned activity.

From the points made above, it will be seen that the first basic problem in budgetary planning is to decide upon the level of activity which will be assumed and from which costs and revenue will be calculated. One way would be to assume that the organisation will produce at its maximum physical capacity and will sell all of that output. Figures for different budgets may then be prepared on that basis. If however the resources of the organisation have been continually underemployed in the past or demand for the company's product has been falling or is expected to fall, this would be an illogical basis on which to proceed.

If there is not any shortage of skilled labour or productive capacity to limit output, then it is likely to be sales which will act as the constraint and which will therefore be the 'key' budget around which all others are formulated.

So, it is usually the sales budget which is the first to be prepared. From estimated sales, revenues and costs throughout the organisation can be projected at that level of activity.

The sales budget

The manager responsible for the sales department will prepare the sales budget. As we have stressed, he or she will work within policy and strategy guidelines laid down by top management.

Sales forecasting, however, is a notoriously difficult operation. One can begin by projecting past trends and incorporating established seasonal variations in sales estimates, but there are no guarantees that trends will remain constant. There may be new products in competition with those of the organisation preparing its forecasts, there may be new pressures on consumer demand or there may have been relative price changes between the organisation's products and those of competitors. All these factors can invalidate the simple projection of past trends.

In an attempt to get a more realistic estimate, market research information may be gained from customers about one's own and competitors' products, salesmen will be asked for their own estimates based on experiences with existing and potential customers, and the effects on sales of variations in price, advertising expenditure, the size of the sales force and other such factors should be analysed and should then bear on the final sales estimate.

Selling, distribution and administration costs

Once the sales estimate has been finalised, the different costs incurred in achieving that level of sales can be budgeted. These will include the sales force salaries, selling expenses, advertising and public relations. They should include also the estimated costs of distribution and the administration involved in the sales process. These may be the cost of operating the sales offices, any retail outlets, insurances, wages and salaries, depreciation and other costs directly attributable to maintaining the sales effort.

When costs are prepared by product, by region and by salesman, this can reveal operations which will not be justified by the sales volume estimated for that product, region, or salesman. This is clearly valuable to management who may decide to alter policy and concentrate on more profitable operations.

Budgetary planning and control

Production

The production budget is linked closely with the sales budgets. Once a sales volume figure for different products has been identified, plans can be drawn up for their manufacture. The production manager needs to decide the production capacity which will be required and whether the current resources of plant and working capital will be sufficient to achieve planned output. Naturally, where the production manager envisages physical difficulties in achieving this planned output, this may have a bearing on the sales budgets. It is as pointless to produce more than it is thought can be sold as to budget for sales greater than can physically be produced. Close co-ordination is therefore necessary between sales and production.

Materials/purchases budget

At this stage of budgetary planning it is possible to determine the quantities and costs of the materials which will be needed to produce at planned levels. The first step is to forecast the volumes of materials needed. Basically these figures will be arrived at after analysis of past usages. Final figures will take into account materials actually used along with the amounts of materials damaged or pilfered, wasted in manufacture, scrapped or rejected in quality control. After volumes have been projected the costs of required materials can be projected on the basis of likely prices and anticipated market conditions.

Labour

Once again here, the first step is to ascertain the quantities of labour of different grades or categories that will be required at planned levels of operation. This can be done for each department or budget centre in the organisation and will be based primarily on past relationships between manpower levels and output. However, once again the task of management is to anticipate change. If production methods are to be varied, or if any new productivity or wage incentive system is to be introduced, then these and similar changes will distort the past relationships. The implications of any such changes will need to be forecast and incorporated in any assessments of labour requirements. Once the quantities of different labour grades or categories are established, they will need to be costed. The rates of pay for each grade, adjusted for anticipated changes due to negotiation, cost of living adjustments and other complicating factors, then need to be established before the labour budget can be prepared.

Administration cost budget

At this stage, administration and overhead costs can be budgeted. The office salaries, lighting, heating, rent and rates will typically be included here.

The cash budget

One of the major concerns of the accounting function is financial management. Profit alone does not guarantee the success of an organisation; if cash flow is mismanaged, then the organisation is almost certain to fail. The cash budget represents a picture of the projected inflows and outflows of cash during the budget period. This estimate depends on estimated income from sales and other miscellaneous sources and all estimated expenditures on materials, capital, labour and expenses.

There are two elements in drawing up the cash budget. First, cash receipts must be projected, followed by the projection of cash payments. Cash receipts are for the most part generated by sales. These sales may be made on a cash or credit basis. The former generates cash immediately, whilst in the case of the latter, cash will be received after a time lag. Depending on policy towards creditors and past data, cash receipts throughout the budget period may be estimated. Cash payments projections also depend on an analysis of timing – some payments will need to be made in advance whilst others will be made retrospectively.

By adding projected receipts to the opening cash balance, cash resources for the period are established. Payments to the labour force, suppliers, Inland Revenue, capital expenditure payments and overheads are then aggregated. By comparing this total outflow for the period with the projected inflow of cash, management can establish the financing that will be needed to cover any deficit over the budget period as a whole or during any shorter period within it.

Flexible budgetary control

The projections in the sequence we have examined are all based on an initial, estimated level of activity usually determined by projected *sales* in the budget period in question. This can create problems because sales forecasting can be very hazardous. There is little point in having a set of budgets for a projected level of activity which is either never achieved or which is exceeded. To avoid the need for constant revisions and adjustments, flexible budgeting is possible.

Flexible budgeting is a process whereby a range of output around a projected figure is established so that different budgets may be based on different percentages of total productive capacity. In drawing up these budgets it will of course be necessary to distinguish which costs are fixed and will not therefore vary whatever level of activity is achieved, and those which are variable or semi-variable and will as a result alter according to levels of production.

Long-term budgeting

An organisation must be concerned with short-term operating budgets, and it must also lay down plans for the longer term.

The name given to the quantitative plan for providing the resources for the organisation in the long term is the capital budget. Despite the fact that the budget period for capital budgeting is much longer than for trading budgets discussed above, basic principles remain the same. The main difference lies in the greater uncertainty which inevitably exists when plans are projected for years rather than months into the future.

In our discussion of strategic planning in Chapter 13 we outlined how management needs to assess and anticipate changes in external environmental or operating conditions.

When drawing up plans for the long term, economic, legal, political and technological changes need to be anticipated and their implications for the organisation and its industrial context considered.

Once future prospects are established for the organisation, forecasting the areas in which growth or contraction are likely to occur, the fixed assets and working capital needed to resource future activity, including the cost of replacing existing fixed assets, can be assessed and plans drawn up for the financing of these resource needs.

Control

Control is one of the basic functions of management. Forecasting and planning alone do not guarantee that objectives will be achieved. Efforts must be made to ensure that plans are implemented effectively and yield the results which were expected. Control is the process of checking actual results against planned results, noting significant variations, accounting for them and taking any necessary corrective action at as early a stage as is possible. Constant monitoring and reporting are therefore crucial to the effectiveness of management control.

Of course, so much of budgetary planning is based on estimates and projections that minor deviations are inevitable and should cause little concern. It is those serious and consequential variations which must be identified early and acted upon. The process of regularly checking actual results against budgets is known as variance analysis.

15.3 Human and motivational aspects of budgetary planning

Budgets are not just another quantitative management tool or technique – they can have important motivating (or demotivating) effects. Planned and implemented wrongly, budgets can be dysfunctional in terms of the quality of management decisions, and can be restrictive and burdensome for the members of a management team.

It is widely accepted that targets, used properly, have a beneficial effect both on individual and group motivation and on task effectiveness. Indeed, it is a principle fundamental to such management systems as Management by Objectives and the model of group effectiveness outlined in Chapter 6. The motivational effect of targets has been shown to be enhanced further where they are established by means which allow for the participation of those who must work towards them. They should be relevant and salient for, and accepted by, those whose task it will be to achieve them. Budgets should not limit managers in terms of imaginative and creative decision making. They should not encourage defensive and over-cautious management. Rather they should guide, assist and encourage managers to work together towards a clear and co-ordinated set of reasonably flexible goals to provide them with the means to exercise effective and intelligent control of limited resources.

15.4 Review

If control is the process whereby the implementation and result of plans is monitored and reported, review is a retrospective examination of the plan itself and the decisions that led to its formulation. The contribution made by the plan to longer-term goals and objectives can be considered and valuable lessons learned for the future. Conscientious and open review can contribute valuably to management experience and expertise and can therefore raise the quality of decision making in the future.

Evaluation

In this chapter we have looked at the ways in which management draw up quantified, fixed-term plans to cover the whole of the organisation's activities for a period. Within the context of both long-term objectives and policy a sales estimate is made, from which estimates of expenditures required to achieve that level of sales are drawn up. Through budgetary planning, each functional area or department has an operating plan to guide decision making. Departmental budgets will be the direct responsibility of each departmental manager; thus, authority is delegated without loss of control. Of course a major danger of detailed budgeting is that budgets can come to be seen as sacred and inflexible in spite of unforeseen, possibly unforeseeable, changes in trading conditions. Budgets are not devised to confront managers with obstacles to imaginative decision making; they should be flexible and should assist rather than hinder management's day-to-day business. Given such an approach, organisations can move forward in a planned and co-ordinated way toward a more secure and profitable future.

Self-test questions

1 What is a budget?
2 Why are sales usually the starting point for budgetary planning?
3 How might a future sales figure or target be established?
4 What other budgets can follow from the sales budget?
5 What is flexible budgetary control?
6 What is a cash budget and how is it prepared?
7 Distinguish between control and review.

16 The marketing function

- Marketing philosophy is ultimately concerned with consumer satisfaction.
- Before any decision is made in marketing, due consideration should be given to all those interdependent activities that constitute the marketing mix.

In the early stages of the factory system of production, demand for products was greater than supply. The main problem facing businessmen was that of meeting the demand for products given the constraints on output. By the later stages of the nineteenth century and perhaps up until the 1930s this problem of scarcity was decreasing and business went through a process of consolidation and rationalisation. Since the second World War a scarcity of markets, even within so-called mass markets of consumption, has become a major problem, partly through the increase in the levels of personal discretionary income. Today the typical mixed economies reflect a market place of fierce competition with a strong need for product differentiation to enable a company to survive.

The actual ideas behind marketing are common sense and as old as the first successful businessman. However, marketing has only been accepted as a formal area of business study since the 1950s in America and the 1960s in the UK.

16.1 The marketing philosophy

Before marketing was adopted, manufacturing business followed several apparently logical stages of trading activity:

- to design a product,
- to engineer a prototype,
- to manufacture as many units of the product as possible,
- to give these to a sales department to sell to the customer in either industrial (firm to firm) or consumer (firm to private end-user) markets.

This approach has been referred to as 'production orientation' and is summed up in the maxim, 'What is good for industry is good for the customer'. It is typified by the early American car manufacturer Henry Ford when he reportedly said, 'They can have any colour they like as long as it is black.'

The stages in the marketing philosophy are more comprehensive and have proved to be more successful:

- to establish corporate goals (see Chapter 13),
- to determine customer requirements,
- to design a product to suit these requirements and evolve a marketing strategy,
- to engineer prototypes,

- to manufacture the product and initiate a marketing plan,
- to give the products to the sales department to sell,
- to ensure adequate after-sales service.

It should be clear by a comparison of these two lists that the marketing philosophy is a wider, more integrated and dynamic approach to business. It aims to ensure that supply is a function of demand and not the converse. The idea of 'consumer sovereignty' has sometimes been used to describe this reorientation. The professional body for UK marketing, the Institute of Marketing, has defined marketing as 'the management process responsible for identifying, anticipating and satisfying customer requirements profitably'.

Although this particular chapter treats marketing as one of the line functions of an organisation, nevertheless it is important to recognise the point that marketing can be seen in a broader context as a total view of the business process. All organisations make marketing decisions, but not all organisations would recognise them as such.

16.2 The marketing mix

Each organisation should select and concentrate on particular marketing activities according to the market it is operating in. For some, price sensitivity is all important, for others mass distribution backed by extensive press advertising is the key to success. Whether the organisation operates in the industrial markets or in the consumer markets it is marketing a product or service and is engaged in certain activities known collectively as the marketing mix.

These activities must start off with sound market research. This is the objective and systematic collection, recording and analysis of information to help the marketing decision makers. They need to know about the market size and strength of the competition, consumer motivation and buying patterns, the product's strengths and weaknesses, advertising effectiveness, and distribution logistics.

In theory there is no limit to what can be researched. In practice, time and costs set limits. The techniques used include secondary research using company data and published sources, and primary or field research where original information is collected through random or quota sampling methods. Although research cannot eliminate business risk, it can reduce the guesswork, helping to reveal a particular target group of potential customers that should be concentrated on.

This target group is known as a market segment. Segments can be classified on bases of age, sex, income, class, personality and location or on a combination of these. Knowing what a particular segment needs leads to the development of a product or service to fulfill that need. These are usually given a brand name to increase awareness and hopefully to create purchasing loyalty. Linked to the brand identity is a pack designed for protection and appeal.

The organisation will then advertise its products to inform and persuade customers to buy them. Advertising consists of impersonal communication techniques through what are called 'above the line media', where the owner of the medium is identifiable, such as in commercial television and radio, the cinema and the press, and 'below the line media' such as sales promotions involving free samples and competitions. Advertising often uses irrational stimuli based on status, sex and humour and is the target of much criticism as being wasteful and creating false demand. Although a lot of advertising is repetitive and apparently excessive (Boots for example spent £6.9m on advertising in 1979), it is argued it generates sufficient demand to create economies of scale for the producer that lead

The marketing function

to cheaper prices for the consumer. Organisations also advertise themselves, as distinct from their products or services (BP planned to spend £2m on corporate advertising in 1980). Linked to this are Public Relations activities such as sponsorship.

A vital decision area in marketing is on how to make products or services available to the consumer. Channels of distribution include direct mail order and indirect selling through franchises, authorised distributors, wholesalers, brokers, selling agents and the retail outlets such as multiple chain stores (Woolworths, for example). These organisations collectively are often referred to as the distributive trades. Many organisations will operate a sales force for personal customer liaison. The representatives' duties include negotiation over terms of supply, advice, merchandising, accounts collection and sometimes even delivery.

Lastly, perhaps the most important mix activity is that of setting a price. Pricing policies must relate to demand and supply and to the organisation's trading position. Pricing tactics include 'skimming', where as high a price as possible is set to cream off large profits in the short term, as was done in the early days of the electronic calculator; 'penetration' where a low price is set to gain a market share, as with the use of 'loss leaders' (goods sold below costs to encourage customers to go to a particular shop); and psychological pricing, e.g. 'Special offer at £4.99'.

16.3 The marketing department

The degree to which marketing is accepted by senior management has a profound effect on the organisation of the marketing department. A conventional method is to co-ordinate activities on a functional basis as shown in Figure 21.

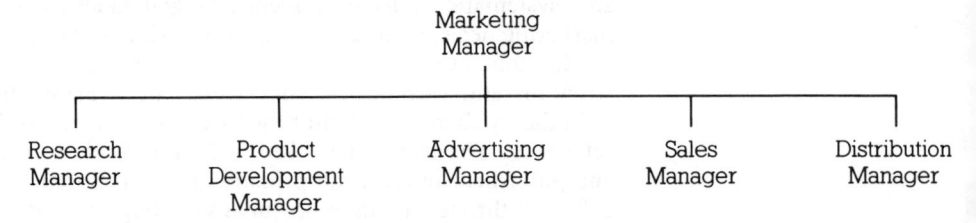

```
                         Marketing
                          Manager
    ┌────────────┬────────────┼────────────┬────────────┐
 Research      Product     Advertising    Sales      Distribution
 Manager     Development    Manager      Manager       Manager
              Manager
```

Figure 21

Certain companies will reorientate the department to emphasise the product, the market or the geographical sales unit (see Figure 22).

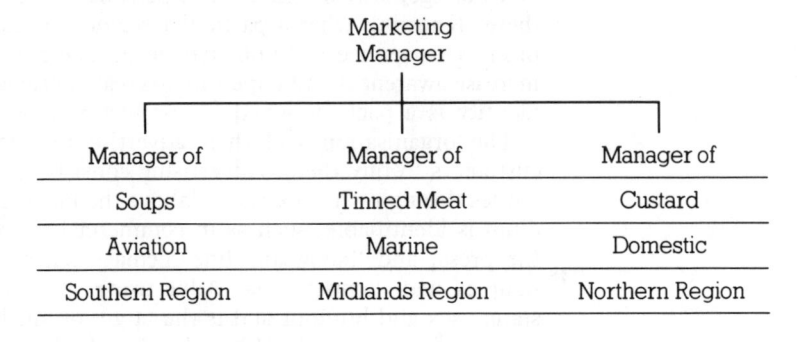

```
                         Marketing
                          Manager
              ┌──────────────┼──────────────┐
         Manager of      Manager of      Manager of
           Soups        Tinned Meat        Custard
          Aviation         Marine          Domestic
      Southern Region  Midlands Region  Northern Region
```

Figure 22

Another alternative is to use the role of Product Brand Manager and adopt the matrix hierarchy as described in Chapter 3.

The marketing department

The design of the organisation structure should be the one that best fits in with the firm's internal and external environments. Chapter 2 detailed the Classical approach emphasis on organisation charts; whilst there is no definitive design, it is important to note that all too often hierarchies evolve through historical accident when they should be planned to accommodate the basics of the marketing idea. Whatever structure is created there will inevitably be a clash of interests with other line and staff departments. Employees committed to the marketing idea will tend to have different priorities from those who do not put the customer first and do not look beyond their own department's localised problems. Conflict might arise for example with the production department over the size of the product range and lack of standardisation, with the finance section over the need to increase the advertising budget. Problems of successfully communicating their objectives are not unique to the marketing department but they tend to have greater significance. The table below lists some of the possible conflicting interests between a marketing department and others in a manufacturing organisation.

Table 3

Function	Marketing priority	Other departments' interests
Finance	Flexible budgeting Access to contingency reserves	Target capital budgeting Tight expenditure control
Accounts	Differential trading terms Flexible credit control	Standard terms Strict credit control
Production	Customisation Short lead-time High product range	Standardisation Long lead-times Low product range
Purchasing	High stocks Customised components	Low stocks Standardised components
Personnel	Rapid career development opportunity	Programmed manpower plans

Evaluation

Marketing, as this chapter has tried to show, looks after the outputs of the organisation or the demand side. The full importance of marketing mix activities has yet to be appreciated by many organisations. Few companies operate fully integrated marketing management systems although more and more are creating a marketing department. Marketing has been misunderstood in the past. It offers no magical formulas for success. However, if an organisation recognises and works towards meeting the needs of its existing and potential customers it will have taken the most important step towards being marketing orientated. Customers do not simply buy products or services, they buy solutions to their problems.

Marketing is far more than an American euphemism for sales. It is, if practised properly, a vital help towards business survival and prosperity.

The marketing function

Self-test questions

1 Can the techniques involved in marketing be applied to political campaigns?
2 Would Henry Ford's decision to offer customers only cars painted black be acceptable today?
3 Is persuasive advertising always also informative?
4 Do you think that psychological pricing, even if recognised as such by customers, is nevertheless effective?
5 Can you identify any franchised organisations in the UK?
6 Draw a matrix structure for a company marketing a range of hair shampoos.
7 Why can it be argued that marketing is the key to successful trading?

17 The production department

- The role of the production department is determined by the technology used.
- The task of production management is to balance the planning and control of the various manufacturing resources within the constraints of the different types of production process.

Production management is concerned with planning and controlling the operation of the department responsible for converting material inputs into product outputs. This chapter aims to give an introduction to the characteristics and problems of production departments in different types of manufacturing organisations.

17.1 Production planning and control

Production planning centres on the setting of output targets which meet criteria of quantity, quality, time and cost, using labour, materials, machinery and production methods to meet them. To ensure proper co-ordination of the workforce the targets are broken down into detailed schedules and decisions are made on what has to be produced, where, how and when. A manufacturing plan forms the basis of instructions issued regarding material specifications and availability, work methods, the allocation of work and workers to machines (machine loading), and delivery dates.

Production control concentrates on dispatching these instructions in the form of works orders and of collecting and recording data through progress reports. The job of production control is to check on when, where and with what aims activity is carried out, and to monitor all work in progress and final output levels. Material and quality control is often carried out by a centralised inspectorate but this responsibility is increasingly being shared with the actual production operatives. Control over plant maintenance to prevent machine failure and breakdowns is similarly divided.

Good production planning should reduce the need for production control. They are, however, really dual functions and in fact are often referred to singularly as production control. The production manager's objective is to reduce waste in material and in the use of machine and manpower and thus to reduce costs. His duties are largely determined by the type of production system the organisation operates. There are four main types, jobbing, batch, mass and process. To illustrate how complex a production department can be, Figure 23 highlights how manufacturing (assembly) is but one sub-section of many.

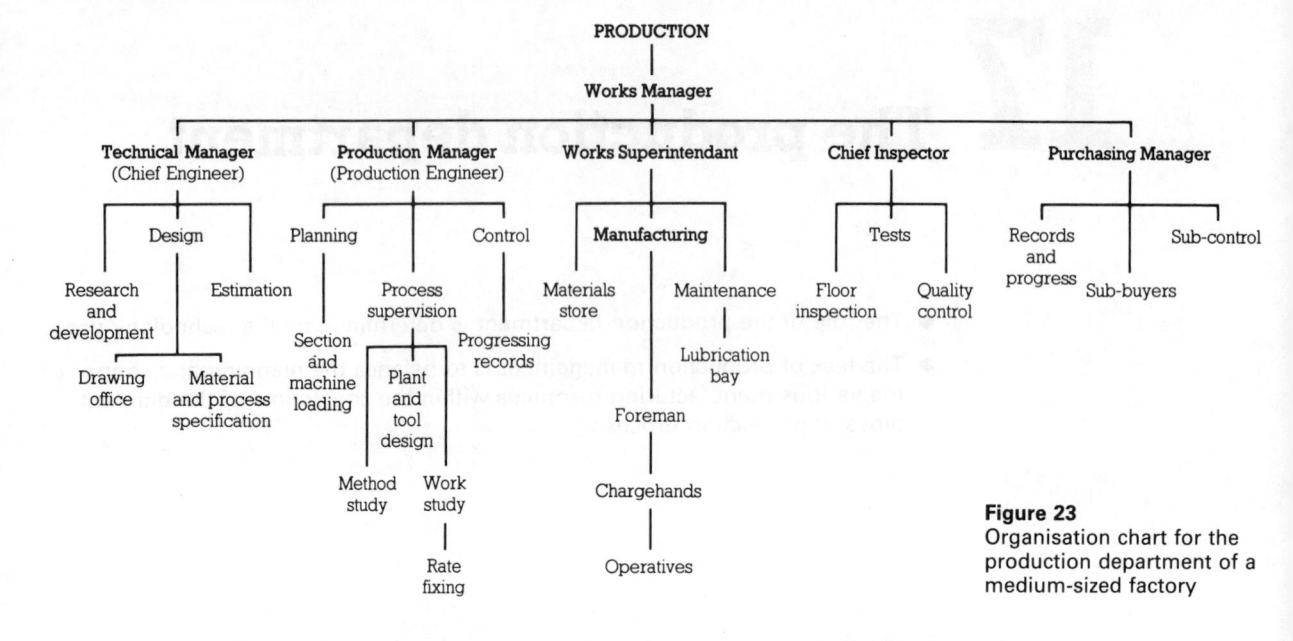

The production department

Figure 23 Organisation chart for the production department of a medium-sized factory

17.2 Jobbing production

Under this type of production small quantities of a particular product are made to meet a customer's specific requirements. Sometimes just one item is 'made to order' as a single unit.

By its very nature, jobbing creates its own problems of planning and control. There is no standardisation in the goods produced because customers require different tailor-made items, and manufacturing equipment tends to be of a general purpose nature. Each order will require different production skills and consequently a labour force of above average skill is employed. Since there is no continuity of output as in larger scale production, it is difficult to plan ahead and organise the workshop layout in a way that will be appropriate for all occasions. As a result production management's function tends to emphasise control in keeping machines and men fully utilised and in maintaining flexibility in operations.

These problems are reflected in the premium price customers have to pay for such an essentially personalised production service. To the organisation jobbing is attractive because the sale of the products made is guaranteed and the variety of work helps to increase job satisfaction.

Many manufacturing organisations started off in jobbing. The typical jobbing company would be a small engineering firm employing up to thirty employees, although jobbing can refer to fixed site production such as bridge building.

17.3 Batch production

Under batch production goods are made not as 'one offs' nor as part of a continuous process but in production runs known as batches. Because of this, batch production falls between jobbing and mass production and carries some of the characteristics of the other two.

Sometimes one customer will require an order of a large quantity that will justify a batch run: at other times the organisation will speculatively produce a batch of goods and rely on several customers placing orders that will equal the amount produced. Whichever tactic is used there is a choice of factory layout. Layout by product is usual in large batch production where one good is made in one location. Layout by process is adopted for smaller batch sizes where different production functions are located separately. Production management's role is equally divided between planning and control. There is the usual need to maintain continuous use of equipment and labour. The preparatory set-up costs for each batch production run and the level of demand for the products are critical. Very often production is done to provide stocks rather than to meet a specific order. These factors necessitate considerable skill in calculating the optimum batch quantity, sometimes referred to as the economic lot or batch size. Production costs must be balanced against stock holding costs. A common formula used for this is

$$\sqrt{\frac{2RS}{I}}$$

where R = annual demand
S = set-up or order cost
I = stock holding cost.

Usually each production run will have a code in the form of a batch number. This helps trace back any problems that might arise; it is important when buying wallpaper for example, to buy all the rolls from one batch in case there is a variance in dye colour between batch runs.

Most medium sized manufacturing organisations, especially electronics and engineering companies, operate on batch production lines. Large batch production is, however, a term often used for mass production.

17.4 Mass production

Mass production in one sense refers to the now widespread use of machines to make large quantities of similar goods. When the term is used in relation to production capacity of one organisation it is usually referred to as flow production or assembly line production. Flow production (as distinct from flow process production), relates to the continuous flow of distinct materials via a series of work stations which are either on the layout by process system or more usually the layout by product system. The typical assembly line is in the form of semi-finished goods on a moving conveyor belt at waist height or hung from an overhead trackway.

Queuing problems arise if the pace at which the products flow past the operatives stationed along the line is not set correctly. Work study techniques help to set the appropriate time margins allowable for each production subprocess. In an alternative type of assembly line, mechanical pacing does not exist and semi-finished products move on to their next stage of manufacture once the previous stage is completed. In this situation it is necessary to have buffer stocks between work stations to prevent wasteful delays.

Production management is concerned principally with the planning function. The key to efficiency is to arrange the factory layout so that the 'flow' is as smooth as possible. Sequencing of the work processes is critical. There is a high degree of capital investment in expensive specialised machinery which must be used as much as possible. This often means round the clock shift working. The labour force is given simple specialised tasks for which little skill or training is necessary. The goods being manufactured are standardised and produced in large numbers. Profit

The production department

margins are often low and the organisation relies on low competitive pricing but high sales turnover. Consequently not working to full plant capacity can result quickly in loss. Because the whole production department is specialising on one product type it is vulnerable to changes in consumer demand. There is usually a strong marketing department to research into demand trends and to ensure adequate sales.

The typical organisation that adopts flow production methods is the car manufacturer, and Henry Ford was in fact one of the earliest pioneers of this technique.

17.5 Process production

Process production is in many ways similar to flow production. The essential difference is that the products are not distinct, separate items but bulk items that physically flow and are measured by volume or weight. Because of this it is easier to plan for a continuous flow, and many of the work processes are automatic with the material being pumped from one section to another. Production management's function concentrates on planning. Output is made to forecast and human control is minimal. The investment costs are higher than for the other types of production not just in processing equipment but also in providing storage facilities. There is therefore a requirement for high and stable demand.

The typical organisations are the refineries producing oil, chemical feedstocks, sugar etc.

17.6 Woodward's research

Joan Woodward conducted research into the organisational characteristics associated with different types of production technology. Although her sample firms were limited to engineering works in Essex and the results are somewhat dated (1965) it is nevertheless interesting to consider her findings. The results were centered on a range of production types from unit and small batch, through large batch and mass production to process production. On this scale it was found that technology was least complicated under unit jobbing production whereas management was most complicated. The number of supervisory levels was highest under process production as was the ratio of indirect to direct production workers, although labour costs were the lowest. Control and certainty in reaching organisational goals was more likely also under process production. The only characteristic where mass production did not average out between the other types was in the span of control of the first level of supervisory staff where it was the highest.

The above is only a selection from Woodward's work but it should be evaluated in the light of her contribution to identifying the significance of technology in the development of the System Approach (see Chapter 3).

Developments in production work

The production department has been the focus of attention in much of the study of organisations, from Taylor's *Scientific Management* to the Hawthorne Studies and Goldthorpe's researches at Luton. Although not all organisations have a resemblance to a factory or indeed produce anything beyond an intangible service, the fascination with the work involved in production continues. There have been many attempts to lower levels of absenteeism and labour turnover and to increase productivity, all features that reflect the fact that production work is not the happiest of occupations. Experiments in adopting the semi-autonomous work group, the cell system of organising operatives to work in self-pacing teams have had mixed success and have often proved too costly to implement. Job rotation schemes have had more widespread success but perhaps the biggest successes are yet to come in the form of better industrial democracy schemes.

Many factory workers are still dissatisfied with their jobs. On the mass production assembly lines, machines still set the work rate. Tasks are still monotonously repetitive and require little imagination. Within the next decade all this should radically change. Although the completely automatic factory has yet to be built (despite Fiat's slogan 1979 'Hand built by robots') the trend towards increasing automation is growing. Silicon chip technology can and will revolutionise the whole production process. The largest manufacturer of industrial robots for paint spraying, welding etc., Unimation of America, sold 15 million units in 1979 at an average cost of £35,000. Their market is expanding. British Leyland has equipped its new Mini Metro factory with many such machines.

The implications of this move towards computerised production are twofold. First, production will become more efficient and many workers will no longer have to do boring jobs. Secondly, unemployment will be increased and measures such as reducing the working week will be only temporarily successful.

Evaluation

Whatever changes do occur in the production department some essential features will remain. Production is that part of a manufacturing organisation that converts raw material inputs into finished products. The scale of production determines its technology and management complexity. This should be clear from consideration of the main production systems, many of which exist side by side in one organisation. Automation will inevitably cause the greatest changes to both technology and operating procedures, especially in mass production. Products will still be made, subject to the continued existence of resources, but employment in the manufacturing sector will decrease.

Self-test questions

1 Which department is more vital to corporate success, production or marketing?

2 Explain how production planning can reduce the need for production control.

3 Give examples other than the ones shown for each of the four types of production system.

4 How can you tell if a product you have bought has been made in a batch run?

5 Why might an employee's feelings of alienation vary depending on the type of production technology adopted by an organisation?

6 Will automation in the factory eliminate only boring jobs or eventually all jobs?

7 What are the economic and social implications of the adoption of micro-technology?

18 The purchasing function

- Purchasing is basically about resource planning, acquisition and control. It demands a variety of skills and experience. Different policies and practices are used by different types of organisation.
- Sound purchasing can make a major contribution to cost reduction, innovation, goodwill and continuity in all functions, especially in the production department.

One of the key inputs into any organisation is that of materials and equipment. The task of acquiring these falls to the purchasing officer. Whatever its formal organisational status, the job is a crucial and often underestimated one. This chapter examines the role of the purchasing function and looks at the positive contribution its effective management can make to efficiency, economy and profitability.

18.1 The scope of the purchasing function

The main task of a purchasing department is, of course, buying. In practice though, this demands a wide diversity of skills. A purchasing officer needs to know what *quantities* and *quality* of materials to buy. He must also decide *when* is the best time to buy, and this in itself can be a complex decision. It will depend on many factors such as current prices, likely movements in prices, current stock levels and so on. Buying too late could lead to delays or stoppages in production whilst buying too early risks depreciation or obsolescence and will commit storage capacity and capital which might in the meantime have been put to better use.

Additionally, a purchasing officer needs to know *where* to purchase the requirements, getting the best terms possible from dependable vendors. As well as actual buying, the regular requisition, purchase, delivery, storage and usage of material involves considerable administrative and clerical work. In most cases, alongside the buying section in a purchasing department will be a clerical section responsible for this work. Here data are recorded and updated and correspondence is dealt with. It is on the accuracy and completeness of these records that good purchasing ultimately depends. Limited or inaccurate records make effective overall purchasing virtually impossible.

A third section likely to be found within a purchasing department is the progress section. Here, the progress of outstanding orders is managed and necessary action taken where delays or difficulties arise. Liaison with the other departments will also be the responsibility of this section.

Being responsible for these different sections, the purchasing officer needs a particular combination of skills, experience and attitudes. In terms of buying and buying decisions, he or she will need to have as wide a knowledge of commerce and industry as possible and to be familiar with the workings of markets and the range of potential suppliers of different materials; also, he or she will need to be able to anticipate supply difficulties and resolve them where they arise. Commercial contacts and goodwill are both important assets in this respect. More than this, the purchasing officer will need to be familiar with the mathematics of ordering and reordering, so as to ensure security of supplies in the most economic way, and finally he or she will need to be able to negotiate terms with suppliers and suppliers' representatives. Experience, imagination and training contribute equally to this special stock of skills relating to buying.

In addition to the skills of effective and economic buying, the purchasing officer is responsible for supervising record keeping and the administrative back-up so essential to organised and efficient purchasing. An understanding of clerical methods and procedures and their importance is therefore as crucial to the success of the purchasing function as shrewd and imaginative buying.

The task of the purchasing officer, then, is to decide what to buy in terms of quantity and quality, when to buy it bearing in mind both physical and economic factors, and finally, where to buy, considering such factors as vendor reliability, terms available, like credit facilities and discounts, and of course, price.

Purchasing practice

Each organisation will have its own purchasing procedures. The aims of the procedure are to ensure a reliable service to the organisation through ensuring the timely purchase and delivery of materials requisitioned, on the most favourable contractual terms. When materials are requisitioned by stores or other departments, the purchasing department will ensure that there is proper authorisation for the purchase and that proper details of what is required are given on the requisition form. To assist in this practice items in use should carry a reference which can be quoted and catalogued.

Quotations may then be invited from a number of suppliers, and the most favourable terms on price and delivery can be accepted by the placing of an order. All details of this order or contract will be filed so that goods received can later be checked against it. After the placing of orders, it is important that the progress section ensures that delivery dates are adhered to. Finally, when materials are received these should be checked for accuracy in terms of quantities and quality of goods for which the organisation contracted and checked also against suppliers' invoices. These checking procedures should ideally be carried out by the receiving department, any discrepancies being reported to the purchasing department.

18.2 Purchasing policies

We have said already that the purchasing officer faces a problem of achieving the greatest economy possible in purchasing without jeopardising continuity of production. What he or she will be trying to achieve is the lowest cost per unit by the time of consumption. This does not necessarily mean *buying* at the lowest unit cost. In a moment we shall examine the factors influencing the most 'economic order quantity'. First, though, it is important to understand the different policies which a purchasing officer can choose and some of the factors which might determine his choice.

The first option open to the purchasing department is to buy as and when goods are required. In other words, only quantities needed for current production requirements are purchased. The most obvious advantage of this method is the saving it achieves in terms of storage space and administration, as well as the fact

The purchasing function

that capital is not tied up in long-term stock holding. Its disadvantages are that buying small quantities frequently is an expensive policy. Quantity discounts cannot be taken advantage of, and additionally, administration and handling costs are increased because of frequent reordering and delivery. Of course, where goods are infrequently used, or in an emergency, the policy is a sound one and the most likely to be pursued. In other circumstances an alternative is likely to be preferred.

A second and very different policy is to buy for a fixed and long-term period. The advantages and disadvantages are virtually reversed. Capital and storage space are committed and therefore an opportunity cost is incurred; on the other hand, administrative and handling costs are fewer and the risks of interrupted production are minimised. Where there is little danger of obsolescence or deterioration and little risk of error in terms of the price negotiated, then this policy is a suitable one.

A third policy which in some ways combines the advantages of these first two is termed contract buying. For materials which will be required over a long period and will be used in some quantity, it is possible to negotiate a contract for continuous supply. The major advantage is that large stocks do not have to be held because delivery can be arranged to coincide with requirements. Examples of materials often purchased on this basis (even domestically), are fuels such as coal and oil.

In terms of policy, the last two options need bear little relationship to actual requirements of the materials or commodities purchased. The first is called speculative or 'bargain' buying. Here materials are purchased in anticipation of future price rises. The objective here may simply be to save money, even considering the costs of storage, or to profit from the later resale of some or all of the commodity. Speculative buying is therefore one of the ways in which a purchasing manager can contribute to profitability not through cost saving, but directly and positively through his purchasing policy. (An obvious cautionary note is that it is possible that prices may fall rather than rise and as a result a loss may be incurred.)

Finally, and similar in many ways, is what is termed 'market purchasing'. Here, the main criterion determining when to buy is market price. Little heed is paid to manufacturing requirements, and the more favourable the price is felt to be, the more of the commodity will be purchased.

So the purchasing officer has a number of alternative or complementary policies which may be pursued. The main aim, remember, is to achieve the lowest cost per unit by the time goods leave the stores. A major determinant of that final cost will be the size and timing of the original purchase. We now move to consider some of the factors which will influence the most economic order quantity.

Achieving economic order quantities

The problems of achieving the most economic order quantity have already been introduced. On the one hand, the less capital tied up in stored goods the better. On the other hand, small purchases are expensive in terms of price and handling costs. The kinds of factors which will need to be considered in determining order quantities for different items will include the following:

- price and possible price movements
- the risk and consequences of stock shortages
- reliability of supply/delivery
- patterns of consumption of the material within the organisation
- any price advantage of bulk purchase
- costs of holding large stocks
- seasonal variation in cost and availability of supplies
- deterioration and risk of obsolescence when goods are stocked long-term

- availability of storage facilities
- costs of purchasing and administration

The actual decision on optimal stock levels, then, is a complex one subject to a variety of influences. In an ideal situation, stocks would be reordered so as to be received when minimum stock levels were reached in order to re-establish a predetermined maximum stock level. In practice things are rarely so easy. Consumption can be far from predictable, deliveries are often irregular, and price movements may make such a policy obviously uneconomic.

18.3 Stores and stock control

The position of stores, in terms of organisation, can vary widely. In some firms they will be under the purchasing officer, in others they will be under the works manager.

The aims of good storekeeping have already been implied in our discussion of purchasing policies and reorder quantities. Primarily, continuity of production must be maintained. This means ensuring that supplies are held which are appropriate to the continuing needs of the production process. In addition, stock levels must be maintained in a way which makes sensible use of the company's resources of working capital.

Items in store will each have a predetermined reorder level which takes into account consumption patterns and the availability of replacement stock as well as 'lead time' – the time elapsing between reordering and delivery. In essence, the main task of stores management is to ensure continuity of appropriate supplies in spite of fluctuations in availability and delivery of materials. Details of current stock levels need to be meticulously maintained if this responsibility is to be discharged effectively.

Location and design of stores

Physical location is obviously an important consideration if the stores are to function efficiently. Stores should be located for maximum convenience and to ensure minimum movements of goods. This may mean that decentralisation of stores will pay dividends, especially where some items are used exclusively by one department.

Layout within the stores should be similarly based on convenience. The most frequently used goods should be most easily accessible and vice versa. In addition, special provision should be made for goods most susceptible to deterioration or fire or which are fragile. Layout should also be based on handling considerations and ease of movement. Whilst they may not be located in separate stores, different items will be classified differently, e.g. raw materials, components, finished goods, and indirect stores for tools, maintenance equipment and indirect materials.

Storekeeping

The procedure followed by the storekeeper must be an exact one. He or she will be responsible for requisitioning those items which are nearing their minimum stock level. On receipt of the requisition, the purchasing department can place an order for the specified materials. Once the order is received, the items will be checked against the original order and placed in store. The storekeeper will record the receipt of all items. Stores will then be issued on receipt of a materials requisition by the storekeeper. This will identify the quantities of each item required and its destination and should be authorised by an approved signatory. Items leaving the

The purchasing function

stores are as carefully recorded as those coming in, in order that accurate and up-to-date records are always available. Periodically, there will be stores checks to ensure that stock control is accurate and effective and that proper stock levels have been maintained.

18.4 The decision-making unit

Before concluding, it should be said that, increasingly, purchasing decisions will not be made by one person alone. Industrial purchases will instead be agreed within what is called a 'decision-making unit' whose members can be drawn from different parts of the organisation and will each have an interest in the choice of purchases of equipment and materials. Typically a decision-making unit might comprise a production or works manager, a buyer or purchasing officer, a finance director, 'users' of the product and possibly people such as a safety officer. It is not hard to see that the priorities of the members of the decision-making unit might be different and that a final decision will need to reflect the views and needs of the various interested parties.

Evaluation

In this chapter we have looked briefly at the role of the purchasing officer and the task of stock control. We began by stressing the importance and breadth of the purchasing officer's responsibilities. His or her effectiveness will ultimately be judged by skills in negotiating contracts which satisfy the two criteria of economy and security of supply. At any time there may be a range of policy options open in the quest for the appropriate balance between the two. Through experience, skills and external contacts, the purchasing officer can make a real and positive contribution to goodwill towards the organisation, continuity of production, materials innovation, economy and general efficiency.

When things are running smoothly, the purchasing department's work is likely to go almost unnoticed; when things go wrong the costs to the organisation as a whole can be immense.

Self-test questions

1 What qualities would you look for in a candidate for the job of purchasing officer?
2 State the different purchasing policies which might be adopted.
3 Summarise the overall contribution to organisational success which can be made by effective purchasing.
4 What records need to be kept by a purchasing department?
5 List the factors which should influence the location and design of the store.
6 What do you understand by the term decision-making unit?

19 Personnel management

- People represent organisational assets. The role of personnel management is to ensure that manpower plans are fulfilled as efficiently as possible.
- To maintain staff efficiently a personnel department is responsible for appraisal, training and payment schemes which call for detailed records and formal procedures.

19.1 The personnel function

Concise definitions of personnel management are difficult because of the diversity of the activities it involves. Essentially though, personnel management is about people and their effective management. The personnel management role involves a number of specialist activities which include:

- manpower planning
- staff recruitment and selection
- performance appraisal
- training
- remuneration or compensation
- industrial relations
- safety and welfare
- maintenance of records.

Before we examine these activities individually, a few general comments on the nature and importance of personnel management are appropriate.

Firstly, good personnel management begins from the recognition that people are *assets* of an organisation. Even though they do not usually appear as such on company balance sheets (though many now argue that they should) there are many parallels between the management of 'people' assets and other forms of company assets. For example, they must first be planned for. Exact present and future requirements need to be established, budgeted and acquired in a logical and systematic way. Similarly, just as the management of a firm needs to make judgements about the nature, quality and quantity of an investment in plant and equipment, so too must they about company manpower requirements. Personnel recruitment, selection and staff placement procedures should be designed to optimise the company's return on its 'people' investment.

Further, like most other assets, people require some form of maintenance and protection. It is in the organisation's interest, having made its investment in personnel, to strive to ensure that they perform consistently and effectively and are protected from 'damage' – either physical or psychological. As a result, personnel management is very much concerned with the range of motivational techniques, with the quality of conditions of work and with the general integration of employees into the work situation.

Finally, like other assets, people must be paid for. It will be the responsibility of

Personnel management

the personnel department to reward and compensate employees for the time, labour and expertise they provide.

Unlike many other assets, people's value to the organisation actually appreciates. The contribution of people at work is not, or should not be, fixed and static. As they gain in skills and experience, so their contribution escalates. Obviously, it is in the interests of the organisation to increase the scope and quality of employees' contributions, and the personnel manager will thus be concerned with training and development based on assessments about employees' potential and capabilities.

Another key area of personnel management is concerned with managing both interpersonal and intergroup relations at work. Maintaining motivation and morale, avoiding, containing, or controlling conflicts as well as industrial relations generally are of vital importance and concern to the personnel manager. His or her overall aim will be to try to establish a climate within which both the organisation and employees can prosper from their relationship and their interdependence, drawing on the whole range of ideas, principles, and methods we have discussed throughout the first three sections of this book.

19.2 Fulfilling manpower requirements

Planning

The purpose of manpower planning is to avoid shortfalls or poor utilisation of labour. In forecasting and anticipating labour requirements, both in quantitative and qualitative terms, manpower plans must start from, and be co-ordinated with, other operating plans. The nature and level of the planned future operations by the company will indicate its likely manpower requirements. Figure 24 shows diagrammatically the different elements comprising the manpower planning process.

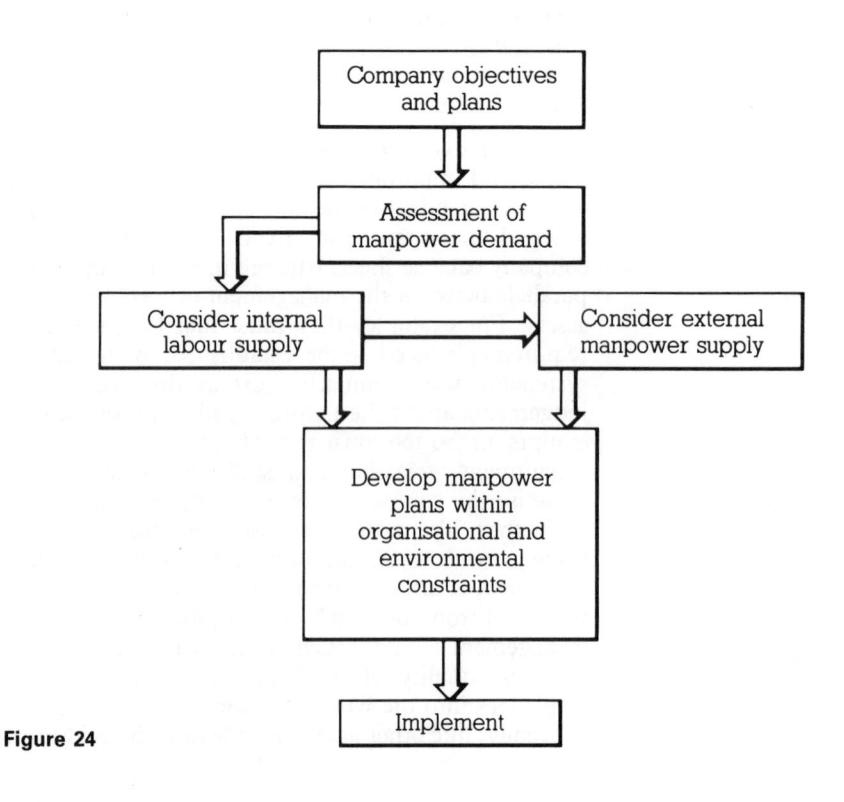

Figure 24

Fulfilling manpower requirements

It can be seen from the diagram that manpower planning begins from the company's objectives and operating plans. The logic of this is obvious – it is the company's plans and forecasts for the future which will create a specific demand within the firm for a particular quantity and quality of labour skills. The same principle holds for all the inputs into the organisation, requirements being based on expected levels of activity.

These plans and objectives must then be translated into manpower terms. This will involve a systematic analysis of their labour implications. In some areas an increase in demand for certain labour skills may be expected: in others, a decline.

Having established, in manpower terms, what the implications of projected company operations are likely to be, the manpower planner can begin analysing current labour resources within the firm. If the analysis shows a shortfall in labour required for the future, the external labour supply will need to be drawn upon. In most cases, a firm will be most concerned with local labour market conditions because for all but specialist staff it will be this that they mostly draw upon. Of course, the analysis might reveal a labour supply greater than that required for the future. Should this be the case, the company will be concerned with the planned shedding of labour rather than its acquisition.

Recruitment and selection

Most usually, manpower planning will result in a number of positions having to be filled. They may be filled internally or externally, but in either case the quality of selection procedures is of crucial importance. Recruitment and selection are complementary to manpower planning. They represent the main means whereby the quantity and quality of labour required are acquired.

To fill new, existing or changed positions within the organisation satisfactorily, the main features of these positions, the responsibilities that go with them, and the skills needed to fill them, need to be carefully analysed and recorded. Once compiled, these records must be kept up to date to ensure their validity and usefulness for the future. For these and other purposes, job descriptions and job specifications are used.

The job description

A job description should give the title of the job it refers to, describe the scope of the job, and detail what supervision is required to be given and received.

The job specification

Job specifications detail both the physical and mental demands and requirements of any job. In addition, they should refer to the working conditions under which the job is carried out, the equipment and materials used and the performance standards which are expected.

Recruitment and selection procedure
Recruitment

Where a new job has been created, or an existing one vacated, it needs to be staffed. It may be filled either from within, drawing on the existing labour force (internal labour market), or from external sources. There is a variety of reasons why internal recruitment may be preferred. Generally, a commitment to the use of the internal labour supply as a first recourse will:

- improve staff morale and motivation;
- lead to better placement of staff because more is known about them than about unknown external candidates;
- reduce problems of induction training and staff 'integration';
- prove easier and quicker than using external recruitment procedures.

Personnel management

In most circumstances however, recruitment from the external labour market will still be necessary, even if only to fill positions vacated as a result of internal recruitment. Access to external sources of labour can be through different channels or media. These will vary in both cost and coverage and should be used discriminatingly by a personnel department. The most common channels for most organisations will usually be:

- general, unsolicited enquiry by job seekers
- access through present employees e.g. recommendations to friends or family
- links with schools, colleges and universities
- job centres
- private employment agencies
- professional bodies
- trade unions
- direct advertising using various media – radio, newspapers, specialist journals etc.

Selection

Whatever the source of job applicants used, the first stage in the vitally important selection process will be to require applicants to complete an application form. The design of forms will vary from company to company and possibly for different kinds of jobs within the same organisation. The aim of any such form should be to gain readily usable information about the different applicants for any vacancy. Once again, a balance has to be found between gaining sufficient useful information about applicants and overburdening them with overlong, complex forms to complete. To some extent the form should be a 'screening' device which allows the most suitable candidates on paper to be invited for interview whilst providing enough objective information about the applicants to justify the rejection of others. The short list of applicants for interview will be compiled with the job specification very much in mind.

So much time is spent in interviewing at an enormous cost in management time, that it is not surprising that a great deal has been written about the procedures to adopt and the pitfalls to be avoided. In an introductory text such as this one, not all of these can be covered and what follows is therefore a list of a few basic points and principles to be remembered. The first thing to be stressed is that frequently people are mistaken in their assumptions about what an interview is. Many people when asked will say that an interview is a method of finding out more, in a face-to-face situation, about candidates for a job as a basis for their subsequent selection or rejection. This view, however, is only partly correct. Just as important as gleaning information about candidates is the passing of information *to* candidates. It is equally wasteful and disruptive to find employees leaving the organisation or being dissatisfied because they were not fully aware at the interview stage of the situation they would find themselves in on taking up the job, as it is to have to deal with an employee who is found to be unsuitable for the job he or she was selected for. Communication in interview situations must therefore be *two-way*.

Recruitment of staff to an organisation involves a major decision both on the part of the organisation and on the part of the prospective employee. It is crucial therefore that interviewing is carried out professionally and systematically.

Personnel testing

It should be mentioned here that in certain cases tests of various kinds may be given to candidates as a supplement to the interview. There are many different types of test, measuring various skills and aptitudes, personality and intelligence.

The use of testing, however, remains slightly controversial and it is important that the tests used are known to be both valid (that is, actually testing what they claim to be testing) and reliable (that is, that the same candidate would score the same on two different occasions or that two people of the same ability would score the same on the same test).

Testing is usually advocated on the basis of its objectivity compared to other methods – certainly, if a test is proven to be both valid and reliable it can have an important contribution to make. In fact though, the obvious scope for bias and prejudice inherent in the type of interviewing described above can be avoided by having more than one interviewer either interviewing successively or as a panel or group.

Once having been selected the candidate must, whether or not a verbal offer has been made, confirm the offer in writing, specifying exactly the conditions on which it is made. Within thirteen weeks of their employment, employees must be issued with a statement of their terms and conditions of employment and other details of their contractual rights and obligations or reference to them.

Induction

Induction is a process which attempts to orientate the new recruit into unfamiliar work surroundings. It will involve introducing the recruit to those people and methods he or she will be working with, acquainting the recruit with all the facilities and practices of the organisation as well as providing the information about the organisation necessary for him or her to do the work required and understand its importance within the wider framework of the organisation's activities. Successful induction will allow the speedy integration of the employee into the organisation and into the work group with which he or she will be involved. This process of orientation is clearly of importance to the individual, but the benefits of early induction from the point of view of the organisation itself should not be overlooked. The sooner familiarity with methods, facilities and procedures is acquired, the sooner the recruit learns where to locate different information, where to take particular problems etc., the sooner he or she will become an efficient and productive member.

19.3 Staff appraisal

Staff appraisal is linked closely to manpower planning. It was mentioned that labour may be recruited either from external or from internal sources. Amongst other things, staff appraisal allows the identification and development of those people who can satisfy different, future manpower needs within the organisation. It will also indicate where labour needs cannot be satisfied from within.

All organisations carry out some form of staff appraisal, but they vary widely in how systematically they conduct it, in how much the employee being appraised is involved in the process, and in the objectives and priorities their systems are designed to achieve. An appraisal can be simply a subjective and personal assessment by a supervisor or superior, or it can be a methodical and comprehensive mutual assessment by appraisee and superiors designed to achieve a number of clear objectives.

Any good staff appraisal system should have the following four types of objectives;

1 reward objectives, rewarding competence and excellence,
2 performance objectives, designed to allow improvements in performance,

Personnel management

3 development objectives, aimed at identifying and developing potential,
4 motivational objectives.

To achieve these goals, however, any system must be carefully designed and implemented.

Traditionally, staff appraisal systems have tended to fail in achieving this range of objectives and have even, in some cases, been destructive in terms of motivation and performance improvement.

Traditional appraisal methods

Fortunately the worst kinds of deficiencies in appraisal practice are being eradicated – at least in larger organisations where appraisal is formalised. At their worst, these systems require an annual completion of a standard appraisal form by the employee's superior where different, usually poorly defined, aspects of an employee's performance are rated for the year past on a scale from, say, one to ten. Supplementary to this might be a rating of the employee's potential where the superior is asked to make judgements as to whether the subordinate is 'promising material', 'very promising', 'unlikely to go further' and so on. A general comment is then usually called for, as is any recommendation for merit payment if such a system is practised. The form will then be forwarded to a higher level of management for comment and/or approval.

Often, without being given automatic access to the form and the judgements it contains, the appraisee will be called for an annual appraisal interview with a superior where general praise or criticisms are offered. These interviews are usually short, fairly ritualistic affairs and will often be little more than a 'pep' talk.

Some principles for the design and operation of appraisal systems

Obviously, appraisal systems have to be designed to be specific to the nature and needs of any particular organisation. Special skills, abilities and potentials will be required in a different mix in different cases. It is possible, however, to elicit a number of general principles along which a system of appraisal might be based. We have already made a case that annual, ritualistic appraisals should be avoided. Line managers must be coached and guided in techniques and methods of appraisal and come to appreciate its contribution to the effectiveness of the organisation.

Interviews designed to improve or discuss performance should not at the same time consider wages, salary or promotion. The roles of judge and counsellor do not go together well and should be separated. In terms of performance improvement, it seems that little is achieved through broad praise or criticism. It is now widely accepted, and has been demonstrated, that performance responds best to specific goals or targets for improvement. This improvement is most marked when the goals to be pursued by the appraisee in the forthcoming period are salient to him or her and have been mutually agreed at an appraisal interview rather than being imposed by the superior on the appraisee. The importance of this 'psychological ownership' of goals has been discussed in connection with motivation and group performance in earlier chapters. It provides the theoretical basis for such systems as management by objectives and has its origins with McGregor's 'Theory Y'. Appraisals should therefore be participative and involving for the employee; they should contain an element of self-appraisal and should be based on open, constructive discussion. They should be constructive too in their contribution to the achievement of manpower plans – to which appraisal must be closely linked. They should be as objective as they can be made, involving more than just the appraisee's immediate superior and, perhaps most important of all, they should be standardised and seen as being fair, across the organisation. One's potential or performance ratings should not depend on who one works under.

19.4 Training

Training, for many reasons, has a fundamental part to play in the efficiency and productivity of the modern enterprise. Apart from the training which is necessary initially to allow recruits to become familiar with the demands and skills their job requires, training is one of the most important means to the accomplishment of manpower plans. It allows a company to employ and deploy its labour in such a way that required quantities and quality of manpower are assured, even when there are shortages of particular labour skills in the external labour market. It allows a company to maintain a labour force appropriate to the demands of different technologies and work methods and it allows performance to be improved and the potential of employees to be developed. Finally, in most cases, the provision of appropriate training can increase job involvement and motivation, especially where training needs for each employee are mutually agreed through effective staff appraisal and counselling.

It must now be said, even at the risk of becoming repetitive, that training in an organisation, if it is to achieve any or all of the objectives above, must be carefully and systematically planned and implemented. Any systematic training approach will begin from manpower planning. Manpower plans should detail when, where and in what quantities different labour skills will be required. The training programme for the company can then be designed around this projection.

In the long term, forecasts will have to be made of the pattern of future company operations, areas of expansion and contraction identified and their technological and manpower implications assessed and linked to a time scale.

In the shorter term, in order to ensure desired standards of performance throughout the organisation and to develop individual skills and abilities, training must begin from an analysis of each job and the different standards of performance which are required in it. Then, only on the basis of some rigorous assessment of employee performance and potential, preferably through a comprehensive and participative appraisal system, should the training needs of each employee be established. Training will thus be designed to eliminate the gap between actual and desired performance. Quite clearly, unless both desired and actual standards are defined and recorded the nature and extent of any deficiency between the two cannot be accurately charted.

Once training needs are agreed, a training programme may be designed or selected to meet those needs. Following training, its effectiveness must be established. It was initially devised to allow certain specified improvements in performance. It must therefore be tested against this objective. In other words, the training given must be assessed for its validity. How effectively has it achieved what it was intended to achieve? If it has not, what are the reasons? Is the deficiency in the content or level of training given, or in its appropriateness in the first place?

Finally, attempts should be made to evaluate the training in terms of cost and effectiveness. The process is a difficult one if it is to be more than a crude comparison of costs and improved performance. The psychological benefit to employees, for example, less absenteeism and lower turnover, less resistance to change, are all possible benefits of good training programmes. These are benefits which should not be overlooked in the evaluation of training given.

19.5 Wage and salary administration

The calculation and payment of an employee's wage may seem a fairly mechanical process – in fact, the design and administration of wage and salary systems can

Personnel management

fundamentally influence the quality of industrial relations, employee motivation, labour turnover, the organisation's ability to recruit, its competitiveness and profitability, and even the quality of what it produces.

Wages and types of wage payment

The term 'wages' is one which is used loosely by many people and thus needs clarification. The term might be used to describe the reward to an employee for giving his time and energy to an employer. This description, however, would also incorporate 'salaries' which are usually distinguished from wages as a system of payment.

It could incorporate too, the different non-financial rewards and benefits which might accrue to an employee of a particular firm. By an employee's wage, do we mean what his actual gross financial earnings are in a period, what he or she actually retains and 'takes home', or do we mean a basic rate for a unit of work? The distinction is an important one because each of these will be significantly different. There is in fact no real definitive description of what a wage is. Conventionally, by someone's wages we mean a payment to a manual worker, before deductions, for a given period of time. Unfortunately, because of such things as bonuses, payment by results and so on, a definition of wages in terms of time alone can be misleading.

Time payments

Time payments are, straightforwardly, payments for units of an employee's time. They are conditional only on that employee's attendance. The unit of time for which payment is made may be an hour, day, week, month or year. A salary is a time payment in pure form. It is a statement of how much money will be paid for a given period of time, usually one month or a year. Manual workers on time payment are paid on the same principle, but will tend to be paid on a weekly basis with that payment being termed a wage. The difference between the two, however, is usually more than a mere description of the interval at which money will be paid to employees. Traditionally there is a status differential between wage and salary earners, with salaried staff attracting, traditionally at least, a greater social and workplace status than the wage earners. There will tend to be differences too, possibly, in the facilities and privileges afforded to wage earning and salaried staff by the company. The salaried worker may not be required to record his exact time of starting and finishing work, may be entitled to use different employee facilities, will usually be entitled to a longer period of notice, may receive more generous pension provision and so on. In terms of security, privilege and status then, there can be real and important advantages to being salaried.

The major characteristic of time payments, as was mentioned, is that they are conditional only on attendance. There is no relationship between effort and reward, output and reward or quality of work and reward (except in so far as these might eventually secure promotion to a better paid position). A second main feature of time payments is that they are secure. They do not depend on fluctuations in output, performance or other variable factors as other forms of payment will.

The second main type of payment system is called payment by results. Again, the basis of the payment systems in this category is suggested by the name. Payment is related directly to work accomplished. It is usually calculated on one of two bases.

Piece-work

Under this system a price is agreed for each unit, and the worker is paid according to how many units he or she produces. Some systems, called group piece-work, pay on the basis of group rather than individual output. The principle, however, remains the same as for individual piece-rates.

Time allowances

These systems time output rather than price it. Basically, a standard time is established for the production of a given volume of output. Payment is then based on the amount of time saved by the worker on this standard time in reaching that volume of output. (Standard time − actual time = time saved.)

Each of these payment by results systems has many complicated variations and bases of calculation, but in each case the key relationship is that between effort and reward.

Advantages of different payment systems

The increase in mass production methods and the emphasis on quantity rather than quality of output was a major reason for the growth of payment by results (PBR) systems. Added to this, new techniques of work measurement (essential to PBR) allowed more workers to be paid in relation to their individual or group output. For these and other reasons, payment by results grew rapidly as a system of payment. It was widely believed to be a panacea for the problems of poor motivation and productivity so symptomatic of repetitive, monotonous work.

In many cases, however, PBR brought many more problems than it resolved. First, for PBR to be a possibility, output must be measurable so that a wage based on it can be calculated. This led to a situation where whilst some workers were able to increase their earnings through PBR systems, other workers whose output or contribution to output could not be accurately established were unable to do so. This created a variety of problems. Some earnings relationships which were either customary or generally felt to be fair were disturbed by PBR.

Inequities frequently arose and customary differentials were disturbed. Often, as a way around these problems, special compensatory payments were made to different groups of workers – a practice which quickly added to the complexity of the system from both the employees' and the administration's view. Errors, inaccuracies and deficiencies of work measurement often led to some jobs being considered 'gravy jobs' – jobs where it was considered easy to increase earnings substantially because of over-generous rates having been set. As frequently, the opposite situation would occur. All these difficulties made for complex payment systems with a high potential for generating conflict. Groups of workers were able to press claims on the basis of comparison with others, rates were frequently in dispute and open to challenge, especially where changes in technology or work practices distorted the accuracy of standards of output. In short, from an administrative and industrial relations point of view, PBR proved rather less than the panacea it had once seemed it might be.

Perhaps surprisingly too, PBR is often unpopular with a workforce. Such systems, in spite of an element of wages sometimes being guaranteed, lead to high uncertainty and insecurity of earnings – a feature which again does little to build stable industrial relations in an organisation.

None of these criticisms of PBR is intended to invalidate its role or value to an organisation, but rather to suggest some of the pitfalls of PBR as it has tended to operate. Where PBR systems are as comprehensive (in terms of coverage) and comprehensible as possible, where they are fair and seen to be fair by different individuals and groups, where they go some way to recognising customary differentials, and where they permit earnings security for the workforce, they can be an effective contributor to productivity and employee motivation. If PBR is to be preferred as a system of payment, this should not preclude other forms of motivation; and great care must be taken to avoid the tendency for systems to 'decay' over time and become so complex that they are virtually unmanageable.

Personnel management

Objectives of a wage and salary system

Whilst different payment systems can be examined out of context and criticised for their general deficiencies and shortcomings, it is increasingly recognised that these different systems will influence a workforce in different ways and that a system should only be designed in the light of a company's nature, objectives and priorities. To take a simple example, PBR is a payment system inappropriate in situations where the priority is quality of products, emphasising as it does, output in quantitative terms. PBR contains no incentive for the employee to safeguard quality. Indeed, it provides a disincentive to do so. With this in mind, we shall now consider what might be some of the objectives of a payment system.

The first function or objective of a payment system concerns the labour market. It must attract, or be capable of attracting labour of different grades and skills from outside the organisation, and it must minimise labour turnover through dissatisfaction with wages or salaries.

Secondly, wages and salaries are a major cost to an organisation and must be controlled along with other costs. A payment system therefore has a role in cost control and in promoting efficiency and productivity.

Thirdly, there are certain 'mobility' objectives of a wage and salary system. Internal differentials should be sufficient to encourage upward mobility within the organisation and will need to relate performance, merit and considerations of equity to the rewards given.

A payment system must meet all these objectives within the additional constraints of customary differentials in both money rewards and status. However, it has been suggested that different systems will be either appropriate or inappropriate to achieving these (and possibly other) objectives, depending on the type of organisation they are operating in. In other words, a payment system should not only be designed with specific objectives and priorities in mind, but should be designed also in such a way that they are consistent with the nature of the company, its workforce and its environment.

The nature of the technology in use in an organisation is a major determinant of the degree of autonomy and discretion the worker has and should therefore influence the basis on which he or she is paid. Some technologies leave little scope for the worker to influence either the pace of work or the quality of output.

The company's labour market situation – the time it takes to fill vacancies, labour turnover for different labour categories, and the scarcity of different workers needed by the organisation – should also shape the system adopted.

PBR systems are liable to decay and erosion after a few years of operation, becoming complex, difficult and time consuming to manage and a source of conflict. The seriousness of this decay and therefore the appropriateness of systems liable to it will be a function of the effectiveness and fairness of the procedures which the firm has for the resolution of conflicts and the implementation of changes which will become necessary over time.

Finally, many structural characteristics of an organisation and its workforce will tend to make one payment system more appropriate to it than another. The occupational structure of the firm, the existence or not of multi-unionism, the nature of wage settlement machinery are all examples of influential features.

In summary, in common with other prescriptive areas of organisation theory it is suggested increasingly that there is no one best system or method, but that the choice should be based on clear objectives and an appreciation of the situation for which that system is prescribed. One form of payment system will work best under one set of conditions, another will be more effective under another.

Job evaluation

We have seen that there are a number of objectives which wage payment systems must satisfy if they are to succeed in the long term. They must take account of market factors externally and any relevant statutory or negotiated rates. They must allow acceptable unit costs to be achieved, and they must provide motivation and feelings of equity through internal relativities which they define. One way of establishing a system of relativities which both encourages mobility and is understood and felt to be fair is to base the system on agreed methods of job evaluation.

Job evaluation techniques are designed to achieve a ranking of the worth of jobs on as objective a basis as possible and thus to formalise them into an appropriate pay structure. The criteria against which jobs are evaluated may then be used to re-evaluate them where changes in them occur and to incorporate new jobs into the structure as they are created.

Because of various influences on pay levels such as market rates, job evaluation cannot be concerned with establishing absolute levels of pay, but it can, through the application of common criteria, lead to conclusions about what one job is worth *relative* to another. Its main aim therefore is to establish relative not absolute pay levels.

There are a number of different systems of job evaluation, ranging from a simple ranking of jobs based on a fairly impressionistic judgement of each job as a whole, to more complex analytical systems which take account of a number of component factors common to the jobs being evaluated, e.g. skill, effort, responsibility, working conditions and others agreed upon, and judge the weight of each of these factors for each of the jobs under study. Compensation, usually in 'points' form, is then made according to the weightings given for each of the jobs.

19.6 Industrial relations

Chapters 10, 11, and 12 consider some aspects of the wide area of industrial relations. An examination of the history, structure and processes of the industrial relations system in Britain is beyond the scope of this book, but what we have examined in our earlier chapters are some of the problems of authority relationships, some of the causes of conflicts at an interpersonal and intergroup level and some of the processes through which those conflicts may be limited or resolved. To appreciate the apparent illogicalities and idiosyncracies of the structure and operation of the wider system of industrial relations as a whole, however, the student will need to appreciate its origins, the unique social, political and economic pressures on its development, and the variable role of the State and the law throughout the modern history of industrial relations. Reference is made to these factors in Chapter 13.

19.7 Employee safety and welfare

Good occupational safety and welfare should be a basic policy of any personnel department. It is estimated that almost two and a half times as many working days are lost through industrial accidents and disease as through strike action. Legislation was piecemeal until the Health and Safety at Work Act of 1974. The Act set up a policy-making commission and an inspectorate executive. It is an enabling Act, which means that new regulations can be introduced at any time, and this demands careful monitoring. It applies to all persons at work, employers, employees and the self-employed and lays down high minimum standards which should be reasonably maintained. The one important difference to previous Acts,

Personnel management

which it supersedes, is that it involves everyone at work. To help do this employees, through their unions, can appoint Safety Representatives to act as the 'eyes and ears' of the inspectorate. Everyone, though, has a duty to take reasonable care, and employers are criminally liable for negligence.

19.8 Maintenance of records

Essential for effective personnel management is a comprehensive and current set of pesonnel records. We have already mentioned the importance of up-to-date job descriptions and specifications; other records and statistics are of equal importance to the personnel department.

First, there should be a personal file on each employee, beginning with the job application and documents relating to the offer and acceptance of that job. To the file will be added over time relevant details about the employee's history and performance whilst with the company.

A personal record will be kept of the personal details of the employee: the date of joining the company and of job movements within it as well as entitlements to holidays, pensions and other benefits. To this will be added details of training undertaken, appraisal details, disciplinary actions taken against the employee and other detail considered relevant, for example a record of absences. Finally, on leaving the company, the date that employment was terminated should be recorded along with any reasons given by the employee.

Information about individual employees is important for many reasons. Employees' suitability for transfer, promotion or training can be assessed on the basis of factual recorded information over the total period of employment, career progress can be planned systematically, evidence can be given when required of compliance with the agreed requirements of any disciplinary procedure which might result in dismissal of an employee, and reasons for leaving can be analysed collectively in an attempt to identify major causes of dissatisfaction within the organisation.

To assist decision making and control, many other statistical records should be held in addition to the personal records of employees. These include:

- a record of accidents, documenting location, cause and relevant circumstances
- details of labour turnover, examined by types of labour and location
- working days lost and a breakdown of their causes
- statistical details required by Government Departments and agencies
- records of grievances and disputes
- records of wage and salary statistics
- training records
- overtime statistics

The reasons for the importance of accurate record keeping and statistics are several. They allow the systematic diagnosis of weaknesses in different areas of personnel management influence or responsibility, which provides a sound basis for planned improvements. They allow also for personnel decisions to be made across the range of the department's functions on the basis of current and accurate data. They contribute to efficiency in each of the areas we have covered in this chapter. As such their importance cannot be overstated.

Evaluation

Personnel management is a specialism. It is one which really involves a process comprising a number of complementary activities. Manpower resources must be first planned for, within the context of the organisation's present and future needs: they must be acquired, developed, motivated and 'maintained' physically and psychologically. This chapter has simply reviewed the considerations and methods which facilitate that process.

Self-test questions

1 What is the overall aim of personnel management?

2 What is a local labour market?

3 Why might it be better to recruit internally?

4 What characterises a good interview?

5 What should be the objectives of staff appraisal systems, and according to what principles should they be designed?

6 What is payment by results and what problems can it create?

7 What is job evaluation? Does it have any inherent limitations?

8 List some of the records that you as a personnel manager would want to maintain.

Case studies on Part D

VIZ-AID

Viz-aid Manufacturing Co. wishes to purchase fans to be used in the manufacture of overhead projectors. It uses 250 such fans a month at present, and has storage for 325. The maximum price it will pay is £2 per fan (as charged by present supplier). Viz-aid is a large company, using assembly line methods and a computerised accounting system. The market for overhead projectors is reaching its peak.

Supplier 1 already manufactures and supplies fans to a competitor of Viz-aid, and specialises in fan manufacture. The minimum price would be £1.50, for a minimum order of 250. The supplier is 20 miles away from Viz-aid, is a small company partly unionized, and has had some union problems in the past. Delivery would be by road.

Supplier 2 manufactures fans, although not the precise type required by Viz-aid, and also makes a wide range of other products. The minimum price for fans as required by Viz-aid would be £1.25, for a minimum order of 300. It is a very large company, fully unionised, and has had no industrial relations trouble for several years. It is 150 miles away from Viz-aid, and delivery would be by rail.

1 What factors should influence Viz-aid in their decision to buy from supplier 1 or 2?

2 What considerations would suppliers make in choosing to do business with Viz-aid?

COOLA LTD

Coola Ltd is a firm of 5,000 employees manufacturing bodies for ice-cream vans.

Bill Smith, aged 50, is Works Manager. He has been with the Company for 25 years and has been promoted up the production line from the shop floor. He has held his present post for seven years. He recently attended a management course on Organisation and Human Relations. He was not fully convinced of its value, and at the time mentioned this view, in conversation, to his Superintendent, Jones.

John Brown, aged 35, an Arts graduate, has spent his last five years as Training Officer, having had seven years' previous experience in the personnel department of a smaller firm.

Arthur Jones, aged 30, Production Superintendent, has been with the Company since starting his apprenticeship and obtained his H.N.D. in Mechanical Engineering three years ago, shortly before his promotion to Production Superintendent. He is very ambitious, and keen to maintain his department's efficiency and productivity.

Jim White is regarded as the best foreman in Jones' department, and has been earmarked for promotion to another department. In accordance with normal procedure, the personnel department has been informed of this.

Case studies on Part D

Company policy, which is to train managers and potential managers in the techniques and principles of management, is based on the belief that such training will benefit both the Company and the individual. It is part of this policy that only in exceptional circumstances should a man be prevented from attending a training course for which he has been selected.

The training department is planning its next three-week internal course for supervisors to commence in a fortnight's time. The balance of the course requires three production foremen representing different departments; Jones's department is required to supply one, and he has reluctantly nominated White some time ago. Two other foremen were also nominated by their superintendents.

As a result of a recent work study investigation, Jones's department's workload has been increased to capacity and the need for close supervision has intensified. A special export order representing three weeks' work has to be completed in White's section within the next month, having been brought forward from the original programmed date.

The training course in question is the last of its kind for six months. It is planned that White will take over a more senior position after training in three months' time. In a telephone conversation with the Training Officer, Smith confirms that White will attend the course. He then informs Jones, who says that in view of the programme alteration in the export order, he cannot now spare White and still meet the delivery date.

1 What is the nature of the problems evident in the case, and which is the company's key failure?

2 What action should be taken in the short term and long term?

3 How sensible is Jones in preventing White from attending the training course?

JETTA LTD

The main problem for the Jetta motor cycle company was, and had been for many years, one of falling sales both at home and in overseas markets. Total demand was increasing but Jetta's share was growing ever smaller. The reasons for the decline of the once extremely successful company were not hard to find. The labour force was not as productive as rival manufacturers', the equipment and production line technology at Jetta was, by modern standards, outdated, and the company had failed to develop any strategy based on trends in customer demand. They had continued to turn out the same products they had always made in spite of an obvious shift in demand towards the lower powered end of the motor cycle market – probably attributable to rising fuel costs. It was obvious to Michael Prover, the new managing director, that if Jetta was to survive it had to establish clear objectives for the future. Production equipment was largely outdated – something had to be done about that. The work force was too large and would have to be slimmed down. A new, modern and appealing product range had to be established to compete with rival products. Productivity, even with new equipment and a reduced workforce, would have to improve substantially. Prospects for the company were so depressing that Prover felt it essential to call together his management team and pool their ideas. If changes were going to be made in technology, manning levels and work methods, he would need the backing and co-operation of everyone from management downwards. There was a real challenge ahead for Jetta, one which would test the skills and abilities of its management in almost every direction.

1 From your knowledge of the functions of management, suggest which will be tested most fully if Jetta is to recover its share of motor cycle sales and give your reasons.

2 Having been given one week's notice of the MD's meeting, what special points would you want to make at the meeting if you were:
   (a) the Marketing Manager?
   (b) the Personnel Manager?
   (c) the Chief Accountant?

PART E

The subject matter of this book has ranged from the technical detailed function of a purchasing officer through to apparently abstruse and ephemeral subjects like individual motivation and the 'nature' of leadership.

The 'practical' manager might pay far more attention to the former rather than the latter – and the 'theoretical' sociologist would probably disagree. But that is the point of this book. Organisation studies must necessarily look at the problems of management combining many different perspectives. It is a measure of our advance in understanding that we cannot now promise blue-prints and do's and don'ts for managers, giving easy answers to all questions. We have begun to understand the complexity of our business life.

This is not a council of despair – managers still have to make decisions; they still have to manage. This section looks at some more practical organisation problems with the aim of showing how *all* of what we have studied does interrelate and does have importance. Having completed this section you will almost certainly still make mistakes, but if you have considered all the factors as you should, you may at least know what the mistake is and, perhaps, what to do about it.

20 The functions of management 'revisited'

Throughout this volume we have said a lot about the problems of dealing with a subject area such as organisation studies. The need to avoid seizing on apparently easy answers to complex problems with many implications has been stressed. We know that many problems in organisations differ in kind from individual to individual and from situation to situation. A problem-solving strategy which works well in one organisational context may well be inappropriate in another. Yet, at the end of the day, managers must manage and produce ideas and strategies for the problems which confront them daily. So – how should the perceptive individual, armed only with volumes of contradictory theoretical perspectives, and aware of the minefield of unique pressures and circumstances, actually set about doing the job?

There are two alternatives. A manager can say: 'Well, all those insights into the behavioural sciences are very interesting but I still can't really see their practical value.'

At work, pressured by deadlines and work load, this type of manager can too easily become heavily 'task-orientated', relying on the use of authority and reward power to 'get the job done'. At the back of his mind, he knows that he is not bringing the full range of his knowledge and expertise to bear on his job. But his uneasiness in this direction can make him and his kind prey to the simple packaged programme or formula to improve involvement or motivation of staff, improve their leadership or create better teamwork. By accepting such a formula, however naive it is, they can thus ease their conscience and then better claim to be progressive, 'all-round', people-centred managers. Unfortunately, faced with poor results, perhaps high labour turnover, absenteeism and obstructive employee attitudes, these managers may eventually convince themselves that their original suspicions were correct – and that there is no practical value in the behavioural sciences. Managers who eventually adopt such attitudes should not be condemned too quickly. It will happen to a high proportion of the management students reading this book.

The second alternative is unquestionably harder to follow. It requires managers to back their *own* judgements of people and situations. Managers who choose this alternative must accept that good management is first about problem *diagnosis* and then about problem resolution. It should be remembered that none of the theories introduced earlier in this book is 'wrong'. Most are based on the evidence of observed results in actual organisational or experimental contexts. What we have learned, however, is that the same results cannot be guaranteed when any theory is applied in varying organisational contexts. A simple example outlined in Chapter 5 is Herzberg's Two Factor theory of motivation. When blue-collar employees were questioned, pay, which for Herzberg's original sample of professional employees was a 'hygiene factor', emerged as a 'motivator'. Similarly, it is clear that different employees will express different aspirations and that different organisation structures seem best suited to particular technologies and operating environments. The list could go on and on to include the need to match leadership style to the specific context within which it will be exercised, and many other such examples discussed throughout our text.

The manager's problem, then, is to attempt to define and understand the situation and *then* to make judgements about which strategy or combination of strategies to apply. If you have been tackling the case study examples in this book, you will have begun to appreciate the vast range of options and implications which each different situation holds: if organisational panaceas existed they would have been used long ago.

In this chapter we look again at the basic functions each manager, whatever his/her specialist role, must practise. Using case study examples we shall attempt to build frameworks to show how different theoretical approaches can and should be incorporated within any approach to the basic management task.

To help you tackle some of the problems and cases we present in this chapter, we shall occasionally suggest the direction you should take in answering them. Usually we have selected one problem from the range given after discussion of each management function.

20.1 Forecasting and planning

If we go back to the basic elements of organisations we can list them as:

- people
- task technology
- structure
- environment

In essence organisation is the continuing process of dividing the total task into smaller units or groupings of work and establishing who will be responsible for those areas of work. The result of this process is an organisation structure deemed appropriate for operating within current social, economic, legal and technological constraints.

As we saw in Chapter 3, certain limitations will be imposed on us by the nature of the technology we decide, or are obliged to employ. Similarly economic factors – like existing market opportunites, levels of consumer demand, and prices of different factor inputs, can lead to a need to expand, contract or diversify certain parts of the business. Naturally, this carries with it organisational implications. Government controls and fiscal policy may have the same effect; statutory provisions, for example, can influence factory and office design, patterns of working and such basic factors as physical opportunities for expansion. So, in first acquiring and then combining our organisational inputs, we need first to have information about the environment we are designing our structure for. The greater the investment of the organisation in people and technology, the more important it becomes to ensure that those investments are appropriate and to look forward to a time when they may no longer be adequate. The small business will tend to be more flexible, more easily and quickly adaptable to changing conditions and may, therefore, need to plan on a relatively shorter time scale.

Of course *external* constraints will not be the only limits on how an organisation is structured. People, finance, past policy, physical resources and other factors will also be a major influence. For Fayol, forecasting was the *essence* of management. If that was true for Fayol at the time of writing – how much more true must it be now that the pace of change has accelerated so much. Let us look at a few short case examples of forecasting and planning problems.

The functions of management 'revisited'

Case studies

A Bulldog Office Equipment

Jim Smethwick liked to back the judgement of his departmental managers; they were a good team and had all done their best to help arrest the decline of his office furniture business. Smethwick had, originally, built the firm with his father on a reputation for solid, reliable, quality products backed by a proficient selling team, skilled at convincing customers that 'Bulldog was Best'. Bulldog now employed 160 people. Lately though, the competition was clearly outstripping Bulldog. Fancy designs and bright colours seemed to be all that was needed to succeed on the furnishing side – stuff that would have made Smethwick's father turn in his grave.

At the morning meeting of the management team of the Personnel Manager, Accountant, Production and Sales Managers, the Sales Manager – Angus Ferguson – had reported that the 'British Bulldog is Best' campaign, designed to counter the appeal of foreign imports and their main domestic competitor, 21st Century Designs, had had only a very marginal effect on sales – partly because Bulldog deliveries had been so erratic – salesmen were complaining of increasing difficulty in selling Bulldog products.

The Personnel Manager voiced his concern at lack of high calibre junior management within the firm; most of those with any talent had left Bulldog for competitors. In addition he was concerned at poor staff morale and attitudes coupled with the effects of rumours of redundancies at a time of high local unemployment.

The Production Manager reported on his work study and rationalisation programme designed to plan out the work for each man within a system of co-ordinated production targets. He seemed annoyed at its ineffectiveness, saying that whilst he knew the equipment was old, he was at a loss to know what more he could do than ensure that each man received detailed instruction and close supervision. Over-capacity and overmanning, which had been long-standing problems at Bulldog, were as bad as ever.

The Accountant's comments were no less gloomy. Productivity was down again and costs were rising. There was little or no money available for reinvestment in more productive equipment. There was no doubting the consensus at the meeting. It was put to Smethwick in no uncertain terms. Something must be done and quickly. Smethwick, as was his style, asked each of his managers in turn what they felt would have to be done and what they expected of him as Managing Director.

1 Evaluate the management approach at Bulldog.

2 What would your advice to Smethwick be, (a) in the short term, and (b) in the long term if you were:
   (i) the Production Manager?
   (ii) the Sales Manager?
   (iii) the Personnel Manager?
   (iv) the Accountant?

3 In broad terms, what information should each manager seek from both internal and external sources in order to justify their recommendations to Smethwick?

4 Draft the key points contained in your collective advice from the management team in the form of an outline action plan for the next three years at Bulldog.

In tackling a problem such as this one, you should first address yourself to the job of problem diagnosis. Read the case study more than once, and on the second reading jot down any clues to what the problems at Bulldog are. Note some of the assumptions and assertions of the Bulldog management.

- What are the real problems and what are only symptoms?
- What are the problems which seem to need tackling first?
- What symptoms of poor performance will then disappear and which might well persist?
- What specialist information can you draw upon from Part D to help you to remedy fundamental problems and to ensure that they do not recur?
- What organisational or management principles might be being misapplied?

Forecasting and planning

Try to draw as widely as possible on the key issues discussed in the different sections of this book. Be creative, be imaginative, build your own solution to the problem as you have diagnosed it; but think hard about the implications of your recommendations and, of course, about their cost.

B
Choose one of the following industries and list the economic, social, political, legal and technological changes which are likely to affect them over the next 10 years. Briefly state, with examples, how organisations within that industry could begin to plan for the effects of those changes.

> Banking
> Motor vehicle manufacture
> Leisure and entertainment
> Education
> Public transport

C
A large foreign company is known to wish to establish itself at a site in Britain in order to manufacture and assemble motor vehicles.

1 Who would be the main interested parties in the company's proposals and what would be their main priorities and reservations?

2 What social, legal, political, economic and technological factors might influence the different parties, including the company itself, with an interest in the decision as to whether and where to locate the factory in Britain?

D
You wish to stage a local Midsummer Carnival in aid of charity. You live in a part of London where there is a public park in which similar events have been staged in the past. You and a committee of nine others are to be responsible for staging the event some time early in July.

At a preliminary meeting you have decided to organise the carnival along the following lines:

> an 'arena' where a number of crowd-pulling events will occur,
> about 20 stalls and sideshows to raise money from those present,
> beer and food marquees on the edge of the 'arena'.

It is intended to raise money also from the sale of printed carnival programmes for 15p each.

One of the committee members knows a member of a stunt motor cycle display team whose programme includes leaps over a row of parked cars and another finale act, jumping through a wall of fire created by blazing straw bales. The team has agreed to perform for expenses only – approximately £125.

Other suggestions for the arena made at the preliminary meeting included a hot-air balloon, which might give rides, a majorette display team, a junior sports competition and a limited-over sponsored knockout cricket tournament between the five local pubs.

You have no capital equipment, although through weekly raffles and a recent jumble sale you have raised £750 which may be used as you like to finance the event and to hire such equipment and facilities as you feel necessary or which you are told you must provide.

1 Decide clearly and in detail, which members of the committee will have what special responsibilities leading up to the carnival, and list the information they will want in order to draw up a plan for the day.

Try to ascertain factual detail where you can, and detail the action necessary before the event takes place and on the day itself. A few of the things you would need to consider might be:

- expenditures, including hire and rental costs
- permissions which must be sought
- legal and social obligations which you have in staging the Carnival

The functions of management 'revisited'

- manpower requirements and responsibilities on the day – manning stalls, administration, etc.
- additional, appropriate, money raising ideas.

2 Design the programme which will be sold to the public.

20.2 Organising

Throughout the different sections of this book we have considered different theories of organising work and the implications of each. Essentially, it is organisation, that is the way in which people and technology are deployed and combined together, which represents the central theme of our total subject area.

From the theories we have considered, it seems clear that there are important links between organisation structure, including job design, and key aspects of organisational efficiency.

These include:

- employee satisfaction
- productivity
- group effectiveness
- productive leadership
- the avoidance of role problems
- effective control and communication

Employee satisfaction

For example, links between organisation structure and employee satisfaction are proposed by Human Relations writers both from the point of view of the social satisfactions they afford or preclude and by the extent to which structure and job design permit challenge, responsibility and 'professional growth' for the employee, allowing him or her to satisfy important higher order needs. Jobs whose structure and content are dictated and limited by mass production technology have also been shown to increase the likelihood of alienation amongst employees. Similarly, when structures permit meaningful participation by employees in decisions of concern and interest to them, then, it is claimed, satisfaction will increase. Provided we do not argue that these causes and effects are inevitable or universal, they are useful indicators of the kinds of implications which different organisation structures can hold.

Productivity

Similarly, whilst a direct positive correlation between satisfaction and productivity is disputed by many writers and researchers, much of the evidence does indicate an important link between the two. But even apart from this, it is obvious that certain forms of organisation design and structuring, alternative ways of allocating tasks and responsibilities, will be more or less helpful in terms of productivity. The principles of management outlined by classical organisational theorists, whilst they can be criticised for their rigidity and dogmatic assertions, were no more than attempts to help managers appreciate the structural variables which can improve organisational efficiency and productivity.

Taylor and the Scientific Management movement were again concerned with identifying structural and job design variables correlating with efficiency. Later writers too, including Systems theorists and Contingency writers, all stress the relationship between structure and productive efficiency, but this time related to specific operating contexts.

Organising

Group effectiveness

Without repeating here models of group effectiveness already considered in Chapter 6 it will be remembered that amongst the many variables influencing group performance were some which could be classified as structural.

How we structure and build groups, when and what we ask them to do and with what resources are aspects of the management function of organising. Together and in combination with other factors they will be major determinants of group effectiveness, measured by the twin criteria of productivity and member satisfaction.

Productive leadership

The later theories of leadership we considered in Chapter 7 highlighted key variables in leadership effectiveness. One of the variables emphasised above all others by the leadership 'style' theorists was the extent to which, either formally or informally, employees' jobs were supplemented with more responsible or varied work. Advocates of democratic styles argue that this opportunity should be increased, allowing subordinates to do work or take decisions which under 'normal' circumstances might have been executed elsewhere or by a superior.

The structuring and allocation of work and decisions is a function of managerial leadership and, as we have seen, existing task structure can limit or constrain leadership possibilities and styles, influencing which are most likely to be effective.

Role problems

Role theory is one of the areas most clearly linked with organising. Breaking the total task down in different ways and allocating authority and responsibility creates the system of formal expectations to which individual job holders are required to respond.

Individuals can be overloaded or underloaded with these expectations; they will often be unsure of them; they may feel they conflict or are incompatible with what they, or members of their role set, expect.

In these cases, role problems are directly attributable to deficient organising and will usually be remedied by changes in the allocation of formal duties.

Communication

Connections between organisation structure and the quality of management control and communication were at the root of early Classical theories of work organisation. The number of levels of authority in an organisation, any superior's span of control, and other structural dimensions of the organisation will either facilitate or hinder the exercise of all management functions especially communication, both vertically and horizontally, and control, which is dealt with later in this chapter and is itself heavily dependent on the quality of information flows between managers and operatives.

Many other relationships with, and implications of, organisation structure have been identified throughout the text – technology, for example, was dealt with in some depth – and we can conclude that since it has so great an influence on organisational performance and employee well-being, organisation is one area where, despite contradictions in the theory, managers must get it right.

Case studies

A

Bill Rowntree was Personnel Manager with Shead Paper Sack Co. Ltd. The firm employed nearly 300 people in their office and factory. Rowntree and his Managing Director had decided to channel company resources into an extensive programme of staff development.

The functions of management 'revisited'

Both were convinced that employees needed responsibility and the chance for personal development and growth. The Company was housed in modern premises, and both office and factory staff enjoyed good working conditions, social facilities and competitive wages and benefits.

Rowntree had approached company management and asked them to nominate three senior staff each from their departments to sit on a staff development committee to meet monthly or as was found necessary. Having convened a preliminary meeting in his office, Rowntree addressed the 15 staff gathered around him.

'We want people who think the way we do', he said, 'senior staff who know the ropes in the Company and who will appreciate the resource limitations I shall have to set before them. Our job – assuming you are all happy to participate – will be to see how we can best use our budget and resources to further staff development in the Company.

'Now, I have some very strong ideas on where we've been going wrong in the past and I hope that in you we've chosen people who see things the same way and share my priorities. I want to get things moving quickly and, as a starter, I'd like you all to come back at the next meeting with a positive scheme or suggestion to make. Naturally, my decision on any go-ahead will have to be final, but feel free to use your imagination in coming up with something positive and practical. I'm afraid we'll have to continue meeting in my office as I need to be on hand, but I'll see what can be done about additional seating for next time.

'Finally, if anyone wants to test out the idea they're working on with me before the next meeting, just pop up and we can have a short chat to see that it fits the bill.

'Thank you all for coming.'

1 How would you have approached the problem of setting up a staff development committee at Shead to give it the greatest possible chance of success?

2 In terms of your knowledge of groups and group effectiveness, where has Rowntree already gone wrong?

3 To provide staff development which meets the real needs both of the Company and individual employees what information would you first require?

B

Choose a job with which you are familiar or for which you have access to a job description and show how it might be enriched. Where might resistance to job enrichment come from and why?

C

Cyril Wilson was a traditionalist. When recruits came to his accounts department he believed that they should begin as he did – mastering the routine work. After a day or two, he could leave them alone knowing that only a moron could make a mistake working at such a basic level. Later, if the Junior had proved satisfactory after an 'apprenticeship' of a year or so, he might move him to work which was marginally more difficult and demanding. It was this thorough, gradual grounding in accounting methods which Wilson believed now made him, as Chief Accountant, such an asset to the Company. Those who left the Company within a year or two of joining his department lacked character as far as Wilson was concerned and epitomised the young generation's impatience and lack of appreciation for a steady job leading to a secure career. He deplored the contrasting methods of the Sales Manager, Cyril Crabtree.

Crabtree's style was entirely different. He threw his recruits in at the deep end. 'No good always telling them what to do and how to do it – never learn for themselves', he was fond of saying. 'People *have* to learn for themselves – learn from mistakes. I never tell them what I expect of them. Let them find out for themselves. They'll soon find out if they've done it wrong and if they can't learn that way they're no good to me', he had said to Wilson over lunch one day.

It gave Wilson a certain satisfaction that Crabtree lost just as many staff in their first two years with the firm as he did. At least he could be sure that his own leavers had lacked character. Crabtree seemed to turn bright new recruits into nervous wrecks. Never mind. Crabtree would learn to change his ways.

1 Evaluate the two managers' approach to managing new recruits and the work they are asked to do.
2 What expectations would you have of your manager/superior if you were a new recruit? What expectations do you feel he or she would be entitled to have of you?
3 Which areas of organisation theory would you recommend Wilson and Crabtree to consider and practice?

D
Refer back to your plan for the Charity carnival worked out under D on page 151. Try to think pessimistically and list all the problems which might arise and things that might go wrong before or on the day of the event. Now test your plan and organisation to see how well they would be able to minimise losses and disruption caused by such contingencies. If, for example, the weather on the day is bad – did you consider insuring against this? Who will decide which events will be cancelled? The advertised motor cycle team does not arrive because their trailer has broken down – what, if any, is your liability? A very young child is brought to you having lost his mother somewhere in the crowd. The stall holders have all run short of small change, etc. Who would have taken what action in the event of these and similar contingencies? Would you now wish to change the organisation and allocation of responsibilities you originally decided on in order better to meet the demands of the task in hand?

E
Your management training includes an analysis of the importance and implications of organisation structure. As part of this training you are asked to evaluate the organisation structure of your employing organisation and to prepare a formal written report summarising your conclusions and recommendations.

You are presented with an organisation chart to enable you to make your analysis and are invited to request additional detail if required.

1 What criteria would you use for your assessment?
2 What additional detail would you request or what more would you wish to observe before drawing your conclusions?

We leave you to decide your own approach to these cases and problems on organisation and how you build in ideas and information from different areas.

Before moving on, however, we briefly consider the kinds of issues you might think about in tackling an apparent problem of organisation.

Problem E above describes a task which management must continually undertake. Regrettably, it is nearly always more complex than it first appears.

In tackling the problem you might for example want to discuss the importance of basic structural dimensions such as spans of control, levels of authority and so on. But remember you should be doing this in the context of technology, environment, communication channels, control considerations, product or task factors and motivational implications. Consider also links between organisation and role theory, informal relationships, group effectiveness and logical specialisation. Remember to consider how both internal and external factors should influence organisation and job design.

20.3 Leadership and direction

There is little point in devising creative and well-researched plans unless they can be effectively implemented and controlled. Both organisation structure and motivation can facilitate decision implementation, but quite clearly the plan must

The functions of management 'revisited'

be communicated 'downward' in order that each person involved in its implementation is clear what has to be done and what is the extent of their own or their group's responsibility. Similarly, activities at different levels and different elements of any plan must be co-ordinated to achieve the specified objectives most economically. At its simplest, direction is ensuring that employees know, and do, what is required of them.

As we have seen, though, there are many ways in which the essential task of direction can be carried out. There are styles and approaches to leadership and direction, different ways of getting people to comply with organisational plans and direct their full energies towards success. Some of these approaches will have a different effect on people's commitment and involvement with organisational plans than others. In some cases the effect is likely to be a constructive and beneficial one; in others it will be to frustrate and alienate subordinates.

As we have seen in Chapter 7, many people believe that leadership is a natural and innate quality or that effective leadership is in some way intuitive. So to what extent can anybody deliberately adopt a particular style or approach to leadership because a situation seems to demand it even when a different approach better suits their temperament or image of themselves as a manager? And if this is possible what has been learned from our study of people and organisations that enables us to diagnose situations and predict the likely effects of particular leadership approaches and strategies?

Certainly there are many different studies into the probable general effects of different leadership styles on motivation and productivity, and there is evidence that effective delegation can motivate and develop subordinates. We know too that where employees are working towards clear and salient goals their performance is more likely to improve than in situations where goals are ambiguous or unspecified or are simply imposed. Here though, we need to put together more specific practical advice for employees faced with the complex task of leadership; we need to look again at the nature of power and authority and how leaders should make use of them.

Etzioni, it will be recalled, demonstrated a relationship between the type of power preferred in organisations and the involvement of subordinates in the organisation and their identification with its goals and objectives. Types of power and types of involvement tended to be paired. That is, coercive power tends to alienate, remunerative or reward power reinforces an instrumental involvement in the organisation, whilst normative power pairs with moral involvement or deep commitment and strong identification with organisational goals. At the same time where a leader or manager is faced with any of these three types of involvement, the source of power with which it is paired is likely to be more effective than either of the others. If this relationship between the use of power and involvement is a strong one then it follows that it matters *a great deal* how a manager draws on the different sources of power at his or her disposal. It is logical to conclude that if managers were to resort to physical power and force their subordinates to get things done, commitment to organisational goals would be non-existent or even negative and hostile. Reliance on position power or managerial authority – 'Do this because I say so and I am the boss' – is likely, though to a lesser extent, to generate resentment on the part of those employees affected.

Even the constant resort first to financial incentives can induce an instrumental approach to work; it can condition a workforce to believe that the main reward for work is money, that their views and their development are neither required nor valued and that their compliance needs only to be bought. It would seem natural that in this context employees will seek the best price in money terms for their continuing co-operation and will lack any real personal commitment to the task itself and the objectives pursued.

Discussion, persuasion and consultation are more likely to be the tools used when managers prefer first to draw upon what we have called personal and expert power, so that people do things without resentment because they can see their logic or benefit, not because they have been forced or 'bought off'.

If we can depend on these assumptions, then we can draw up a rank order of management styles to be used to create a healthy and creative involvement with the organisation and its goals.

The problem, unfortunately, is more complex than this. It depends whether one is prepared to take the long-term or the short-term view. Few leaders enjoy the luxury of being in a situation where they are starting from scratch. Situations and attitudes are likely to be long standing, and attitude change is a notoriously difficult exercise. Maybe, existing deep-rooted types of employee involvement can be changed by the long-term, consistent use of personal and expert power as a first resort. But if results are required in the short term perhaps we should be best advised to note the arguments of theorists like Fiedler, who assert that results will come when the leadership approach is applied according to the existing dimensions of the context in which it will be used.

The position power of the leader, the originality or ambiguity of the task, and the relations between leader and subordinate will together determine the styles of leadership and direction which will work best. Other 'best fit' or contingency theories have modified and extended key, determining variables. The danger, of course, with these approaches is that recourse to the style of direction dictated by, amongst other things, subordinate attitudes and involvement is that whilst a leadership style may yield the best possible short-term results it can reinforce adverse situations where task commitment is low and leader–subordinate relations are poor.

These, though, are judgements best made by the leader himself. In reality it is quite likely that, say, technology precludes much real scope for employee identification with the task or product.

You may now like to consider the situations outlined below and propose how you might respond to them.

A. More important things

Jack Brown ran the General Office in the main city branch of a national bank. It was the largest department of all, most of the others being smaller, specialist departments.

Sometimes he really thought that his leadership task was virtually impossible. The department was too large for him really to get to know his staff individually – many of them working in the office for only a year or two as initial experience immediately on joining the bank. The real problem was the diversity of tasks and subordinates he was responsible for.

His section heads and senior staff were not the greatest problem. They were well into the career structure of the bank, secure in their work and with good prospects. They were really self-motivating, conscious of the need to gain a favourable annual appraisal and, Brown thought, encouragingly competitive in their pursuit of limited promising opportunities. Margaret Brophy worried him occasionally but she was so expert at her job that he found it hard to criticise her in specific terms. She had been in the bank far longer than Brown but just didn't seem able to win the respect of her staff and to get the best out of them.

She worked with Ron Pickering and three grade one juniors – their first job in the bank after leaving school. Ron was something of a character. Fifty-five years old and still doing a job with no responsibility and now, for him, no prospects. It didn't worry him, in fact he made no secret of the fact that it suited him. He was one of life's jokers, easy going and good company. The trouble was that no one really ever knew where he was. That was one of the perks of the queries section. One often had to be away from one's desk quite legitimately. Ron's productivity, however, in terms of queries dealt with didn't really justify his prolonged absences.

The functions of management 'revisited'

Margaret and Ron, for two people so completely different, got on famously with each other, even to the point that she would frequently cover up for Ron whenever he was required or enquired after.

The three youngsters on her section were learning the job. They had no real experience and were in need of patient guidance. Naturally, they were often high spirited but were fairly keen and co-operative. They agreed on one thing, however. First, there was no need for Brophy to be such a stickler with them and to explode whenever they made mistakes or took too long over their work. They resented the licence she gave Ron whilst being so finickity and disciplinarian with them.

She was fond of telling them that they were not at school any more and couldn't expect to be spoonfed. That would have been all right if she had given them time to work things out for themselves. If they asked questions she clearly showed her displeasure at being interrupted and would simply tell them to leave the query they were working on in her tray and 'get on with something else'. Ron was no help. He would just say that there were more important things in life than work and queries, smile, and saunter off across the banking hall.

The girls in the machine room were a different proposition. Their work was routine, monotonous and largely machine paced. There was no real job interest, and turnover and absenteeism were both high. The jobs were graded lowest on the job evaluation system and because of the nature of the work there was little by way of avenues for promotion. The girls regarded their main perk as being allowed to listen to music all day whilst working the machines.

Brown's other intake of staff were the A level and graduate entry, again coming to him for an initial training and orientation. Most made no effort to disguise their resentment at having to perform routine clerical duties but, being as inexperienced as other joiners, were told that they would just have to learn the hard way like anyone else. Brown sighed and reflected that perhaps Ron had got it right, there were more important things to worry about than work, and anyway, he was taking his own retirement in a couple of years.

1 Summarise Brown's problems in terms of motivating his department. How far should any manager in his situation delegate this task?

2 What action, if any, should Brown take to resolve the problems on the Queries Section?

3 Design an appraisal form which could be fairly applied to the diversity of staff within the department and upon which future movements of staff could be based.

4 Is there any room for manoeuvre as far as motivating and involving the machine room girls is concerned? What implications do your suggested alternative(s) carry with them?

5 Should the A level and graduate entrants be treated differently to others?

B. How would you do it . . .?

Describe briefly the approach(es) you would be most likely to use in the following situations.

1 Addressing a group of soldiers prior to a military engagement.

2 Addressing a meeting of trade unionists, advising them to take industrial action in support of workers in another of the Company's plants.

3 Addressing a workforce and persuading them of the need for 20 per cent redundancies and a zero wage increase in the coming wage round.

4 Addressing new employees on an induction course in an attempt to persuade them to participate fully in the firm's joint consultation scheme.

5 Dealing with a problem of recurring lateness by some individuals.

6 Meeting with the supervisor and another member of the same workgroup who have a personality clash which is clearly destructive in terms of other group members.

7 Addressing a group of employees in an attempt to end consistent petty pilfering.

8 Attempting to deal with high labour turnover and absenteeism in a technology-dominated work situation without recourse to financial incentives.

9 Trying to eliminate sloppy and careless work.
10 Introducing job evaluation.
11 Resolving a problem of role overload without denting an individual's pride and self-esteem.
12 Dealing with the playful but hurtful teasing of one employee by members of his workgroup.
13 Explaining your decision to appoint an outsider to a senior position to two long-serving staff who might have expected to be promoted to it.

In these 'How would you do it?' questions, you obviously lack full information which you might have in the real-life situation.

Each problem, though, is reasonably typical and says enough to suggest what might be the most fruitful leadership strategy to adopt. In tackling the problems, always consider what it is you are *using* to gain acceptance or compliance or to convince the parties involved to act in particular ways. Is it persuasion, position power, threats, money, rules and regulations, or an appeal to some 'higher' ideal? Similarly, think through the implications of your decisions.

Taking question 5 as an example. Possible (though not necessarily sensible or cost-effective) options include:

- threats and formal disciplinary action
- loss of pay based on time lost with or without an additional penalty
- the introduction of a 'clocking in' system
- introduction of flexitime or similar systems of working
- informal discussion and persuasion
- moving the individual on to a output-related payment system
- arranging for the individual's workgroup to be paid on a group bonus system, or moving him to one which is, thus leaving informal group pressures to 'discipline' the employee.

Naturally, some of these options are more desirable than others. Think which represent an increase in the closeness and visibility of general control and what the implications of that can be. At the end of the day which options you choose, reject or create should depend upon the cost, benefits and possible repercussions of each.

20.4 Control

When a task has been subdivided into smaller tasks and different, often isolated, individuals are made responsible for them, the need for some co-ordination of activities and checks on progress towards a final objective or set of objectives is obvious.

If direction mainly involves the downward communication of plans and objectives, control is the key management activity of gaining the information necessary to check actual against planned progress and to account for and remedy deviations as they are identified.

The obvious relationships between structure and control have already been considered. Like the other functions we have discussed in this chapter, however, there are styles of control. They can be either productive or destructive. They can complement other features of good management practice or totally undermine them. Control links not only with the structural dimensions of the organisation but with the human and managerial aspects too. Control styles, like leadership and direction, can alienate or motivate and challenge.

The functions of management 'revisited'

A. A matter of trust

Brian Gresham had quite enjoyed the management course he had attended. He didn't agree with some of the ideas and methods he had been told would improve his managerial effectiveness, but at least some of it had been useful.

He had, above all, made up his mind to delegate more. Inside, he knew that this had always been one of his weaknesses – always trying to do, or at least check, everything himself. He had particularly appreciated being told on the course that delegation of some routine work would free him to take more of an overall view of things and to concentrate on the planning and broader management of the work of his department. Additionally, he had been told, the delegation of work to subordinates would have important effects on their motivation and job satisfaction. It was worth a try, he had decided.

He made up his mind to speak to his three section heads about his ideas and begin his new style of management as soon as possible.

Gresham told the section heads that in future they would be responsible for some of the decisions which previously had been left to him, and that he expected them to operate a similar policy with their own subordinates. To make sure there was no loss of effectiveness on the sections however, Gresham went on to tell the section heads to prepare detailed instructions to all delegatees, spelling out what they were being asked to do, precisely how they should set about doing it and instructing them to take all their work to section heads for checking when it was completed. Subordinates would need closer supervision in their new tasks and should not be left alone for too long with a problem.

This after all, said Gresham, was what he would do with the work he delegated to the section heads. Delegation, he speculated, was all very well provided there was no loss of control.

1 Does delegation imply loss of control and greater risk of error?

2 Lack of trust in subordinates' abilities is usually cited as a major barrier to delegation on the part of many managers. At the same time most employees respond to situations where they are trusted by superiors to carry out work of a responsible nature. Has Gresham shown trust in his subordinates by his decision now to delegate work; if not, how might you have implemented Gresham's decision to delegate more without losing control effectiveness?

B
List the ways in which organisation structure should facilitate effective control.

C
What role problems can delegation create and under what circumstances?

D
Explain the relationship between control and each of the other functions of management.

E
Briefly explain how the following might influence the nature and style of control exercised.

1 The level of expertise of subordinates

2 A bureaucratic form of organisation

3 Routine, machine-paced work-flow production technology

4 Leadership style: authoritarian, paternalistic, democratic, laissez-faire

5 Task structure – high or low (as Fiedler – see Chapter 7)

6 Group size and member characteristics

7 Stage of development of the group

8 Type of payment system

9 Size of organisation

10 Voluntary and non-voluntary groups or organisations

11 Position power of the delegator

Control

Exercise E lists a number of situations or variables which might lead a manager to adjust the style of the control measure he or she uses.

Think through each of the items and try to list the reasons for your answers to each.

Take the first, 'The level of expertise of subordinates'. A number of points might come to mind. If an employee is experienced or skilled:

- should they be left unchecked for longer?
- should standards be agreed rather than imposed?
- would they be more likely to resent close control?
- should more of the total control process be delegated to the employee?

If your answer to these questions is an unqualified 'yes' what then does this imply for less skilled staff:

- close supervision and control?
- imposed standards?
- constant reporting back?

Clearly, the correct approach is likely to be rather more complex than one's initial thoughts often suggest!

Index

above the line 119
accounting 112–17
achievement need 33
Action approach 21
action-centred model 46
activity levels 4
Adair 46
Adams 35
advertising 119
alienation 75
alienative involvement 65
appraisal schemes 137–8
Argyris 29
articles of association 6
authority 7–8, 62–7
authoritarian style of leadership 47
autonomous work groups 77–8

batch production 124–5
below the line 119
best fit leaders 48
Blackler and Williams 31
Bolton report 110
budgetary planning and control 112–17
   motivational aspects 116
   planning 113–5
budgets 112–4
buffer stocks 125
Bullock Commission 75, 78, 82
bureaucratic organisation 7–9
Burns and Stalker 21
buzz-word generator 101

calculative involvement 65
capital 105–11
   structure 109
capital budgeting 115
channels of communication 88
channels of distribution 120
charismatic power 7
civil servants 6
Classical approach 10–15
classification of organisations 4–9
co-determination 76, 81
coercive power 65
collective bargaining 76, 81
commitment 64
communication 84–93, 153
   channels 87–90
   media 85–7
   problems 85
   process 84
   system 90
community 96

conflict 68–74
   dimensions 71
   distribution 72
   management 73
   organised and unorganised 71
   underlying causes 72
consultation 80
consumer sovereignty 119
Contingency approach 21
contingency leadership 48
contract buying 130
control 66, 115, 159
customers 96
Cyert and March 20

debentures 107
decision-making school 20–1
decision-making unit 132
deed of partnership 5
democratic style of leadership 48
discounted cash flow 109
Donovan Commission 81

economic lot size 125
economic man 26
economic order quantity 130–1
economic sectors 6
employees 97
employers' associations 97
environments of organisations 3, 94–100
equity capital 109
Equity theory 34
Etzioni 65, 156
Expectancy theory 35

Fayol 10–12
feedback 84, 88
Fiedler 48–9
finance 105–11
financial management 101–9
fixed capital 109
flow production 125
focal person 52–3
forecasting and planning 149
formal groups 40
Fox 37, 68
French and Raven 63–4
functional structures 13
functions of management 11, 148–61
   control 159
   forecasting 149
   leadership and direction 155–6
   organising 152

162

Index

gearing 109
goal divergence 73
Goldthorpe and Lockwood 21, 32
Gouldner 21
government 97
grapevine 89
groups 39–44
    characteristics 40–1
    cohesion 43
    defining 39–40
    effectiveness 42, 153
    formal, informal 40
    involvement 43
    membership 41
    uses 42

Handy 49
Hawthorne effect 16
Hawthorne studies 15–16, 27
health and safety 143–4
helicopter factor 46
Herzberg 29–30, 148
hierarchies 13–15
hierarchy of needs 28
Human factor industrial psychology 15
Human Relations approach 15–17
hygiene factors 30

individual development 29
individual differences 32–8
induction 137
industrial relations 143
influence 63
informal groups 40
in-plant factors 32
instrumental orientation 33
interest groups 95–8
intrinsic satisfactions 33–4

Jacques 34
jargon 40
jobbing 124
job: description 135
    design 79
    enlargement 29
    enrichment 78
    evaluation 142–3
    extension 78
    satisfaction 29–30
    specification 135
joint consulation 76, 80

kinetics 87

laissez-faire style of leadership 47, 48
Lawrence and Lorsch 21
leadership 45–51, 153, 155–7
    defining 25
    styles 47–8
leadership and direction 155

least preferred co-worker 48
legal rational authority 8
legal structures 5
legitimate power 66
lenders' finance 107
leverage 109
Lewin 47
liability 50
Likert 50
limited companies 5, 106
line and staff 14
line structures 13
logo 86

McCarthy 80
McClelland 33
McGregor 28
machine loading 123
management 148–61
management accounting 112–17
management by exception 91
management sciences 21
managerial prerogative 80
managing system 19
manpower planning 134–5
manufacturing 123–7
marketing 118–22
    department 120–1
    mix 119–20
    philosophy 118–19
market purchasing 130
Maslow 28
mass production 125–6
matrix structures 14, 120
Mayo 16, 28
mechanistic type of organisation 21
memorandum of association 5
mixed economy 6
moral involvement 65
motivation 25–38
motivators 30
Myers 15

National Enterprise Board 6
need-fulfilment 16
needs of workers 25–31
Neo-Human Relations approach 17
net present value 109
networks 90–1
non-verbal communication 87
normative power 65
norms 40

obedience 7
objectives 99–100
operations research 21
oral communication 85
ordinary shares 106
organisation charts 13–15

163

Index

organisations 2–9
organising 152
organistic type of organisation 21
orientation to work 32

paralinguistics 87
Parkinson's Law 9
participation 75–83
    forms 76
partnership 5, 106
payment by results 141–2
penetration 120
perception 34–6
Perrow 15
personnel management 133–45
    functions 133
    induction 137
    industrial relations 143
    manpower planning 134–5
    records 144
    recruitment and selection 135–7
    safety and welfare 143
    selection 136
    staff appraisal 137–8
    testing 136
    training 139
    wage and salary administration 139–40
Peter Principle 9
phenomenological actionalism 21
piece rate 10, 140–1
planning 99, 112
pluralistic view 68, 70
power 8, 62–7
    authority 62
    coercive 64, 65
    expert 64
    legitimate 64
    normative 65
    referrent 64
    remunerative 65
    reward 63
    sources 63–4
preference shares 106
pricing 120
primary departments 14
primary groups 39
primary task system 19
Principles of Management 11–12
private sector 6
process production 126
product brand manager 14
production 123–7
    batch 124–5
    jobbing 124
    mass 125–6
    process 126
    planning and control 123–4
production orientation 18
productivity 152

profit sharing 82–3
progress section 128
proxemics 87
psycho-economic equilibrium 34
public sector 6, 107
purchasing 128–32
    scope 128–9
    policies 129–30
    practice 129
pyramid of power 13

Qualities approach 45–6
quality control 123

rate of return 109
rational-economic man 26
recruitment 135–7
reference groups 41
referrent power 64
remunerative power 65
reward power 63
rights issue 106
risky shift 43
Roethlisberger and Dickson 16
role: theory 52–60
    ambiguity 57
    applications 56–7
    conflict 56–7
    definition 53
    incompatibility 56
    overload 57
    problem diagnosis 54–5
    underload 57

sales budget 113
scalar principle 12
Scientific Management 10–11, 26–7
secondary departments 14
secondary groups 39
secondary system 19
segments 119
selection procedures 136
self-actualisation 28
selling costs 113
shareholders 96
share ownership 82
shares 106
shop steward 53, 80
Situational approach 46
size of organisation 6
Silverman 21
skimming 120
social man 27
Socio-Technical System approach 18
sole trader 5, 105
span of control 12
speech 85
speculative buying 130
staff appraisal 137–8

Index

staff relationship 14, 88
stakeholders 70, 95–7
stock 106
stores and stock control 131–2
strategic planning 99
structural functionalism 18
substantive agreements 81
suggestion schemes 77, 79
synergy 42
Systems approach 18–20

tactical planning 99
Tannenbaum and Schmidt 48
task of management 28
task systems 19–20
Taylor 10–11, 26–7
technology 7, 18, 127
territory 72
testing 136–7
T-groups 42, 92
Theories X and Y 28, 138
think tanks 42
time payments 140–1
trade credit 107

trade unions 69, 97
traditional leadership 8
training 139
Trist 19
two-factor theory 29

unitary view 68–70
unit production 124

valence 35
vertical job loading 78
visual communication 86
Vroom 35

wages 140
Warr and Warr 76
Weber 7
Wilson Committee 110
Woodward 18, 126
worker directors 82
working capital 109
works councils 76, 81
work study 26, 125
written communication 86